the
ELEMENTS
of
RITUAL

About the Author

Deborah Lipp (New York) was initiated into a traditional Gardnerian coven in 1981, became a High Priestess in 1986, and has been teaching Wicca and running Pagan circles ever since. She has appeared in the A & E documentary "Ancient Mysteries," on MSNBC, and in *The New York Times*.

To Write to the Author

If you wish to contact the author or would like more information about this book, please write to the author in care of Llewellyn Worldwide and we will forward your request. Both the author and publisher appreciate hearing from you and learning of your enjoyment of this book and how it has helped you. Llewellyn Worldwide cannot guarantee that every letter written to the author can be answered, but all will be forwarded. Please write to:

Deborah Lipp
⁒ Llewellyn Worldwide
P.O. Box 64383, Dept. 0-7387-0301-X
St. Paul, MN 55164-0383, U.S.A.

Please enclose a self-addressed stamped envelope for reply,
or $1.00 to cover costs. If outside U.S.A., enclose
international postal reply coupon.

Many of Llewellyn's authors have websites with additional information and resources.
For more information, please visit our website at:
http://www.llewellyn.com

the
ELEMENTS
of
RITUAL

AIR, FIRE, WATER & EARTH IN THE WICCAN CIRCLE

DEBORAH LIPP

2003
Llewellyn Publications
St. Paul, Minnesota 55164-0383, U.S.A.

First Edition
First Printing, 2003

Copyeditor: Liz Tufte
Cover photo © by Digital Stock
Cover design by Kevin R. Brown
Interior illustrations by the Llewellyn art department

Library of Congress Cataloging-in-Publication Data

Lipp, Deborah, 1961–
    The elements of ritual : air, fire, water & earth in the Wiccan circle / Deborah Lipp.—1st ed.
      p.   cm.
    ISBN 0-7387-0301-X
     1. Witchcraft. 2. Neopaganism—Rituals. 3. Goddess religion. I Title.

BF1571.L56 2003
299—dc21   2003044669

Llewellyn Worldwide does not participate in, endorse, or have any authority or responsibility concerning private business transactions between our authors and the public.

  All mail addressed to the author is forwarded but the publisher cannot, unless specifically instructed by the author, give out an address or phone number.

  Any Internet references contained in this work are current at publication time, but the publisher cannot guarantee that a specific location will continue to be maintained. Please refer to the publisher's website for links to authors' websites and other sources.

Llewellyn Publications
A Division of Llewellyn Worldwide, Ltd.
P.O. Box 64383, Dept. 0-7387-0301-X
St. Paul, MN 55164-0383, U.S.A.
www.llewellyn.com

Printed in the United States of America

Acknowledgments

There are more people to thank than I can possibly name. Everyone I have ever done ritual with has made a substantial contribution to this book—if I tried to name you all, I'd surely omit someone. For starters, all the members, friends, and guests of Stormcircle Grove—even if you only attended one circle, I promise I remember you! Also, the members, friends, and guests of the Jersey Shore Pagan Way, Circle Web, Primavera Grove, Gnosis Heart Grove, Coven of the Fiery Swans of Bhrighid, and Coven Lotus Flower.

Special thanks are due to Barbara Giacalone, Nial Hartnett, Constance Doane, Lesley Carey, and Isaac Bonewits, all of whom performed rituals that influenced me strongly, and from all of whom I may have stolen inspiration. Nial and Isaac also read portions of this book for me. Janet Farrar gave brief but appreciated help. Patricia Monaghan has been my friend and role model. Donald Michael Kraig and the late Scott Cunningham did more than encourage me to write, they demanded it. Thanks, too, to Jeff Rosenbaum and the folks at A.C.E., who have been making space for me to teach for darn near twenty years. Thanks to my brother Daniel Goldfisher, you have been an invaluable source of legal advice as well as general support.

Triple portions of thanks to Isaac Bonewits, who has taught me so much, and who has been as understanding and helpful as it is possible for an ex-husband to be. Arthur Lipp-Bonewits has tolerated more than any child should, with two parents echoing that same refrain, "Not now, dear, I'm writing." The fact that my son admires my work makes me very proud.

Dedication

For Susan Carberry
Dedicated High Priestess and mentor, beloved friend…
I owe every word to you.

Contents

Chapter One

THE WICCAN CIRCLE STEP BY STEP

Wicca is one of the fastest-growing religions around. Interest increases every year, and information, once scanty, is everywhere. Walk into any bookstore and you'll find two dozen books that tell you how to cast a Wiccan circle. Probably because most of these are still geared toward the beginner, they don't really bother to tell you *why*. *The Elements of Ritual* takes a unique approach to ritual; when you finish reading it, you'll know far more than how to cast a circle (and how *not* to cast a circle). You'll know what every step of the circle-casting ceremony means, why it's there, and what it accomplishes. You'll know several alternative approaches to each step, and you'll be empowered to write your own effective, powerful ceremonies using sound magical, theological and pragmatic principles, and avoiding common mistakes.

Every Wiccan ritual follows a pattern, and that pattern exists for a purpose. The ritual flows from one step to the next, and each step, and the order of steps, makes sense and is part of a cohesive whole. The reason for this is simple—a Wiccan circle casting exists in the context of an entire religion. A religion *should* be consistent, functioning as a whole. Its rituals should flow from its theology, its theology should flow from its myth, and vice versa, all around in a circle of wholeness.

Certainly there are religions out there—even very popular ones—that are jury-rigged together like the engines of the Enterprise ("I can barely hold her together Captain!"). There are theological doctrines that seem little more than *post facto* justifications for meaningless or questionable practices. There are saints who were invented by the Church, to justify the worship of Pagan deities who predated them.

I think any religion that cobbles itself together like that is at risk of collapsing under its own weight. Many religions, though, feel they have no choice, being unwilling to adjust established or entrenched practices or beliefs. Sometimes belief outstrips ritual; sometimes either of them outstrips myth. Historically, dominant or invader religions have absorbed local or conquered religions—and the result limps around with a third leg. The ancient Egyptians struggled to create an overarching system based on dozens and dozens of local cults, and hundreds of years of gradual changes, and the results contradicted themselves in innumerable ways.

In Wicca, we're in the unique position of having *options*. We can tailor the ritual to be more consistent with what we actually believe. We can adapt the ritual to the stories we tell. We can reexamine our beliefs in light of our practices or our stories. We can bring all these religious activities together in harmony.

Ritual should be consistent with the religion of which it's a part. Ritual should also be consistent with *itself.* It should be obvious, but perhaps is not, that to enact a ritual is to make a statement—in fact, to string together a series of statements. Some of these are statements of belief, some are statements of intention, and some are statements of mood. Those statements should not contradict each other: I should not say "This is solemn" and "This is silly" in the same sentence (unless I'm doing a ritual about paradox). I should not say "There is only one Goddess" and "There are many goddesses, each unique" in the same ritual.

So, when looking at a pattern for Wiccan ritual, we'll look at the ritual as it exists in the context of what Witches believe and say, at what the ritual itself seems to believe and say, and also at plain old practicality. What makes sense? Some things are awkward, some are boring, some require more props than will fit in the room. There are mundane, earth-based considerations in every ritual, and those should be examined as well.

Finally, we need to ask a question that is rarely asked—does the ritual *work?* Do we touch the gods? Are we elevated and exalted by it? Does it satisfy our spiritual needs? Some of these questions are remarkably practical—if we place the steps in the right order, the meaning will shine through with a mystical strength.

The first thing that we're going to do is review the basic steps of Wiccan circle casting—not as a ritual script, but as a series of principles. We'll spend most of the book discussing various ways to turn each step into a script. Once we have an outline, we're going to shift gears briefly to discuss one of the most important concepts of Western magical thought: the *four elements* of Air, Fire, Water, and Earth, what they symbolize and what they mean to Wicca. The elements are, in my opinion, the building blocks of any occult education. What better way, then, to analyze, dissect, experiment with and experience our ritual pattern, than by using the elements? Each element has its own qualities, and so each step of the ritual will be looked at, in turn, by each elemental quality. When we're all finished, there will be a sample ritual script, based on the pattern we've worked out.

First, though, let's start with the pattern itself:

The Steps of Ritual

1. Preliminary Steps
    A. Preparation (before you begin)
        a. Preparing the Location
        b. Preparing the Participants
        c. Preparing the Ritual Space
    B. Grounding and Centering
    C. Declared Opening
    D. Stated Purpose

2. Making the Space
    A. Sacred Preparation: Consecrations
    B. Casting the Circle: Making the Space
    C. Calling the Quarters

3. The Center
    A. Invoking the Gods
    B. Giving Offerings to the Gods

      C. Cakes and Wine (Receiving the Blessings of the Gods)

      D. Using the Blessings

         a. Acts of Magic

         b. Rites of Passage or Season

         c. Teaching or Play

         d. Divination

4. Closing: Reverse the Steps

      A. Thanking the Gods

      B. Dismissing the Quarters

      C. Uncasting the Circle (optional)

      D. Reversing the Grounding and Centering (optional)

      E. Declared Ending/Reconnecting to Earth

You'll notice that there are sections, or phases, to the rite. There's the Preliminary Phase, in which we get ready to begin, and then formally begin. In the next phase, the sacred space is created, and we'll see that this phase has mythic properties, as creating the circle recapitulates creating the universe itself (tall order!). Phase Three is the "Center," which I almost called the "Mystic Center" but rejected the phrase on grounds of corniness. Corny or not, the central phase is the mystical core of the rite, and the heart of Wiccan religion. This is where we meet the gods, in a complex and beautiful interchange of energies. Eventually, we wind down from that, and then it's time for the final, closing phase.

Before we can proceed with examining the ritual more closely, let's learn about the four elements, because we'll be using them on practically every page thereafter.

Chapter Two

THE FOUR ELEMENTS

The Universe in a Nutshell

To a Wiccan, the four elements of Fire, Water, Air, and Earth describe the universe and everything in it. *Everything* can be understood as taking part in one or more elements. Everything that is whole contains all four, and can be understood more deeply by dividing it into four and viewing it through that lens.

From a scientific point of view, the Periodic Table of Elements describes the building blocks of the universe, and Wicca doesn't reject science. But from a magical point of view, both simplicity and symbolism call for only four.

Here is a small list of things that can be, or already are, sorted into four elemental components, or are used to symbolize the elements:

- Parts of the self
- Personality types
- Seasons
- Time of day
- Wiccan altar tools
- Directions
- Astrological signs

- Tarot cards
- Magical techniques
- Geographical locations
- Colors
- Animals
- Magical beings ("Elementals")
- Methods of raising power
- Herbs
- Gems
- Aromas
- "The Witches' Pyramid"[1]

Why are the elements important? They give us a way of thinking about the world. They give us a structured approach to knowing the unknowable. They provide us with a system of interrelations, and magic is all about interrelations.

One of the basic principles of magic is *sympathy*, which means that anything similar to a thing has sympathy with that thing, and can be used to represent that thing. A Voodoo doll is a sympathetic object; it has a similarity to the person it represents. A doll has a direct relationship, like a picture of a person. Elements have an indirect relationship. A candle is not *the same as* a lion, but both represent Fire.

As we see the interrelatedness, the sympathy, of all of life, more than our magic is enhanced. Our sense of connection with life is deepened, and our connection to Spirit is expanded.

The Qualities of the Elements

Air

In the natural world, Air is associated most closely with the sky, wind and clouds, as well as birds of all kinds. Hawks and eagles are especially associated with Air because they fly so very high, and make their nests at such high altitudes. A stork or duck, by contrast, would make less powerful symbols of Air because, although these birds fly, they live in and near the water.

In a person, Air is associated with *thought* and with the intellect, corresponding in the Witches' Pyramid to *To Know.* Ideas are said to come from Air, as is *inspiration*—which also means to breathe in. Logic and scholarship are Air functions, which is perhaps why academics are said to live in Ivory Towers as opposed to Ivory Basements. People who spend all their time thinking "have their heads in the clouds," and if they're *airheads*, they mistake imagination for real life and are impractical (because practicality is an Earth quality).

The direction of Air is the east, and since the sun rises in the east, Air is associated with the morning, with the spring (the beginning of the agricultural and astrological year), and with beginnings of all kinds. Anything that "dawns" is a thing of Air. The things in our lives that dawn, be they projects, creations, or careers, dawn with *an idea.* Often inspiration feels like the sunrise: a bright beginning full of promise and possibility. Since seeds are beginnings, and are associated with the spring, seeds, too, belong to Air.

For Wicca and magic, we need to look at Air's symbolic associations. Its colors are sky colors—white and sky blue. The magical entity of Air is known as a *sylph.* The astrological Air signs are Gemini, Libra, and Aquarius. The Tarot suit of Air is Swords, although this is an interesting story.

In 1910, Arthur Edward Waite published his book *The Pictorial Key to the Tarot,* and his "Rider-Waite" Tarot deck. Waite was a Kabbalist and member of the Golden Dawn magical lodge. His was the first deck to give all 78 cards unique illustrations, and the first to draw associations between the Tarot and the Kabbalah. The Rider-Waite deck became the most popular and influential Tarot ever created, and its influences are seen in the vast majority of decks available today.

However, Waite's membership in the Golden Dawn included an oath of secrecy, and so he hesitated to reveal too much in his deck or accompanying book. He decided to switch two of the elemental correspondences in order to preserve his oath. He couldn't very well change the association of Cups to Water, since that's a pretty obvious one, and Pentacles are mostly depicted as coins—again, the association between money and Earth is very useful and straightforward. But Swords and Wands are abstract tools, not in common usage at the turn of the last century. The Golden Dawn associated Air with Wands and Fire with Swords—Waite reversed those two and filled his deck with Fiery Wands and Airy Swords.

If you're a Tarot reader, it's hard to break the mental picture Air/Sword, Fire/Wand. Every Wand has little flames, salamanders, and orange colors. Every Sword has prominent clouds, sylphs, and a lot of light blue. Perhaps because most Witches read the Tarot, most associate the sword or athame[2] with Air.

On the other hand, the original association used by the Golden Dawn and others made a good deal of sense. The sword is the stronger and more destructive tool, and fire is more destructive than air. The wand is the tool of the intellectual magician, but the sword is the tool of the willful warrior (Fire is associated with Will). Once you get to know the tools, it's hard to escape the conclusion that a person wielding a sword means business (has Will), but a person holding a wand might still be just thinking it over.

So, on your altar, you will have to decide for yourself which tool to assign to which element. And your decisions aren't over! Tools are assigned to elements the way directions are assigned, and colors are assigned; they don't *represent* the element. Every Wiccan altar also carries representations of each element. Most groups use incense for Air. I'm a big fan of incense, and that's what I use. Others, however, use a feather or feathered fan.

Fire

In nature, Fire is *itself* first and foremost. Fire has always been set apart from the other elements, because Fire alone has no natural home on the Earth—Air has the sky, Water the sea, and Earth the land, but only Fire stands apart from geography. The Druidic cosmology even emphasizes this, by using a "3 plus 1" system rather than a system of four. The Druids see the world as broken down into groups of three, with a fourth set apart, such as Land/Sea/Sky and Fire, or Workers/Warriors/Priests (groups of people) and The King (only one). In nature, Fire is the outsider; it is out of control, it conforms to no known rules.

The place Fire is most connected to is the desert, and the Fiery animals are distinguished by their fiery color and disposition—lions and tigers. Salamanders are also associated with Fire, both because of their bright orange color, and because of the way that licks and curls of a fire can come to resemble salamanders—and that is how the magical being of Fire got its name. Other natural things associated with fire burn—like chilies and cumin, or are orange-colored—like fire opals.

The personal quality of Fire is *will*, and in the Witches' Pyramid, Fire is *To Will*. Willfulness burns hot, and the will to get things done is a spark that ignites. Temper is also associated with Fire; a fiery person is a hothead, and lust is Fiery—you *burn* with desire. All of these things are closely associated with the life force itself: the "spark" within that fills us with life. For that reason, healing is a thing of fire; a person who is losing his spark needs Fire magic to re-ignite him.

Fire resides in the south. It is associated with noon, the hottest and brightest time of day, and summer, the hottest and brightest time of year. In terms of endeavors, just as beginnings and ideas are Air, things that are "on fire" are Fire. As Air is the seed, Fire is the sprout, emerging. Fire takes the original seed and gets it going, gives it force. Lots of creativity gets stuck in Air; it needs an application of Will to turn on the power.

Fire can be a transformative force; in fire, the old is burned away and what comes out is utterly different. The blacksmith transforms ore into steel using fire, raw meat becomes delicious in fire, logs become embers. Transformation by fire is sudden and total.

In Witchcraft, Fire is orange, red, and yellow. As mentioned before, its magical entity is the salamander. Fire signs of the Zodiac are Aries, Leo (another lion association) and Sagittarius. As discussed under Air, the tool and suit of Fire can be either swords or wands (I use swords).[3]

The representative of Fire on your altar is another variable, one of those little things people like to debate. The obvious choice is a candle, or perhaps an oil lamp. A flame on the altar is a pretty intuitive way to represent Fire—can't argue with that! However, I prefer to use the burning incense to represent both Fire and Air.

In a ritual, the "female" (yin) elements Earth and Water are combined, and the salt water is used to represent them both. Therefore, it makes sense, and is more balanced, to represent the two "male" (yang) elements by combining them as well. Ritually, the other elements are *used*, the circle is sprinkled with the salt water, and censed with the burning incense. If a candle, and not the incense, represents Fire, then fire just sort of hangs around; it isn't enough of a flame to warm the circle, and if it's providing light, one candle isn't enough (I tend towards four or five candles with different symbolic meanings—and *that's* enough light). Finally, if a candle represents the Goddess, and a candle represents the God, then a candle representing Fire itself seems, again, unbalanced.

As you see, my effort here is to have a cohesive symbol system—we'll come back to that idea again and again. However you choose to arrange your altar, choose in a way that makes sense, not just for the one item, but for the overall whole. Air, Fire, Water, and Earth combine and become One, and that One should fit together as perfectly and seamlessly as a wooden puzzle box—the kind that is hard to take apart again, because it looks like a solid block.

Water

The natural forms of water are myriad. Not just the sea, but every body of water from a little creek to the Great Lakes. Water is also found in our bodies; in the clichéd "blood, sweat, and tears"; in mother's milk; and, perhaps most importantly, in amniotic fluid. Just as life first evolved in the sea, the fetus swims in salt water as it "evolves" and develops. Since all bodies of water have tides, the moon is also associated with water, and many lunar qualities are also Water qualities.

Sea creatures—both plant and animal—are connected to Water: fish, eels, shells, coral, seaweed, sponges, and driftwood all partake of this element. Dolphins and whales are often the creatures most associated with Water, although I suspect this has more to do with our affection for them than with any natural or symbolic imperative.

The personal quality of Water is *feeling*. Emotion flows, following its own path, which may meander. Emotion runs deep, with mysterious depths not visible on the surface. Emotions bring forth secrets like sunken treasure. Emotionality and mood swings are, of course, associated with the moon as well, as are secrets—those things visible just a little bit, lit by moonlight and not exposed in the Sun. In the Tarot, the card The Moon is full of watery images; crustaceans crawl up from water, and the card's meaning is rooted in secrets, mysteries, and hidden knowledge.

The Moon is the menstrual cycle, and Water is childbirth as well, making Water perhaps the most feminine of elements. Since moon phases are cyclic, ending where they began, and beginning where they end, it makes sense that Water is also associated with death, and its not surprising that many people's folklore depicts death as a passage over water. To make the cycle complete, Hindus refer to rebirth as an ocean.

All of these things: The moon, feeling, depth, birth-death-rebirth, and mystery, combine to associate Water with dreams and the subconscious, and from there to altered states in general—trance, vision, and transformation coming from these things. Transformation by water is visionary, and may take the quality of a journey—which is probably why the Hero Journey generally begins with a passage over water.

Watery people are weepy and over-full of feeling. They are dramatic and sensual and otherworldly. They can be draining to be around—wet rags. They can also be the opposite: joyful and full of love—their cup runneth over. The generosity of water flows forth abundantly, and people in love feel love towards everyone.

Water's direction is west. Sunset in the west is associated also with death, with the end of things, and with transformation. Twilight is an in-between and mysterious time—so is autumn. Neither seed nor sprout, Water is the sap—flowing through flora just as blood flows through fauna.

In our creative/becoming process, we used Air to get the inspiration, and Fire for the get-up-and-go. Now we need to let creativity flow through us. If you've ever written or played music or painted, you know there's a time to let go and let it happen. That's the Water time. Intuition has to play a part in any endeavor, and a "go with the flow" attitude has to allow us to take advantage of opportunities we could never have predicted in advance. Because this is daring, in the way that closing your eyes and letting yourself fall is daring, Water corresponds on the Witches' Pyramid to *To Dare*.

For magical symbolism, Water has ocean and lunar colors—deep blue, sea green, and silver. The magical *undine* is Water's entity. Water signs are Cancer, Scorpio, and Pisces. (Cancer's crab and Scorpio's scorpion both appear on The Moon in the Tarot). The magical tool of Water is the cup, which is the Holy Grail. On the altar, Water is always represented by a simple dish of water—some people add a seashell. I like the seashells that double as water dishes, although they tend to be a little prone to spillage.

Earth

Finally we reach Earth. In nature, well, Earth *is* nature. Earth is the substance of the body of our Mother, Gaia, the Earth Herself. Earth is manifest in all things that are *solid*, or *fertile*, or both: rocks,[4] green fields, rolling hills, and soil. Caves and other buried places are quintessentially earthy. Most people consider the bear the animal of Earth, although pigs, boar, and cattle are apt as well.

A human being's Earth is her *body*. From Earth come solidity, stability, and commitment. We call Earth our home, both the home of all life that is Mother Earth, and the house we live in. By extension, Earth is hearth and family and all those qualities that make us feel "at home." To be an earthy person is to be pragmatic, realistic, and tactile. Good Earth qualities in a person make her "the salt of the earth," but an excess of negative Earth qualities make her a "stick-in-the-mud." Earth is that deep, solid, immobile place—both in the negative sense of stubborn and in the positive sense of patient; the Witches' Pyramid understands Earth well when it names the attribute of Earth *To Be Silent*.

Earth is located in the north and is associated with midnight—because north is opposite the noon of south and because subterranean places are dark. Winter is in the north—the coldness of midnight, the coldness of deep soil, and the stillness and silence of waiting for spring. To be solid is to be patient and to hold still. Contrarily, Earth is also fertility—pregnancy, fruit, the physical manifestation of our labors. In endeavors, Earth is completion—the finished project—the *thing* that results.

The colors of earth are brown and black for soil, and deep green for fertility. *Gnomes* are the magical creatures said to inhabit the Earth, and its signs are Taurus, Virgo and Capricorn. The Tarot suit of Earth is Pentacles[5] or Disks, which represent money—that most physical of possessions (since it provides all the other physical possessions). Wealth and *buried* treasure are things of Earth. The elemental tool of Earth is also the Pentacle, which is a disk or plate with a pentagram inscribed on it (some traditions inscribe other symbols as well). Since a plate also holds food, and since food is also of Earth (the physical product that is the outcome of farming—the sustenance of the body), the pentacle is a doubly good symbol. (Triply good, really, since the pentagram on it represents wholeness.)

The representation of Earth on an altar is usually salt. Salt is considered an exceptionally magical symbol; it was once used as money, and is also used as a food preservative—preserving the body through winter, and driving away harm. Salt is also convenient; it dissolves in water and can be sprinkled about indoors without having to be picked up afterwards (pebbles would be a nuisance in that regard). If you're doing your ritual outdoors, you have more options, and for handfastings (Wiccan weddings) it is my custom to replace salt with flower petals.

Air-Fire-Water-Earth

By now you've noticed how the four elements combine to make cycles, like circling the compass (east-south-west-north), or the seasons, or the time of day. They can make abstract cycles, like the cycle of an endeavor or creation we described: idea, then empowerment, then intuition, then manifestation/outcome. A romance, too, can begin with an idea (an observation, a crush, a hope). Next comes fiery lust, then watery love, and finally earthy commitment. In Wicca, we know that every cycle ends at the beginning—midnight is followed by dawn, winter is followed by spring, and the manifestation of a creative process gives birth to the inspiration for the next process. In ritual, we try to complete circles whenever we start them, both to acknowledge this process and to be ready to start the next thing. You'll see cycles throughout our ritual discussions.

Pentagram

Is There a Fifth Element?

The Hindus have five elements—Air, Fire, Water, Earth, and Spirit *(akasha)*. Most Wiccans go along with this view. In fact, the pentagram—the supreme symbol of Paganism and Witchcraft—is said to represent the five elements. Each of the points of the pentagram represents one of the elements according to this view, with Spirit on top.

I was taught that Wiccans place Spirit on top of the pentagram, but Satanists place Spirit on the bottom of their inverted pentagram. The idea is that Spirit is either above or below matter. Personally, I think a religion focused on the Earth Mother has no business separating Spirit from matter—the idea that either is better than the other necessitates the belief that they're forever separate. If the Earth is a goddess, then how can matter be separate from sacred spirit?

"Spirit on top" is all about Spirit being better than the "base" elements. It's consistent with a religion that wishes to be released from rebirth (Hinduism), but entirely *in*consistent with a religion that *celebrates* birth and rebirth (Wicca). It also implies that the other four elements never partake of Spirit.

Wicca is an *Earth* religion, and it's appropriate to think of the elements in an earthy way; as real, as a part of us, as foundational. The time came when I asked myself if I couldn't derive a theology of the elements from Wiccan ritual—if the way the elements were treated in circle could tell me more about what they are.

A circle is set up with a candle or torch at each of the cardinal points (east, south, west and north), representing the elements, around the perimeter. Traditions vary as to

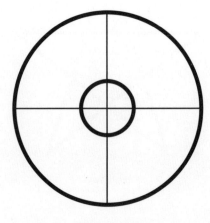

Squared Circle

where the altar is placed, but I was taught to place it in the center. I began to see the altar's placement as having mystical value. The ritual is a "squared circle," marked at the quarters, and the altar is the meeting point of the elemental points.

The squared circle illustrated, then, is the mystical sigil that depicts a circle—not the pentagram (which has mystical significance in its own right). At the center of the circle is the altar, drawing exactly balanced energies from each of the four quarters. What's on the altar? Why, the altar is where the representations of the *gods*, the idols, are placed. Doesn't that make the altar the place of *Spirit?*

The answer that I discovered, what I now believe, and what I teach, is this: Spirit is what happens when all four elements meet and combine. Spirit is the *quintessence*, the "fifth essence," the magical whole that is greater than the sum of its parts. Elementals have only their own qualities: Gnomes will only be Earth, and are incapable of acting in any way but earthy ways; they won't feel or be willful. Salamanders will only and forever be Fire, we cannot ask them to be stable or exercise self-control. But *people*, and other beings with Spirit, have the capacities of all four elements, and the freedom to grow and explore in any direction.

Squaring the circle also represents wholeness; balance. Just as nature is balanced, every person should be balanced in the elements—neither an airhead nor a stick-in-the-mud, neither a hothead nor a sob sister. Rituals should represent that balance; ideas, projects, and theories that don't reflect wholeness are probably missing the boat.

That being the case, it should follow that religion itself, which is an idea, an institution, a *whole* thing, should be balanced in the elements.

The Elements of Religion

Religion can be divided into three basic activities, and one unifying experience, which make up the four elements (and also connects to the three plus one of the Druids). I use the word *activity*, instead of *function*, *component*, or some other inanimate word, in order to show that religion is not static. Religion is not a table with four legs; it is a living, holistic flow.

Since *Air* is thought and intellect, *theology* and belief are the Airy parts of religion—the parts of the mind. Theology can be defined as "rational inquiry into the nature of deity and religious truth; or an organized, often formalized body of opinions concerning deity and religious truth."[6]

Air activity in the religion of Wicca is in something like The Wiccan Rede ("an' it harm none, do what ye will") or the belief in reincarnation, or in speculation about the nature of deity.

Earth, being physical and real, is those things that we *do.* The *doing* part of religion is *ritual.* Ritual is "The prescribed form or order of conducting a religious . . . ceremony . . . [or] A ceremonial act or a series of such acts . . . [or] the performance of such acts."[7] In Wicca, casting the circle is an Earth activity, as is spell-work.

The flow of *Water* is intuition; the state of knowing without understanding—like a dream or symbol, water is fraught with meaning without making linear sense. The Watery part of religion is *myth.* Myth is sacred or archetypal storytelling, or an example of such a story. It has a "recurring theme, or character type that appeals to the consciousness of a people by embodying its cultural ideas or by giving expression to deep, commonly felt emotions."[8]

Fire is the unifying component. We have already discussed Fire's otherness—Fire is separate from and permeates the others. The activity or experience of religion that is Fiery, that bursts forth chaotically like a blaze, that isn't dependent upon location in any one world, is *mysticism.* Fire is the mystical experience: vision, enlightenment, nirvana, or oneness with the Godhead. The mystical experience can occur during, or as a result of, any activity or combination of activities. Nirvana could be achieved through the ritual of meditation, or while discussing the fine points of belief, or listening to sacred stories. Or, enlightenment could occur while ritually enacting a myth, or analyzing the theology of a ritual.

Mysticism can be direct contact with the gods, and that isn't "religion"—it comes *before* religion. The same deities can be worshiped in multiple forms; the same vision can give rise to multiple religious paths. A vision isn't dependent on a religious practice—it can come to anyone. So the Fiery part of religion is the part that is religious without being a part of the religious structure. The mystical experience in Wicca seems to be similar to mystical experiences everywhere. In as much as mysticism is a structured part of a religion, it is apart from the mainstream of that religion—Sufism, Kabbalism, the Rosicrucianism[9] all stand separate from their parent faiths, and all have more in common with one another than with those parents.

Each of the activities that make up religion overlaps the others to a certain degree, and each has its proponents, who struggle to demonstrate that their particular discipline "is" religion. Some theories of myth, for example, say that myths are stories that explain rituals. Other mythologists answer that the opposite is true: rituals enact myths. Some folks say that theology explains myth or ritual, while others argue that rituals and myths are devised to enact and depict a people's thoughts about the nature of deity (theology). It's like each activity has its fan club. Fan clubs for elements don't make any sense at all if you understand the squared circle. All elements are necessary—you can't have life—Spirit—without Fire *and* Water *and* Earth *and* Air.

Elemental Structure of This Book

In the coming chapters, we'll look at each phase of Wiccan ritual in the following ways:

Earth: How do we do this step, what are different ways of doing this step, what is needed to do this step, and what are the practical considerations? By confining each Earth section to "just the facts," it can be used later, as a reference—just flip back to a step and read the Earth section for the how-to tips.

Air: Why do we do this step, and what is the meaning behind it? What are the beliefs and theology that inform this step, and is there a philosophy behind it? Again, this can serve as a reference; once you know what you're doing, you may want to refer back to the thinking part.

Water: What is the mythology behind this step, or what story is this step telling? What is the metaphorical meaning of this step? What is the emotional impact of this step?

Fire: What is the mystical meaning of this step? In what way are the gods involved in this step? Meditation is connected to mysticism, and topics for meditation are suggested in this section. Meditations are essentially homework assignments—I can talk about the results of my own meditations, but the most important results are *yours*. Flipping through the Fire portions of each chapter will give you a wide assortment of meditations that will aid your spiritual growth.

---

1. The Wiccan name for a magical saying originated in the Golden Dawn. It goes: *"To Know, To Will, To Dare and To Be Silent, these are the four tools of the Magician."*

2. The black-handled, double-edged knife that is the Witch's personal tool.

3. However you decide to view swords, athames and swords must go together, as they are essentially different versions of the same tool.

4. I have a rock that I found in Lake Ontario. It is very smooth and flat, obviously water-worn. I use it in the west to represent Water because of its appearance and origin. My coveners, bless them, were always getting mixed up and putting it in the north, since rocks are obviously Earth.

5. A *pentagram* is a five-pointed star. A *pentacle* is an object with a pentagram on it.

6. Adapted from the *American Heritage Dictionary*, with editing to remove sexist and monotheistic language.

7. Also *American Heritage*. Thankfully, no editing needed on this one.

8. *American Heritage* was nearly hopeless here, but I managed to cull some sense from it.

9. In order, mystical movements of Islam, Judaism, and Christianity.

Chapter Three

PRELIMINARY STEPS

Here are the preliminary steps in performing a ritual:

- Preparation
- Grounding & Centering
- Declared Opening
- Stated Purpose

Preparation

These are the things you do before the ritual, most of which aren't particularly ritualistic, so we'll be spending most of our discussion with Earth—the practical stuff.

Earth

The things that need to be done prior to starting a ritual can be broken down into:

- Preparing the location (surroundings),
- Preparing the participants,
- Preparing the ritual space.

Preparing the Location

This is the preparation of the house that the circle will be held in, or the park, back-yard, rented hall, etc.

In any location, you should clean thoroughly prior to the ritual. Carpets should be vacuumed and floors swept. Open windows if it's stuffy; close them if it's chilly. If any-one will be taking a ritual bath, or doing other ritual cleansing, then clean and prepare the bathroom with special care. Obviously, tub and sink should be spotless, and towels fresh and clean, but also make the area just a little Witchy, with incense and candles, and perhaps an idol or even flowers.

Examine the safety and comfort of the areas where people will be sitting, standing, or walking. If you meet in a living room, remember that nothing is more disconcerting in a ritual than suddenly stepping on a Lego or sitting on a squeaky cat toy. If you're holding your circle outdoors, walk the perimeter for large sticks, stones, and dangerous holes. If the ground is very uneven or treacherous, save your ritual dance for another time and just warn people.

Review any issues that may distract or disrupt you, such as privacy or noise. At home, lock the doors as soon as everyone has arrived (this is very easy to determine if you're Circling solitary). As a High Priestess, I have historically been quite strict about starting time. Waiting indefinitely irritates everyone, and sooner or later the doors must be locked and the ringers on the phones turned off. At a rented location, make sure well in advance that you know the parameters of your stay. Don't rent someplace that has to be vacated the minute you're done—if you think you'll be done at ten, rent until midnight. A looming deadline will break your focus, as will an unexpected guest.

Unexpected guests are very hard to avoid at outdoor locations, even if they're on private land. Plan to post a guard who will stay outside the ritual space and watch for intrusions. You should know well in advance if you need a permit for a public outdoor space, and have it at hand.

Do not have audible phones, beepers, or alarms (unless there's an emergency rea-son—and obviously, a smoke alarm is the exception). Don't have visible distractions—lights, electronic displays, and most especially, *no clocks*. People can leave their watches with their street clothes, but stationary clocks have to be covered—especially glowing ones, such as on a VCR. The *mystical* idea of timelessness is best left for *Fire*, and the emotional and psychological issues for *Water*. For now, just note that timepieces have no place in ritual space.

You may want to keep track of time, perhaps to judge the right length for a silent meditation. This still won't necessitate a watch or clock. Rosary beads as a prayer device were invented as a way of keeping track of the number of prayers or chants without consciously counting or using any kind of timer. Other ways to use a timer in ritual without disturbing the space with a clock might be to use a piece of recorded music, to watch until a candle burns to a particular point, or to wait until a particular piece of incense has burned up.

Preparing the Participants

There may be only one participant (you) or there may be a crowd. If there's only one, you can skip the briefing. Otherwise, people *really appreciate* knowing what's expected of them. If all you say to them is "This will be completely spontaneous" or "There will be surprises," you've still given them something that will help them feel at ease.

If there are songs or drumbeats that people should know, review them ahead of time. If there's an expected call and response ("When I say 'Blessed be,' I want you all to say 'Blessed be!'") let them know. If they're to have something in their hands ("Bring your athames,") or *not* have something in their hands ("We'll be handing out special cups, please don't bring your own,") let them know.

If there's something that everyone *must* have—like a blue robe, or a beaded necklace—telling them in advance isn't enough. Keep extras around so that you'll be sure everyone can participate.

If you're serving food or drink in the ritual, then check about allergies, and if you're serving alcohol, have an alternative available for those who need it. People who need special foods or drink can be in charge of bringing their own; there's no need to burden one person.

My experience is that there can be confusion over what food and drink can be consumed when. Unless you fast before a ritual, and if your rituals are also social occasions, then there will probably be some snacking and drinking before the ritual. There will also be the "Cakes and Wine" portion of the ceremony, and (as we'll discuss when we get there) anything used for Cakes and Wine should not be opened or sampled beforehand. The best solution is to clearly label everything that's in the refrigerator (or elsewhere). If children are coming, even that may not be enough, and I suggest a little creative subterfuge.

Speaking of food and drink, have you done your shopping? There's nothing like a last minute trip to the supermarket after you're already in your robe. You end up with the limpest, most unwanted bouquet of flowers ever—the Charlie Brown Christmas Tree of bouquets—and very questionable wine ("Have you ever heard of Beaujolais Guido?") That's *if* you can get wine at all—every U.S. state has different liquor laws, but generally you can't buy alcohol as late into the night as you can buy other things, so you don't want to leave it to the last minute.

To fast or not to fast? I find, personally, that fasting makes me too lightheaded to get through the focused preparation portion of the evening—I suppose I could do it if someone else were in charge, but after fifteen years in the driver's seat, it's not something I count on. I also admit that my blood sugar tends to fluctuate, and a person without those kinds of ups and downs might find a fast beneficial rather than debilitating. It also depends on the length of the ritual; I'm rather reluctant to have people passing out, but if a ritual was very short and to the point, there would be little risk of that.

On the other hand, eating too much is at least as bad. Passing out in the circle is embarrassing, but drowsing off is even more so. Red meat is a bad main course the night of a ritual. After years of experimenting, I decided to stick with "carbo-loading." Running a ritual seems to use energy in a way similar to running a marathon, so taking a page from that book, I have a nice big plate of pasta before ceremonies. My energy doesn't flag, but I don't feel too heavy or earth-bound.

To drink or not to drink? As with fasting or eating, there's no hard and fast rule in Witchcraft about this. If you already don't drink, it's not a question, but there are others who do sometimes drink, and might want to know if it's appropriate prior to ritual. Again speaking personally, I find that being mildly intoxicated—as in, one glass of wine—is about right for increasing my relaxation and ability to "get into it," but not enough to impair my focus or ability to function. That's the range you want to look at—the benefits of an alcohol-enhanced ritual experience are a decrease in inhibition, a suspension of disbelief, an ability to shrug off the mundane world, and an increase in psychic sensitivity. The down side is lack of focus and concentration, forgetfulness, awkward motor coordination (tricky around candles and knives), and perhaps a disregard for the importance of what you're doing. You'll have to gauge those pluses and minuses individually, both for yourself and others in your group (if you lead a group).

Finally we come to the issue of ritual cleansings and perhaps anointings. Some groups have each member take a ritual bath prior to the circle. Others use a basin of water for a ritual "splash." The water in either the bath or basin can have added ingredients—consecrated salt, special herbs, perhaps an essential oil. These ingredients can have a ritual or practical significance—they can be oriented toward magic or they can be oriented toward aromatherapy or muscle relaxation. The cleansing can be balanced in the four elements—a salt water sprinkle and a censing or smudging. Anointing can be done with a consecrated oil, with salt water, with spring water, or some other substance. Any or all of these substances may be ritually consecrated prior to use.

Bath salts can be made or purchased with herbal ingredients, and they nicely dissolve rather than floating on the surface of the water the way fresh herbs do. (If, however, you have very old pipes or very hard water, go easy on the *amount* of salt used.) Essential oils don't leave mineral deposits, but some people do have bad reactions to them—real essential oils are intense, and can cause the skin to redden and raise. If you're putting oils in a bathtub, and especially if you have children, scrub the tub out thoroughly before its next use.

It's important that whatever be done be taken seriously. I hardly think a ritual cleansing has any real worth if it's followed by a discussion of rush hour traffic. The best thing to do is probably to use the cleansing as a cut-off between "how ya doin'" socializing and preparing for the ritual. You also need to decide how far the cleanliness is to be taken. Of course, clean towels are a must. Most people wear robes or go skyclad (nude) for Wiccan rituals, but if you're changing back into street clothes, should they be a fresh, clean set of clothes? Some people would say so. The point is to decide how much the symbolism of cleansing needs to be backed up by the reality of being really clean.

There's also the issue of *where* the cleansing should take place. If you're using a basin, you could place it either in the room used for the circle, or the room used for changing into ritual garb. If you're using a full bath, you have to decide if people will be bathing before leaving the house, or at the covenstead (the home where circles are held). If it's a large group, you're simply not going to have enough hot water in a private home. (If it's a *very* large group, skip the idea entirely.) On the other hand, if someone is driving a long way, perhaps in traffic, then bathing prior to facing the stress and tension of the road seems like a waste of a good bath. On occasions when my group has used ritual baths, I've insisted that everyone who *can* bathe at home do so, and that still left three or four who would bathe at my place—because they had a long drive, weren't coming straight from home, or had a stall shower instead of a tub.

Preparing the Ritual Space

There's a bunch of stuff you need for your ritual, and my Number One Piece of Advice is this: *Write it down.* Draw a diagram of what your altar should look like, and next to the altar, list the extra items that are needed. I cannot emphasize enough how useful this is. It gives a point of reference for every member of the circle, so that anyone can set up the room (or help), rather than just the High Priest/ess. It prevents last minute attacks of forgetfulness. It is a useful teaching tool. It can be updated whenever you think "Gee, next time I'd really like . . ." so that you don't have to reinvent the wheel every time you have a circle. Your little altar diagram is your friend, so darn useful that I will write the rest of this section with mine in front of me!

There are certain things to do every month (or however often you meet). You can conveniently schedule them for the day after the ritual, or the day before the next ritual. They are as follows:

- Remove melted wax from everything and everyplace. It manages to get on the altar, on all the candle holders (of course), on robes, and on the carpet. Wax can be easily removed from most objects if you put them into the freezer for about a half-hour first. That doesn't work on the carpet! For floors and carpets, the trick is to place a newspaper over the wax and *iron* it. The hot iron melts the wax and the paper absorbs it. Keep moving the paper to a fresh spot until no more wax comes away.

- Review the contents of the "magic box" (its contents are described on the following pages) and make sure it's fully stocked and in good order.

- Polish all the silver, brass, or copper ritual gear (which may include the pentacle, the altar candles, the cup, and any ritual jewelry you may wear).

Your altar layout is a combination of symbolism, aesthetics, and practicality. Different groups have different altar tools and symbols, and that will affect the overall picture. So will the altar itself.

For purpose of this discussion, we're going to place the altar in the center of the circle, facing north, with you or whoever sits behind it seated in the south.

Many people use a coffee table or end table as an altar. If you're going to buy or build a piece of furniture for the purpose, first assemble everything that will go on it and look at the size. Too big is awkward for passing wine or cakes around, but too small is dangerous—there's nothing like having an athame fall to the floor, or the candles too close to the flowers ("What's that smell?"). My firm rule has always been that the altar itself is a ritual tool, and therefore only ritual (preferably consecrated) things go on it. To follow this rule, you need to decide where the *non*-ritual tools (like matches and a corkscrew) will go. An altar with a bottom shelf or a drawer is therefore exceptionally handy.

Once you have an altar, you can decide whether or not to use an altar cloth. The High Priestess who trained me always used one, and they have many advantages. They protect delicate wood, they can be appropriate colors, and they can be decorated with fitting symbols, for different occasions. They're easily washable, and the ironing trick works just fine on the wax that they'll inevitably absorb. An altar cloth is easy to make, or a large scarf or sarong can be used.

Why then have I never used one? Years ago, I acquired a lovely cast iron table with a hand-painted tile top. It's been my altar ever since. Tile is easy to clean, and of course the painting adds a unique and beautiful element. The table even has a bottom shelf. The only disadvantages have been that it's a little bit too small, and, being iron, unbelievably heavy to move.

I keep a "magic box" in my circle, on my altar's bottom shelf. The box has all of the small emergency supplies I need, plus a compass. I use the compass to align the quarter candles and altar along the cardinal points. As we go on, I'll mention things that I keep in my magic box.

CANDLES

Candles serve both a symbolic and practical purpose—they are the preferred source of lighting for Wiccan ritual and can be used to symbolize various things. Depending upon how many symbolic candles you have, you may want an additional pair of "altar candles" for extra light—they'd go in the far corners of the altar (northeast and northwest). However many candles you have, have *one spare for each.* If you use four white votives, two white tapers as altar candles, a red taper for the Goddess, and a green taper for the God, then you need at least one spare white votive, and one each red, green, and white tapers. Candles sputter and die, are defective, have wicks that get screwed up, or end up in front of open windows or fans and burn down suddenly. Better safe than sorry. Have the spares *unwrapped* before putting them in the circle—plastic wrap all over the place is unattractive.

Some people use fresh candles each time, and some people use the thick pillar candles as "perpetual" candles for some purposes. If you're using a fresh, new candle for the circle, trim the wick, make sure it fits in its holder, and light it for one moment before blowing it out, just to make sure the wick is good.

In the magic box, I keep spare matches (at least two books),[1] a candle shaver, and a "utility taper." The extra taper is for lighting candles—instead of burning your fingers on a match when lighting a recalcitrant candle, it is easier and more glamorous to light a taper and bring it to every other candle that needs to be lit. In particular, this is a much better way of lighting quarter candles. If you walk to each quarter to light its candle, that's four matches, any of which could be a problem, or too short for the wick it's trying to reach—using a taper is a more elegant and efficient solution.

Candles that may be used:

- One candle for each quarter is fairly universal. Quarter candles are placed at the perimeter of the circle. They can be on stands, in sconces on the wall, or on the floor. If they're on the floor, don't place them until everything else is fully set-up—I can't count the number of kicked-over candle accidents I've witnessed.

- Two altar candles, but this may be skipped if your altar has lots of other light.

- Some people use one candle each for the Goddess and the God, although there are other ways of representing Them. Some people add a third candle, representing the Unity of Goddess and God.

- Some people use a candle for Fire, other people use the lit incense, as discussed in chapter 2.

- Some occasions have extra candles associated with them, and so do some spells. For example, you might light an extra candle to represent your "Yule log."

INCENSE

Stick, cone, loose, or smudge? Cones are small and portable, but they don't look very dramatic and they're awkward to carry for censing. Sticks are readily available, and there are lots of great-looking incense burners available to accommodate them, but they're not very smoky. Smudge is, to me, best when doing specifically Native American rites. It has the disadvantage of going out often, and there's no way of varying it—it's sage or nothing. My choice is loose incense. There are several benefits: It's easy to moderate the amount of smoke in the circle at any given moment—smokier when actually censing, lighter at other times. Unlike other kinds, it can be custom-made; you can mix your own easily using various herbs and other ingredients. This enables you to add herbs for specific occasions, or magical purposes, or aromatherapy, and you can adjust the recipe based on allergies or just preference. It also has the advantage of looking and feeling quite impressive; swinging a censer is dramatic and effective. Loose herbs are easy to find, and many excellent books provide recipes and magical associations of herbs. However, charcoals can be hard to come by,[2] and both the charcoals and the herbs have to be kept dry (Tupperware is good for that). Charcoals can also be hazardous to use if they get damp, so they should always be lit *before* the circle has started; if soot and embers are going to start flying around, better that it happen when it isn't disrupting a solemn moment.

If you're using a censer, it needs something in it to cool it, so that it won't burn the altar. Clean kitty litter actually is perfect for this, although some people will find that an unpleasant thought. Sand or dry soil will work just fine. After the first time you use a censer, the bed of ash will help (and looks nicer than kitty litter). The censer you use should be cool enough to be carried, or have a handle. The charcoal, as mentioned, should be lit a few minutes before the circle begins, both to test it and to have it at full heat by the time you sprinkle incense on it. You need spare of whatever incense you're using—extra cones or sticks, extra loose herbs and charcoals.

One of the most useful tools I ever added to my altar was a little pair of silver tongs that I bought in a consignment shop. They were probably originally used on sugar cubes, but I find them ideal for handling hot charcoals, as well as lifting sunken candle wicks out of pools of hot wax.

I keep extra charcoal, in aluminum foil or Saran Wrap, in my magic box. I also keep one or two cones of incense, also wrapped. That way, if *all* my charcoal fails, I still have a backup. This actually happened when a charcoal package came open during a rainy spell. The combination of the lack of wrapping and the humidity wiped out my entire supply. Wiccan ritual calls for a balance of elements, so I like to keep incense going at all times. The cones act as a *second* backup (backup to the backup); they can be lit even if they're a bit damp (if you're stubborn).

Dishes

You may never have thought of dishes as altar tools, but you'll be using several of them, and it's nice if they're pleasing to the eye. They should be set aside for ritual use, so you're not dumping tea bags or candy corn out of them fifteen minutes before you start your circle. You can have a matched set, or each one can be unique. They should be metal, ceramic, or some other natural material; as with cigarette lighters, glass is too modern—it just doesn't go with the theme. They should be small, about ashtray-size, so that they fit nicely on the altar. The one for water should be deep enough so that it doesn't spill when being carried about.

The dishes needed will be those on the altar: one for water, one for salt, and one to hold the incense before it's lit. You'll also need a serving plate for cakes and a libation bowl for offerings. My personal favorite for a libation bowl is a chip-and-dip bowl, the kind with a small bowl inset into a large one. The reason for that is, both liquid and solid offerings are made; both wine and cakes. If you drop the cake offering into the wine offering, and then use the bowl for offerings again later, you'll be greeted by the sight of dissolving cake bits floating in the wine. Yuck. Get the chip-and-dip bowl, put the cakes in the dip part and the wine in the chips part.

You'll need one final dish: an ashtray or refuse plate, discreetly *off* the altar, for used matches, wine corks, and the like.

IDOLS

It's traditional to represent both a (the) God and a (the) Goddess on your altar. At one time, books on the Craft gave you advice on how to find appropriate items to use as God and Goddess representations. Now there's an abundance of Pagan art readily available. Statuettes and pictures from every pantheon abound. Keep in mind that, for the duration of the ceremony, the God and Goddess used are a "couple," they should be compatible in sensibility, culture, and aesthetic. What I mean is, if you're using Aphrodite, don't pair Her with Coyote. Use two deities from the same culture, or with similar personalities, and use two images that look good together.

There are several options for representation available other than statues and pictures. For the Goddess, a mirror is traditional, as is a bouquet, a seashell, a string of pearls, or an egg. For the God, a phallic symbol, a pair of horns or antlers, or a pine cone can be used.

BASIC TOOLS

You need the four basic tools—wand, pentacle, cup, and sword/athame. If you don't have a sword, use your athame, although having both on the altar is fine. You need the representations of the four elements: I use a water dish, a salt dish, a dish of incense, and the censer. Some people add a white-handled knife, a scourge, a staff, or a bell, and Wiccans from the Frost's line use an ankh as a tool.

EXTRAS

One more item to place on the altar is a vase of fresh flowers. If you're seated on the floor, pillows or blankets for sitting on are very nice. If you're working skyclad, a shawl or sarong in case of chill is handy. Musical instruments are a wonderful extra—drums, rattles, a sistrum, klava sticks, a tambourine, even a recorder.

JUST BEFORE YOU START

Where are the pets? Some animals enjoy ritual and are very peaceful during ceremonies. Some are very magical and act like a "canary in a coal mine," alerting you to shifts in the magical energies. I had one cat who was very unusual; I called her my secular humanist. She stayed near me most of the time, but as soon as a ritual began she'd absent herself to another part of the house—she didn't like magical energy *at all*. All these aside, there are many pets who are just nuisances during ritual, or who will jump up on the altar or knock over candles, and they need to be put away.

Where are the children? If you're planning on leaving children out of the ritual, make triple sure they're peacefully asleep before you begin.

I circled in a finished basement for a few years, and many were the last-moment sprints upstairs. Are the beverages and the cakes at hand? Have you remembered both wine (if you drink it) and a nonalcoholic drink (if needed)? *Is there a corkscrew?* Do yourself a favor and get a spare corkscrew to keep in the magic box. Then, uncork the wine before the ritual anyway.

Is there water in the water dish? I don't know why that is such an easy item to miss, but many empty water dishes have ended up on "finished" altars.

Some people light the quarter candles before they begin, and some light them ritually as part of the ceremony.

When everyone is assembled and you're ready to begin, *say so.* Don't just turn out the light—someone will be startled and jump.

Air

We've now covered a whole list of practical considerations, many of which have theological justifications that we've jumped right past. Rightly so, since we were in Earth—but now we're in Air, and we want to know the *logic* behind our ritual. Let's start with ritual cleansings and ritual anointings.

Ritual Cleansing and Anointing

In Wicca, to cleanse is far more than skin deep. Cleansing is similar to purification, although the latter is more intense. In cleansing, we remove from ourselves anything that doesn't belong to the ritual.

Wicca is not a religion that believes in sinfulness. Many people would say that there is no such thing as sin in Witchcraft, but I don't think that's true. To violate life is to violate the Goddess, so I would say that murder and rape are every bit as sinful in our religion as in others. Another example of something that might be considered sin is ecological destruction—because the body of the Goddess is the Earth itself, Gaia, then to violate the Earth is considered by some to be desecration—sinful. But even though there are things that can be defined as sin in Wicca, Wicca doesn't focus on the sinful part of life, and doesn't look at sin as a natural state. We believe that *goodness* is a natural state, that most of what we do is good, and that which isn't good can be improved.

Now, if you believe that people are born into sin, and that all of their natural thoughts are sinful or potentially sinful, then the need for ritual cleansing hardly requires an explanation. Wicca is different, and in Wicca, it certainly *can* need an explanation. What is being "washed away" in the ritual bath? Not real sin—if a real sin has been committed, a bath isn't going to fix it. If you've harmed someone, then you need to make amends for that harm, and/or pay whatever the consequences of that harm turn out to be. Even the forgiveness of the Goddess Herself doesn't free you from that.[3]

The Hindu concept of *karma* is one that most Wiccans accept; it fits comfortably with our philosophy. Karma is the balance of existence, the fact of every action having a reaction, the cause and effect of the universe. Karma isn't judgment, punishment, or reward. Karma is as free of opinion as this: If you hold a cup above the floor and let go, the cup will fall and break. The broken cup isn't a punishment for the wrongdoing of letting go; an intact cup isn't a reward for the goodness of holding on. Actions simply have results, and the concept of karma is that those results come from *all* actions, all the time, and follow us from incarnation to incarnation.

Now, somewhere later in Hinduism came along the idea that you could wash away some of your karma, and pious Hindus often bathe in the (filthy, polluted) waters of the Ganges, because that sacred river is said to have just such power. The whole thing is similar to Catholics going to confession, and receiving penance and absolution. The problem, if you ask me, is that these techniques of "cleansing away" karma *or* sin violate the principles of karma. Actions have reactions, and no ritual should be able to bypass that circuit.

In Judaism, before you can ask God to forgive your sins, before you can pray for atonement at Yom Kippur, you must first make every effort to atone to the persons against whom you sinned. Judaism is very clear, for example, that if you've stolen, prayer is not an atonement until and unless you return the stolen property or make fair compensation for it. This dovetails ethics to religion and is very in tune with karma. It requires that the result of the action be responded to, before the action *can* become the business of God (or the gods).

So, ritual cleansing definitely does not remove sin. What it *does* is remove ideas about sin, and feelings of sin, either real or imagined.

There's a leap between our day-to-day lives and meeting the gods. There's a shift that has to happen inside of us. We have to come to accept ourselves as people who can face the gods. In order to enter the ritual, we must confront the conflict between a religion which tells us that we partake of the gods and they of us, that gods are immanent within us; and a daily life which tells us we aren't much, aren't good enough, and have screwed up again. By bathing, we can use the potent symbolism of water and washing to remove the inadequacies, criticisms, and self-hatred.

This is essentially a mystical act, the purification of the self, but it's written up under *Air* rather than *Fire* because it is supported by a powerful foundation of Wiccan theology—a theology that has often been left unexamined. First is the belief in immanent deity—when we are meeting the gods, we are, at least in part, meeting ourselves. That belief leads naturally to the next—that we are inherently worthy. Whatever we are washing away, then, is not an essential or necessary part of us; it's dross. We are gods (*all* of us) and not pitiable, pitiful things. We are not separated from deity by a huge ocean of sin and imperfection; we are as near as the knowing—and part of the purpose of ritual is that knowing. Also springing from the theology of immanence is the theology of inner power—the source of Wiccan magic. We believe that we have both the power and the wisdom to do the things we need to do, and that includes washing ourselves free of the barriers to self-love, self-acceptance, and the worship and work that brings us into a higher state.

Bathing also removes distraction and allows us to focus fully on the ritual. Just as we believe we have inner power, and that we should improve ourselves by the use of that power, so we believe in concentrating our minds. Isaac Bonewits likens ritual cleansing to washing your hands between cooking a main course and cooking dessert. You probably don't want your apple pie to taste like your pot roast—even though your pot roast is wonderful. Just so, you could have had the best day of your life, full of success, rewards, and fun, but you don't want to be thinking about it when it's time to think about ritual and the gods. Wash away the last course to prepare dessert!

Recall the different ways that cleansing might be done:

- A ritual bath.
- A basin of water for a ritual "splash."
- Adding salt, herbs, or essential oils to the water.
- Balancing the cleansing in the four elements by adding earth, air, and fire.
- Anointing with oil, salt water, spring water, or some other substance.
- Possibly consecrating any or all of these substances.

Each of these variations has meaning—or at least an implied meaning—and so the decision as to which to use is meaningful.

To use a basin and just rinse the hands and face is to use these parts of the body to represent the whole person. "Head, heart, and hands" is a phrase often used to describe the whole person and everything she does. This is obviously connected to the elements (the head is Air, the heart is Water, the hands are Earth, and Fire is set apart, as usual). To make sure that the "symbolic splash" fulfills this, rinse hands and face, and then splash a drop over your heart.

To fully immerse yourself, on the other hand, implies that your *whole self* must be cleansed. If you're doing a bath, therefore, use at least symbolic full immersion, by wetting the hair and face. The bath has a closer relationship to real washing than the basin does, but you shouldn't combine the two functions—get into the bath with your body already clean. Any herbs or oils that you use for more than symbolic effect are more effective when used in the bath, as they're given more time and more skin contact. Hot water itself, of course, also has a relaxing and mood-altering effect.

What might you add to the water? Salt creates a womb-like effect—the salt water of the ocean of our birth, of amniotic fluid and, not coincidentally, of isolation tanks. The idea of returning to a place of birth and origin is consistent with a ritual that honors the Goddess of Creation. Herbs, on the other hand, connect to the idea of the *Earth* Mother, and to all gods and goddesses of growing things. The advantage of essential oils is that their purity (because they are so heavily distilled) is a strong symbolic connection to the purification being achieved.

When you cleanse using just water, or just water with an added ingredient, you're working with the idea of washing something away. That "something" can be as small as distraction or as big as self-loathing, but you are becoming clean by *removal*.

When, on the other hand, you balance the cleansing ritually by using all four elements, you are using the concept of *restoration*. You are both adding and removing, at least potentially. The idea here is that part of the unclean state is a state of imbalance, and when all four elements are used, the missing or under-represented element(s) are corrected. If you anoint, you are specifically *adding*, not removing or restoring. You are taking something—usually something blessed—and adding it to the person, either to give him energy of a particular kind, or blessing, or to alter his consciousness. Since anointing is an addition, it should only be done *after* cleansing.

I should repeat here that neither cleansing nor anointing is required, and there are many traditions that don't do this at all. The circle itself will be censed and sprinkled, and many groups consider that enough. Some groups cense and sprinkle participants at the same time as they do the circle, and this would have a similar effect as the pre-ritual bathing and anointing.

Placing the Altar

The next question that came up while going over set-up was where to place the altar. We breezed past it pretty quickly while discussing layout of the altar, but its location and orientation have a great deal of symbolic meaning.

As I said in chapter 2, I was taught to place the altar in the center, and I have come to see the center as a highly charged place, the place of Spirit within the squared circle. To me, this is the proper place for the altar, because the altar is a thing of Spirit—it is that which holds all the other elements (elemental tools) and, most importantly, holds the images (idols) of the gods. It also makes sense to me that Witches gather around the altar in a circle—a circle within a circle—and that everyone is as equal as possible, facing each other and having relatively equal access to the altar.[4]

There are some impracticalities to placing the altar in the center, not least of which is that it's impossible to perform the traditional *spiral dance* with such a placement. Some people have suggested that the altar placement can't really be traditional if a traditional dance can't be performed around it. Alexandrians traditionally place their altar in the north, which, being the locus of Earth, is very appropriate for an Earth Goddess religion. It is perhaps for this same reason that Gardnerians have their (centered) altar *facing* north.

Some people put the altar in the east, the place of beginnings, because that is the place from which the ritual begins. Ancestor altars—those devoted to the honored dead—are traditionally placed in the west, which has many associations with death. On Samhain, the festival that honors the dead, some groups move their altars to the west, and others have two altars.

The important thing here, and we'll come back to this point often, is to make a choice that makes sense to your ritual, and is consistent with the rest of the ritual, with your beliefs, and with your mythos. Over and over, we're going to see that the structure of ritual needs to be a consistent and cohesive part of the whole of your religious life. When you've finished making all your ritual decisions, beginning to end, about everything you're doing and saying, and in what order, go back to the beginning and review it for consistency. If the center has a special significance in one part of the circle, is that same significance given to the north later on? If so, time to rethink and rewrite.

All About Candles

Now that we've placed the altar, let's get back to candles for a few minutes. Candles are used in a wide variety of symbolic ways, and can represent just about anything—people, elements, deities, abstractions, events—you name it. Candles are both vivid and convenient and have many advantages—they are colorful, eye-catching, and sometimes scented, so they stimulate the senses. They are easily personalized for special purposes, by anointing, engraving, or decorating, and can even be homemade. For magical purposes, they don't leave a "disposal" problem, as a poppet, for example, would. They are readily available at the supermarket, card shops, and housewares stores. For all of these reasons and more, candles are a ubiquitous part of Wiccan life.

Candles can be overused—I have seen covens using four candles (appropriately colored) to represent the four elements. This strikes me as silly, lazy, and uncreative. *Water* should represent Water, not something fiery. This is a case of people forgetting the meaning behind the symbol.

On the other hand, it is easy to see why candles are appropriate to represent people, other living things, and deities—being fiery, they clearly show the "spark" of living essence. Candles are also excellent to represent beginnings and ends in ritual—like turning on and turning off a light, they can mark the entering and departure of a presence. You might, for example, invoke the Goddess, then light Her candle. At the end of the ceremony, you could then thank Her, and snuff Her candle.

A proper symbol should have a real, overt connection to the thing it symbolizes. This is for two reasons: One, part of the purpose of ritual, part of "what it all means," is to connect us to the things we symbolize and enact. Remember, the gods are within—we don't technically "need" to perform ritual in order to reach them. Yet we find that, day-to-day, they are hard to reach. Ritual is the methodology by which we make ourselves into beings who *connect*. We connect to the gods, we connect to our own power, to each other, to magic. And part of how we connect is with symbols. If our symbols aren't potent, our psyches don't respond, and the connection is as dry as reading about it in the newspaper.

Secondly, these kind of symbols work on the basis of *sympathetic magic*, which means that something that has a connection to a thing, *is* that thing. Sympathetic magic is based in the understanding that all of the universe is interconnected, like a vast web. In order to reach a thing, we need to find a strand of the web that connects to it; and everything has a vast array of strands, reaching out from it, to a virtually infinite number of other things. We are all part of this vast web of connection. For example, I am connected to a strand via my own writing—this book connects you to me. I am connected to former parts of my body—the locks of hair and nail clippings that are so famously a part of the witch's storehouse. I am connected to my possessions—the jewelry used by psychics. I am connected to images of me—Voodoo dolls are another famous magical tool, as are photographs. I am connected to my astrological sign, my place of residence, my name, my phone number—a massive weaving of strands emanates from me into every corner of the world. Should you need to make a connection to me, you merely need to choose one of those strands or, better yet, several at once.

Back to candles—a candle is excellent to use as a symbol when it doesn't contradict that which it symbolizes, such as Water, or when something else wouldn't be far more obvious. You can weave multiple strands into the symbol by using color, anointing oil, perhaps engraving a symbol into the candle, or even using a symbolic candle holder.

Remember again that *consistency* is a necessary element of your symbol system, and let's see what candles can symbolize, and how.

Start with quarter candles—many people use a symbolic color at each quarter. Every Wiccan group I've ever heard of has used quarter candles or torches (weather permitting). These candles are primarily *lights*—and are part of "turning on" and then "turning off" the quarter (the meaning of the quarters will be discussed later). The *primary* symbolism of the elements is done through the elemental symbols and altar tools, so the use of candle colors would merely be an "extra." Some people will want colored candles anyway, to maintain consistency with the idea of dividing everything into its elemental associations. However, other groups will want all four candles the same color. This is seen as unifying, and symbolizing that the circle is a *whole*. Since the candles mark the perimeter of the circle, and contain it, some people believe that they should represent the *one* (circle) that is formed of many (elements). In this case, all four candles are the same color, and the color can be used to represent the purpose of that circle: white or silver for lunar circles, symbolic colors for holidays, and black for funerals.

Representing the Gods: Candles and Idols

Candles can also be used to represent the Goddess and God. These vary in kind, number, and color. By kind, I mean what kind of candle—slender tapers are good if you wish to change your candle each time it's used, but a pillar candle is better suited to long-term use. A large pillar can be used as a "perpetual" flame, as you can renew it with votives.

When we get to the point in the ritual where we invoke the gods, we'll spend some more time getting into the theology of who and what the gods are. We can get started here by saying that the color and number of the candles that represent the gods (if you use any) should reflect your beliefs about them, as well as their relationship to each other. This is mostly seen in the stories told about the gods, and so we'll leave this to the Water section, where myth is addressed.

How we represent the gods is a *choice*, and more than one choice might be acceptable, consistent, and empowering.

Remember that in Wicca, it's okay to hold multiple beliefs; our metaphysics accepts multiple realities. We can accept a reality in which gods are each separate individuals, and also accept that, in the words of Dion Fortune, *"All gods are one god, and all goddesses are one goddess, and there is one initiator."*

When there is only one God, there is only one right, and everything else is wrong. Monotheism is also mono-truth, mono-real, and mono-moral. In Wicca, where deity is both immanent and plural, there can be plural truths, plural realities, and situational morality. We can know that our belief doesn't define an absolute, and we can still fully embrace that belief.

So I encourage you to look at all the different ways of representing the Goddess and God—as two, as many, as ultimately joined, and realize that, in a way, you might believe in *all* of them. You'll still have to choose *one* way to represent them on your altar—otherwise your altar will be hopelessly crowded, and your ritual hopelessly confused. The depiction of deity on your altar represents your focus, your paradigm, your narrative structure—not the Only Truth, because in Wicca, there is no such thing.

There are graceful ways of depicting multiple levels of reality. One elegant solution to the contrast between multiple deities and an underlying oneness is to use split candelabras. Three candles arising from a single stem is an attractive way of showing that Maiden, Mother, and Crone are truly one goddess underneath it all. There are even candles with multiple wicks to represent the same thing.

Some people believe that there is an underlying oneness—the Tao, if you will—behind or above any and all gods. This singularity can also be represented by a candle. Whoa, that's a lot of candles. Well, the Goddess and God don't *have* to be represented by candles—you might use idols or icons instead (or in addition). If that's the case, then a single "unity" candle between the idols makes a clear statement of belief in an uncluttered way.

The belief in a unifying single force is by no means universal, but it is extremely common. If we are all interconnected on a vast web, as described earlier, then the One is the web itself. This One, this Tao, is not a *personal* deity, such as the Goddess or Jehovah, it is the *context* that holds and surrounds all other deities. The Tao has been described as a river, through which all life flows. You and I, and the gods, are part of the web, the water that flows in the river—we are bound together by the river itself.

Shiva Nataraja

Most altars have idols (statuettes) or icons (pictures) or other representations of the gods as well as, or instead of, symbolic candles. Idolatry, the use of idols as objects of worship, has gotten a bad name for five thousand years; I think it's high time we Pagans reclaimed the word. Jewish thought, in particular, depicts idolatry as ignorant and small-minded—"how can someone think that a god is in that little bit of clay?" But in fact, idolatry represents a sophistication in thought, and a deep faith in the reality of the gods.

Idols aren't gods, but for the duration of ritual, they *become* gods, and they retain a bit of that essence the rest of the time. In ritual, we act as if the idol is in fact the deity, just as we act as if the picture or lock of hair is the person in a magical spell. The sophistication is in allowing our minds to be in several places at once, understanding that a deity is large and otherworldly, and also within ourselves, and also fully inhabiting the little statue before us. The faith is in understanding that it is utterly possible to be in the presence of deity, of trusting that yes, when I speak to this idol my words do, indeed, reach the god or goddess it depicts.

An idol is a visual and tactile conduit through which you contact a deity. As you use the idol, your contact becomes easier, both because you've become habituated to it, and because the idol has become charged with the energy of your worship. The deity becomes accustomed to reaching you through the idol, and to the feeling of that particular idol. With traditional idols, that have long histories behind them, such as Shiva Nataraja—the famous Lord of the Dance in a ring of flame—the deity is already familiar with that image, and accustomed to imbuing the image with His or Her energy. Offerings placed before the idol reach the deity, and boons asked of the idol are heard by the deity.

I suggest maintaining a relationship with your idols between rituals—keep them clean, in an honored place, pause before them to clear your mind as you walk past, and give them small offerings throughout the month—don't just bring them out at the full moon. Your contact with the gods can be on-going and in this way can deepen.

Magical Tools and Their Meaning

The essential tools of Witchcraft are the four elements and the four elemental tools. With those eight pieces, you have all the magical implements needed to cast a circle. There are more tools than these essential eight—some more practical, some almost entirely symbolic.

> *Earth and water, air and fire,*
> *Wand and pentacle and sword,*
> *Work ye unto our desire,*
> *Hearken ye unto our word!*
> *Cords and censer, scourge and knife,*
> *Powers of the witch's blade—*
> *Waken all ye unto life,*
> *Come ye as the charm is made!* [5]

I've often used this little poem as a mnemonic to make sure I've remembered everything for the altar. Let's go over each tool in the order presented above.

Earth and water, air and fire . . . You'll use something of each element, such as a dish of salt, soil or stones for Earth, a dish of water, incense or a feather or fan for Air, and a flame or burning incense for Fire. Together they represent the building blocks of the microcosm of the circle, the miniature reflection of the macrocosm of the universe. These building blocks are the origins of life; they're all that the gods needed to bring about creation, and so they're all *you* need to make a circle. They also represent balance, and it's vitally important, once you've decided to represent the elements, that you represent *all* the elements, in a balanced manner; Wicca walks in balance with the universal cycles.

It is these elements that bring their elemental quality into your circle. Without Water, your ritual will be heartless and cold, without a symbol of Air (the incense, a feather) your ritual will be thoughtless and ill-considered. Without Fire (the lit incense or a candle) your ritual will lack will; it will be aimless and meandering, and without Earth your ritual will not be grounded; it will be impractical and spacey.

Incense is especially important, and not just for its elemental correspondences. Throughout the world, and throughout history, incense has played an essential part of religious and magical ceremonies.

The Rising Smoke

It is an ancient belief of many Pagan peoples that our thoughts can reach the gods when carried to the heavens by rising smoke, either of incense or of sacred fires (Since Air is cognate with thought, this is especially fitting). The ancient Greeks, for example, believed that the gods "consumed" sacrifices by inhaling the smoke of burnt offerings—this had the advantage of allowing the people to eat the meat, while still appeasing the gods, and is typical of sacrifices throughout the ancient world. When an animal was sacrificed, it was first burnt at the sacred altar, with proper prayers being said. The smoke, aroma, and prayers all reached the gods and were considered acceptable sacrifices. A symbolic portion of meat was also generally set aside for the gods—either something inedible or unappetizing to humans, or something that the priesthood would have for breakfast the next day. The remainder of the slain animal was then feasted upon, so a large sacrifice called for quite a party.

Gods are often considered of finer substance than humans. The sense of smell is also considered fine, and so gods and other spirits respond very well to pleasant aromas, and pay careful heed to them. Incense, then, gets the gods' (or other beings') attention, and once gotten, carries our messages to them. (It is also easier, quicker and tidier, in most settings, than barbecuing steaks!)

If gods and spirits are attracted by pleasant scents, they are equally repelled by unpleasant ones. One of the basic principles of banishing, or exorcism of demons, unwanted spirits, or just plain bad luck, is to use incense to drive away the undesirable entities. Unfortunately, the incenses called for (such as asafoetida) will usually also drive away house pets, your best friend, and the mail carrier. They tend to produce both foul odors and huge quantities of billowing smoke.

A well-known example of the use of aroma for banishing is hanging fresh garlic about your neck to keep vampires away. I am not the first to point out that this technique keeps the living, as well as the undead, at a distance!

ALTERED STATES

Incense helps produce an altered state of consciousness, an important part of any ritual. The ordinary mind, focused as it is on job, laundry, and orthodontist bills, is in poor condition to participate in a spiritual or magical procedure. The early stages of ritual especially focus on altering the state of mind of the participants, allowing them to relax, to let go of worry, fear, and concern; to disconnect from these mundane matters and direct their attention inward. Some ceremonies may require intense concentration, others may call for excitement, still others may need a dreamlike trance—all of these are altered states.

The smell of incense cues the mind that it's magic time and begins the process of opening the psychic centers. This is particularly effective if a group or individual has one particular item, such as cinnamon or myrrh, which is always present in the incense mix used. The smell of myrrh (or whatever) will then act as a trigger, much like post-hypnotic suggestion; as soon as the aroma is sensed, the mind begins to become ready for ritual. The longer you practice using the same cue, the more automatic and effective this becomes.

This effect is not merely psychic or cerebral. Some of our most intense emotions are aroused by aroma—something of which perfume manufacturers are well aware. Aroma can arouse or relax, soothe or confuse, depending upon your memories and associations with that aroma. Many of us instantly feel warm and safe, for example, when we smell hot cocoa on a cold day.

Intoxicants can be used in incense, and this is a very ancient practice. The diffused smoke of an intoxicant produces a milder effect than smoking or eating it, and the intoxicant is fed continuously onto the censer, working like a time-release capsule. Some of the substances burned for this purpose are legal in the United States, and some are not, and I am neither recommending nor discouraging the practice. However, this should *never* be done without the informed consent of all participants.

Any incense, no matter what it contains, will very slightly impair breathing, making it shallower in some cases, in other cases unusually deep. (For this reason, great care should be taken when working with asthmatics or people subject to fainting spells.) Such altered breathing can parallel yogic exercises, such as the *Breath of Life*, in which the yogi's breathing techniques produce an altered state by changing the amount of oxygen that reaches the brain. (The Breath of Life involves extremely deep and rapid breathing, almost to the point of hyperventilation. It is often used in *ashrams*—Hindu monasteries—in order to begin the day in an invigorated state.)

Either an increase or decrease in oxygen will have a mind-expanding effect, providing it is done safely. Using incense is a mild, low-intensity way of experimenting with this effect. If you wish to begin such experimentation, start with very small portions of incense. Keep water nearby so that you can douse your incense if you become uncomfortable. Work with at least one other person present—if you become dizzy and accidentally knock something over, a partner can help. Don't try such experiments if you have any kind of breathing disorder or low blood pressure, or if you are pregnant (which tends to cause shortness of breath anyway).

Herbalism

Every herb, flower, and plant has its own planetary and elemental associations, and many have special magical properties as well. Some are protective (such as frankincense); some bring love (cardamom); and some ease depression, calm nerves, or draw money. All of these qualities can be taken into account when preparing incense—either for a specific ritual occasion or for general use.

For example, a coven might have a general purpose incense that combines herbs associated with fellowship, good feelings, and happy homes (perhaps catnip or hyacinth), as well as herbs or plants traditionally associated with magic and Witchcraft (such as ragwort), and perhaps a pinch of protection as well.

If you were doing a magical rite on behalf of someone having legal problems, you might start with cinnamon or citron for general well-being, add sassafras to draw money (often an issue when lawyers are involved), some hickory for its specific relation-ship to legal matters, and perhaps something associated with the astrological sign of the person in question. You would also want to make sure that, all symbolism aside, your in-cense still smelled good. Even sweet-smelling plants can smell bad when burned (and vice versa), and different parts of plants have different aromas. If you want to use a par-ticular plant, and don't like the way the leaves smell when burned, try the stem or roots.

It is important to remember that you are not just using the physical qualities of the herb when you burn incense during a ceremony, you're using its *associations* as well. A particular leaf may be healing in a tea, but have no physical effect at all when burned. It is still *psychically* associated with healing and could be helpful in incense. If you've stuffed a poppet with certain herbs because of their magical properties, when conse-crating or using the poppet, the incense could contain those same herbs. In both the poppet and the incense, it is the associative property of the herbs that is being used.

Once you've gotten the idea of using herbal properties and associations in your in-cense, it becomes a matter of a little research and a little creativity. For example, sup-pose you were doing a magical rite to save the whales—your incense should contain something associated with the sea. If you were casting a spell to protect the ecology of a particular region, your incense should use plants native to that region—cactus flower is not going to help you end a drought, but seaweed might. If you were meditating in order to send healing energy to someone suffering from glaucoma, herbs associated with the eyes should be used. The possibilities are endless.

In summary, incense combines four important effects: The *elemental* properties of Air and Fire; the magical and spiritual use of *rising smoke*, which reaches deities, spirits, and other entities; the psychological and emotional ability to *alter consciousness*; and the specific physical, psychic, and magical *qualities of herbs*, which can affect anything in the environment that comes in contact with those herbs. These different effects make incense one of the most powerful and important components of any ritual.

Wand and pentacle and sword . . . Three of the four elemental tools are mentioned in this line, the fourth is the cup. These tools were discussed in chapter 2. One of the things these tools represent is gender polarity, which deserves a new paragraph.

Wiccans see life as a product of polarity—the union of opposites. Oneness, the un-differentiated whole, is everything and nothing; there is no up because there is no down; there is no distinction at all. Mythically, the first distinction, the first "other," is

Yin and Yang

the Goddess and the God; They are the original pair of connected opposites. Scientifically, matter and energy is a more likely pair. In religion, the best known polarity is yin and yang; the opposites that are intrinsically and infinitely connected to each other. Yin has a bit of yang and vice versa, as seen in the dot of opposite color in each side of the symbol. Darkness contains light and light contains darkness. Furthermore, every pair of two things has its own yin and yang relationship. If two things are dark, the lighter of the two becomes the yang of the pair, so that even a yin thing is yang in the right context. Polarity is also a system that does not define one pole as good and the other bad; both are necessary and equal.

Male and female is the biological bottom line of polarity. We perceive gender before we perceive almost anything else about a person. That isn't sexism or stereotyping, it's a fundamental and universal reality. We can know this, and still choose not to stereotype. In Wicca, we speak of the Goddess and the God in essentially the same way that a Taoist speaks of yin and yang: the Goddess taking the female, yin characteristics and the God, the male and yang. It's important to remember that this is an attempt to understand a universal pattern, and not an analysis of men and women. Men may be from Mars and women from Venus, but both are from both the Goddess and the God. It would be foolish, and falsely restrictive, to try to fit complex human beings into the broad categories of a polarity system. Instead, we must view our internal polarities as the Taoists view yin and yang—each of us contains a part of our opposite at all times.

Polarity has a profound impact on Wiccan thought, because it is part of the perceived structure of the universe. It also has a great deal of magical impact. Batteries and magnets are mundane demonstrations of the importance and power of polarity. Keeping opposites in perfect balance makes the energy harmonious and brings both types of power to bear, creating a whole greater than the sum of its parts. Separating opposites creates tension and anticipation, raising the hairs on the back of the neck. Most ritual uses the harmony a lot more than the tension, but both can be valuable.

The four elemental tools are a perfectly balanced set, and it is no coincidence that, in the Tarot, the Magician is shown having all four tools on his altar—the true Mage must be able to master all four.

The *sword* is masculine and male; it is phallic in shape and aggressive in nature. Steel and iron are considered male metals, and if the handle is wooden it should be a male wood, such as oak. The meaning of the sword is rooted in power and mastery. A sword represents rulership, and so it is said that "whoever holds the sword rules the circle." Of course, a sword also *cuts*, and so a sword is used to divide one thing from another. In Wicca, both the athame and the sword are traditionally double-edged, signifying that a sword "cuts both ways," and keeping us mindful of the dangers and abuses of power, even while we wield it—power must, in the Wiccan view, be accompanied by equal quantities of compassion.

The *wand* is feminine and male. It is phallic in shape, but passive in nature. Traditionally, the wand is made of a female wood (like willow). It is used in a less aggressive way than the sword; the sword summons by command and the wand summons by request. The wand balances and tempers the sword, teaching that there are other ways to use power besides directly and forcefully, and that the feminine can still thrust itself out into the world.

The *cup* is feminine and female. It is female in shape, receptive in function, and traditionally made of a female material (silver, pewter, or clay). A ceramic cup should be a female color (blue, silver, and pink are examples). The cup is the tool most associated with the Goddess, and in the ceremony of Cakes and Wine, it is the tool by which blessing is transmitted. The purpose of the cup is to receive, to bless and to share. The cup symbolizes love.

The *pentacle* is masculine and female. Its roundness is feminine, but it is flat, so it lacks the womb-like receptivity of the cup. It is traditionally made of a male material— gold or brass—or painted a male color (gold, brown, or green). The pentacle acts as a counterpart to the cup in the ceremony of Cakes and Wine—holding the cakes while the cup holds the wine. It teaches us that the masculine can still be receptive.

Cords and censer, scourge and knife . . . The *cords* are used by a minority of groups, usually for binding or measuring. In binding, the cord is wrapped around something as a spell of restriction, or to let it loose later. One such "binding" is done by making a knot; you "tie the spell up" in the knot, and then, when it's time for the spell to reach its fruition, the knot is dramatically loosened. There are many such spells; it is even said that medieval witches knotted strong winds into cords to be taken to sea. One loosened one knot for a light breeze, two knots for a stronger breeze, and so on. Untying nine knots on such a cord would bring a devastating storm. Cords can be used to measure lengths in the circle (circumference, diameter) and are important to those groups which emphasize sacred geometry (such as used by the Masons). By making a cord of a specific length (which was presumably measured by other means), you have a consecrated tool in the circle that can be used to measure its length, half its length, and so on. In some traditions, cords are also used to denote rank or degree, and are worn as a kind of insignia in the circle (one cord for first degree, two cords for second degree, etc.).

The *censer* contains incense and combines Air with Fire. It is both male and female, as it is a container, and also rises out into the world.

Like the cords, the *scourge* is a tool that is rarely used, although often the subject of whispered conversation. It is a small whip, not unlike a cat o' nine tails. It is used to simulate the "ordeal," or passage by fire, that has been associated with initiations cross-culturally, for thousands of years. The symbol of suffering in Wicca is a potent one, especially since Wicca is often thought of as a hedonistic religion. How can a symbol of pain fit in with a religion which says "All acts of love and pleasure are my rituals?"[6] The answer lies in the religious view that encompasses and embraces *all* of nature.

There are many religions that view God as wholly good, and therefore have to deal with a "problem of evil." Evil is either the product of another entity (Satan) or of error in human beings (sin or accumulated karma). Wicca, however, embraces nature and natural cycles in all their permutations. Earth provides us with a great deal of pleasure and sensuality, and we celebrate that, but She also provides us with tragedy—earthquakes, droughts, and disasters—and we embrace these as well, and even celebrate them as much as we are able. We recognize that the entire cycle—from day to night, from summer to winter, and from pleasure to pain—is part of Her sacred circle.

We also recognize that life is full of "growing pains." My son is at an age where he frequently has deep aches in the long bones of his legs—aches from getting so much taller so fast. We accept these pains as best we can; I try to teach him how to ride out the discomfort and move past it. In giving birth to him, I had my share of pain as well; pain I embraced willingly as a side effect of the effort and power of bringing life into the world. It's not true that nothing good comes easily—there are lots of small pleasures that are easy to have. But none of the really *big* good things come easily—not growing up, not giving birth, not falling in love, and not initiation into the ways of the Goddess.

The scourge, despite the power of its symbology, has fallen into nearly complete disuse in the Craft today. Only a small percent of covens possess a scourge, and most use it merely as a symbol to place on the altar.

The *knife (athame[7])* is the primary and essential Witch's tool. The athame is a black-handled, double-edged blade. Its symbolism is almost identical to the sword; the athame can be used for any function of the sword. The difference is that the sword relates to the coven, and the athame relates to the Witch. The athame is the tool of the individual, and in addition to all its other symbolism, denotes that any one Witch alone can cast a circle and do magic. For this reason, many Witches keep their athames with them all or most of the time, even sleeping with them under their pillows.[8] The athame channels the Witch's energies, extends her powers, and focuses her will. In many cases where your hands alone might be used, the athame can be used instead.

MORE TOOLS

It is useful to have a tool specifically for cutting. Most Wiccans consider it unthinkable to cut with the athame, which would dilute its specific and vital purpose—that of directing energy. So many Witches use a *white-handled knife* (which is single-edged) or a *sickle* for cutting herbs, trimming wicks, and other functions that straddle the border between ritual and practical.

Another "practical" tool occasionally seen is the *aspergillum*, something used specifically for sprinkling water. You can tie a bundle of fresh herbs together for this purpose, or even use whole flowers, but some people use a more permanent device. A brush can be used, or a special handle to which the herbs or flowers are attached freshly each time.

The *staff* is to the wand as the sword is to the athame—it's the large-scale version. Many people today are uncomfortable with using the athame to represent the male principle, especially during parts of the ceremony that have specifically phallic symbolism. They use the wand for many of the purposes I'll assign the athame to—as the primary tool to direct energy, as the male symbol, and to cast the circle. There are two arguments for this. First, a knife is too harsh and violent a symbol, it is "killing a fly with an elephant gun," and it has even been called patriarchal. Why symbolize the phallus as a weapon, as if the only way to be sexual is by force? This, at any rate, is what some people say. I see the athame as forceful *energy*, like adrenaline, and not as weaponry (a wand can be a weapon too, after all), but others disagree. Furthermore, the argument goes, if you're going to represent the phallus, wouldn't it be better to use something that could actually be *used* for penetration? I suppose that part of it is merely aesthetic. For myself, I see a knife as a direct, visceral symbol—obvious and in-your-face. The wand doesn't strike me that way at all—one could look at a wand and not know what it's for.

If you wish to use the wand as the primary male energy tool, then you might prefer to have a staff for the coven instead of a sword.

Another tool used by some is the *bell*. Sound, especially beautiful sound, *especially* musical sound, is said to reach the gods on a higher frequency in much the same way that aroma does. Sound was considered to have a higher vibrational rate than matter long before the science of sound was understood. Sound is considered by many to be that which caused creation to be: "In the beginning was the Word." The Hindus even honor a goddess who is the original sound that created the universe—*Vac*. Indeed, Hinduism is especially concerned with the mystical power of sound, and the Aum is believed to be the original sound that caused creation; it contains all other sound and has many mystical properties, which is why chanting it can bring enlightenment. In Tibetan Buddhism, the bowl gong is used for the mystical qualities imparted by its tones, and the bell is an object for deep meditation. In Catholicism, the bell has the power of beginning and ending, as in "Strike the bell, open the book, light the candle."

The bell is used in conjunction with summoning; the lovely sound is attractive to gods and other entities, attractive both in the sense of being appealing and in the sense of attracting attention. The strike of a bell can be a call to wake up and pay attention on a spiritual as well as auditory level. It is therefore also effective to mark beginnings, endings, and other clear-cut transitions.

Most Wiccans will find a *broom* necessary, if for no other reason than its long association with witches and witchcraft. Like a staff, a broom is best propped up next to the altar, unless your altar is exceptionally large. A broom has many uses; like a staff, it can be seen as a large wand, a representation of the male principle. You could use it to cast the circle if you are orienting your male polarity around the wand instead of the blade.

The broom has a long history as a phallic symbol. The hobby horse or riding pole was part of an ancient fertility rite, in which women took a pole or staff, with one end carved as a phallus, placed it between their legs, and rode it in the fields. This use of *imitative magic* showed the fields how they were expected to behave. The magic imitated the proper action, thus encouraging it—the women behaved in a fertile manner, and the fields presumably got the point. Later, though, the Church's influence spread, and it became scandalous, even dangerous, to have such an obviously Pagan implement as a phallic pole in the house. So the phallus end was covered over with broom or straw, and an incriminating tool became an ordinary household object. The next time you see a picture of a witch riding on broomstick, remember that the sweeping end belongs up between the legs, not on the ground. (The horse-head on a child's hobby horse covered the same lewd carving.)

Riding the broom, then, is a fertility rite; a rite of increase. It is associated especially with the holiday of Beltane. Riding the broom is also associated with deep trance, as the witches' flight of medieval legend was apparently a hallucinatory trip. Old recipes for flying ointment contain hallucinogenic ingredients, leading many scholars to believe that tales of witches flying were tales of drug-induced trance. The broom could therefore be used in conjunction with trance or astral travel. (I don't know anyone who does this, but it *could* be.)

Ankh

The most common use of the broom as a magical tool, though, is for sweeping. Sweeping is a powerful metaphor for removing the unwanted, for cleansing, and for starting fresh. Sweeping the circle can be used to remove unwanted influences, be they psychic, astral, or psychological. Sweeping as part of a spell can remove something unwanted from your life—a symbol of the unwanted can be placed in the circle and swept out. The use of the broom for sweeping is most associated with the holiday of Imbolg (February Eve), which is the time of the year for spring cleaning. Clean the house physically and finish by sweeping the perimeters (inside and out) with a consecrated broom, then sprinkle and cense.

The final use of the broom is to jump over it at a handfasting, symbolizing the couple beginning their new life together.

The last tool we'll discuss is not commonly used, although from time to time you'll hear of it: The *ankh*. An ankh looks like a cross with a loop at the top. In ancient Egypt, the ankh was a sacred symbol of life. Like a pentagram, the ankh could be drawn, inscribed, or sculpted. In Wicca, we distinguish between the pentagram, which is a symbol, and the pentacle, which is the corresponding object. There is no such distinction with the ankh; a necklace with the symbol, or a tool made in the shape of the symbol is still called just an ankh. (I guess "ankhacle" sounds funny.)

Some Wiccans put the ankh on their altar simply to represent life. In groups that use five elements (four plus Spirit), an ankh can be used as a symbol for spirit (a quartz crystal might also be used). The symbol is often seen as representing the union of Goddess and God—the loop at the top is yonic, or womb-like, and represents the Goddess. The vertical line is phallic and represents the God. The horizontal line is their union or is a symbol of knowledge.[9]

Using Your Magical Things

What do you do with your magical tools when you're not doing magic? An answer to this seemingly simple question is based upon your understanding of what Wicca is and how energy works, and will affect a number of different areas. Basically the question is this: Is sacredness something to be set aside, or is sacredness something to be brought into daily life? This question is practical as well as theological; will it *work* to treat magical things in an ordinary way?

As in so many cases, I don't have an either/or answer. My own practice isn't one hundred percent in either camp. The question is nuanced, and instances often have to be reviewed individually. What it boils down to is this: Are you sacralizing the mundane, or are you demeaning the sacred?

Previously, I recommended using your idols between rituals—but I recommended using them in a way that is reverent and empowering—not as doorstops! Perhaps you, like me, have *many* idols in your home—I have at least one in every room, and even in my car, in large part because I like to think of the gods wherever I go. Obviously, not every one of the thirty-plus deity figures I have has a special altar or nook; many are simply on shelves and would look like knick-knacks to the casual observer. Perhaps I sometimes treat them that way as well, walking past them without pausing to think about how special they are. Often enough, though, their simple presence can awaken my inner connection to the gods. One trick I've learned is to move them around—don't leave the same ones in the same spots for more than about six months—so you don't become inured to the sight of them; they don't fade into the background.

Idols, however, are in some ways an exception. Between rituals, I'm not hiding them away, but the only nonmagical use you could accuse me of putting them to is decorative—they're simply visible. What about things that actually have a mundane purpose? These range from knives to jewelry to goblets to robes, and each case is a bit different. But before discussing the specifics, let's look at the generalities of both sides, starting with reasons to treat magical tools in an ordinary way.

Wiccans are the inheritors of a tradition of folk magic which was ordinary, daily, and accepted. The "kitchen witch" cooked her magical potions in the same cauldron in which she prepared her dinner, and made little distinction between the two. She was practical and frugal, and having two of *anything* where one would do would have struck her as wasteful. The idea of separating magic from daily life would be far too "fancy" for her; folk magic was (and is) efficient and to the point.

Our folklore of the Burning Times tells us that hiding magical tools as ordinary household implements was protective coloring, and many modern Wiccans wish to emulate such customs in honor of this portion of our heritage. One example of this "hide in plain sight" policy is the broomstick, as discussed earlier.

So, the first reason to treat magical tools in an ordinary way is as part of our connection to our heritage—there's that web again; many strands of which are those of history. Another reason is for the power and blessing it brings.

Objects acquire magical and spiritual energies. In fact, objects acquire *all sorts* of energy. The psychic art of *psychometry* is what's going on when someone gathers impressions and information from an object—often a piece of jewelry. People, events, even places, have a personality, a "fingerprint" that gets left behind. Part of this can be explained by our understanding of the web that connects us all, but there's more to it than that. Different things absorb energy at different rates—minerals (gems, metals, stones) are more absorbent than wood or plastic—this leads me to believe that there is a *physical* effect. It may be something in the aura; it may be bio-energetic. The answer isn't known and the question isn't likely to produce many research grants. Whatever it is, *something*, something palpable and real, is left behind on objects of all kinds, and magical ones in particular.

The residual charge on an object can be empowering, or soothing, or energizing; in short, it can be useful in day-to-day life. The necklace you wore in circle on Saturday is still vibrant with the blessings of the Goddess on Monday, and if you wear it to work, it could conceivably improve your day.

What then are the arguments *against* using magical objects in mundane life? Primarily, they revolve around this question: Is taking mundane advantage of the magical charge on an object using it or squandering it?

Using the charge on a magical object dissipates that charge. Remember that the charge comes, in part, from the web of connections; it has strands that connect it to magical and spiritual events. If you use the object in other ways, it establishes additional connections, to nonmagical events. This dilutes the intensity of the connection. Look at it this way: Suppose I put a quarter in a jar every time I used a tool for magic, and a pebble in the same jar every time I used the same tool for a mundane purpose. If I use my tool only for magic, every time I close my eyes and reach into the jar, I'll find money. The more pebbles I put into the jar, the less likely I am to pull out something valuable later.

Part of an object's magical power also comes from the psychological focus it creates. When you use your athame, you know that this is your quintessential magical tool, you *know* it. That knowledge does two things: First, it makes the occasion of its use special, like bringing out the good china on holidays. Second, it acts as a post-hypnotic trigger, telling your mind that it's time for the magic to start, time to establish that connection to the gods. Both of these effects are diminished or lost if the tool is used between rituals.

So, what do you do? Surely both arguments are reasonable, but they contradict each other. My solution has been to set up a kind of hierarchy of exclusivity. The most important tools are one hundred percent exclusive—the athame, sword, and wand would *never* be used under mundane circumstances. Some things can be used *in proximity to* ritual—I can continue to drink out of my ritual goblet after the circle has closed (although it is clean and untouched until the ritual). I can continue to wear my ritual robes after the ceremony is over, and I might bring ritual garb to a Pagan festival, wearing it in a religious but non-ritual context.

Finally, in order to bring the magic out into my workaday life, I don't bring ritual things *out* of the circle, I bring mundane things *in.* I will wear (and encourage others to wear) mundane jewelry, as well as my magical jewelry, into the circle. This allows me to use a bit of magical blessing in my daily life without compromising the integrity of my tools.

Related to the idea of using magical things in mundane life is the idea of replacing disposable magical things—like candles and salt. Do you dispose of candles after a single use, so that a fresh candle is used for each ritual, or do you reuse the candles? Some of the same arguments apply; a reused candle is acquiring a build-up of energy, and is becoming connected to the ritual space. On the other hand, a fresh candle increases the sense of specialness of the occasion, and the unwrapping of the new candles can be part of the post-hypnotic cuing. I know people who reuse candles right down to their stubs, and others who are firm about purchasing or making fresh ones for every ceremony. Both concepts are justified, and it's up to you which concept you'll choose. Personally, I am in favor of reusing whenever it doesn't seem shoddy to do so. I don't see the virtue in having a half dozen candles to throw away, or use outside of circle,[10] every month. I don't think a religion devoted to Mother Earth should be quite so wasteful; it's simply not ecological.

Fire

There are several mystical points that need to be covered in this section. First of all, let's talk about the mystical qualities of cleaning.

Mystic Cleansing

There's a lot of cleaning in preparation for a circle, from doing your housework to the ritual bath or basin. I use both external and internal cleaning as an opportunity for meditation. Housework is repetitive and often mindless. To scrub something involves a repeated motion with little or no thought involved. Such mindless and rhythmic conditions are perfect for meditation, for letting your mind go into a quiet state where it can find the small, still voice. Here are some questions for meditation during preparatory cleaning:

- What does it mean to be clean?
- If I clean the outside (my house, my body), what does it mean to the inside (my spirit, my heart)? How can I clean the inside?
- What is there within me that needs to be cleaned?
- What would it feel like, look like, be like, if I were cleansed in spirit?

Meditation for ritual cleansing (the bath, the basin, the anointing, or smudging) should be more affirmative. Tell yourself, "Now I am clean, now I am purified," and ask the small, still voice what that feels like. By dividing meditation into these two phases—the questioning and then the affirming—you can truly experience the mystical aspects of ritual cleansing and purification.

Why Can't I Wear My Watch?

What is timelessness, and why does it matter? First, we have to accept that time is an illusion; something upon which both physicists and mystics agree. Time is a construct by which we organize our experience of events in a linear fashion.

Let's compare time to space. Space is experienced all at once—when you look at a room, you visually take in all of the space of that room simultaneously. But a blind person, who cannot see the room, takes the space in linearly—one piece at a time. As the blind person enters the room, he experiences first the doorway, then the coffee table, then the couch. His brain organizes these items in a linear fashion—if he was born blind, and cannot cross-reference the experience with a memory of sight, he will not come up with a mental concept of the room "happening" all at once. In blind people whose sight was surgically restored, this turns out to be a huge, often insurmountable problem. The newly-sighted person simply cannot accept, cannot get his brain around the idea, that space is happening all at once. Yet to the sighted, the simultaneity of space is a given.

Imagine, now, that there's a "sight" by which *time* can be perceived as simultaneous. We lack that sight, but it exists. Our brains cannot quite wrap around the imaginative task of picturing time as simultaneous, but let's just postulate that only a form of time-blindness prevents it. If time *is* simultaneous, it certainly explains a lot of the occult arts, doesn't it? Clairvoyance is perceiving something that is actually happening now. It's in the linear future, but it's part of the simultaneous now. Past life recollection is actually *simultaneous* life *perception*. And magic is effecting a change in a future that *doesn't really exist.*

The shift is huge, and we will only achieve it in bits and pieces. The circle will still have a beginning, middle, and end. Things will be done *before* or *after* other things. We cannot fully escape time, but we can dampen it.

When the circle is cast it is placed "between the worlds," meaning between the world of mortals (us) and the realm of the gods. Time does not exist in this mystic space, which falls between the cracks of normal perception. This is so important, and so very effective once achieved, that we will make all kinds of extra effort on its behalf.

We will ban time in the circle by not allowing watches, covering any clocks that are fixed in the room (wall clocks, displays on VCRs), and forbidding conversation which references time specifically (just try to keep dates and times out of conversation; it's okay to refer to circles in the past or future).

Sacrifice

The final bit of mysticism that is involved in preparing the circle has to do with the fresh, cut flowers. I was pretty specific about that, but I snuck it past you without an explanation. The explanation is simple but profound; the flowers are a sacrifice.

Mahatma Gandhi considered ritual without sacrifice a sin. Sacrifice is deeply mystical because it involves your most intimate connection with the gods. What you give to the gods and how it is received is a communion far beyond the ritual forms.

There are many ways to sacrifice to the gods, and many kinds of sacrifice are acceptable. Everything from fasting to celibacy can be seen as a sacrifice.

At one time in the ancient past, life itself was considered the most proper and appropriate sacrifice. Every religion performed a life sacrifice at some point in its past, and some still do today. In Santeria, a blood sacrifice is still made, whereas in Christianity, the spiritual surrogate for the sacrifice of the blood of Christ is wine. Behind each of these sacrifices is the concept of surrogacy; an animal's blood for our own, wine for Christ's. The Wiccan surrogate sacrifice is the bouquet of flowers. These flowers are cut, they will die (a plant, in soil, is not a sacrifice).

Religious sacrifice is not an expression of bloodthirstiness. Rather, the worshippers are expressing an ultimate sort of willingness. "Here is everything I have, everything I am." Another part of sacrifice is that we become participants in that part of the life cycle which is most distasteful to us.

As Wiccans, we are supposed to embrace the entire cycle of birth-death-rebirth. But we're only human, and the death part tends to be a bit sticky. When we lose someone we love, or when we face our own mortality, it's hard to achieve any kind of perspective. In any religion, a loss of a loved one can bring about a deep-seated doubt; a "dark night of the soul." We can curse the gods, we can reject their ways because those ways took our loved one from us. In any religion, a sacrifice is an act of siding *with* the gods, of fully accepting their ways, and demonstrating that acceptance by participating in them. We do what the gods do when we sacrifice life, therefore giving our spiritual approval to the fact of death.

We are civilized people, so the sacrifices we make are necessarily symbolic, but somewhere there should be life, whether real (the flowers) or surrogate (communion wine). We must sacrifice, though, both to give deeply and to accept that the gods take. Sacrifice is at the core of a spiritual life, it is what differentiates religion from self-indulgence.

Water

There's not much mythology apparent in setting up the circle, but it's there, underlying the decision as to how the gods are represented on the altar. In order to decide how to represent Them, you have to know what story(ies) you'll be using as your mythic focus.

Who Are the Gods Being Represented?

If you're using candles, you could simply have one candle for each. This could symbolize that God and Goddess are balanced—yin and yang, eternal opposites and complements. In a group that emphasizes polarity, as many Wiccan groups do, this would be a fitting representation. The story behind it would be one of the many that tells of the marriage or romance of the Goddess and God.

If you had one or more candles for the Goddess, with none for the God, that would not represent polarity, but instead might represent Her primacy among deities. It wouldn't necessarily mean that you don't believe in, and use, polarity, but it would place the emphasis differently. You'd focus on Goddess as Original Source, the Prime Mover, the infinite from which matter emerged. Hindus know the story of the birth of Devi, the Goddess; when the universe was threatened by a terrible demon, all the male gods took a bit of their inner power, their *Shakti*, and they combined them together. The Shakti is a female energy that is the creative and energizing force within all that lives. The combined Shakti of all the gods was mixed by Shiva to become Devi—the Goddess. A flame for the Goddess alone would be a Devi flame.

On the other hand, a single candle representing the God would emphasize *His* singular role in Creation. It is He, many believe, who first worshiped the Goddess, creating *separateness*. It is said that in the beginning everything was a single, undifferentiated whole. Then the God, because he so loved the Goddess, separated Himself from the oneness in order to adore Her. This was the Big Bang, the beginning of individuality, which was born out of Her, but caused by Him. This is what Aleister Crowley meant when he said *"I am divided for love's sake, for the chance of union. This is the creation of the world, that the pain of division is as nothing, and the joy of dissolution, all."*[11]

The God, in other words, is the original spark, the seed, the igniter of the flame of life which then gestates within the Goddess. It is fitting, in this context, to represent the God with a single flame, and even to light the Goddess candle(s) from this flame.

This isn't the only way to view the God. Often, the God and Goddess are paired as double and triple; the two-faced god and the triple goddess together combine to create the five points of the pentagram.

The Dual God

The two-faced god appears in numerous guises in numerous myths. The simplest version is Janus, the Roman god who literally has two faces. His image is found in doorways, and the month of January is named for him. Janus is the god who teaches us that every beginning has an end, and every end is a new beginning. At New Year's, he faces both ways, ending the old year and ushering in the new.

Another example of the two faces of the New Year god is seen in the secular image of old Father Time/old year and the baby New Year.

The dying and resurrecting god is also seen as dual; death and rebirth, dying and born; these two phases of a single god are often seen in myth, from Tammuz to Jesus. There are also many pairs of gods who are seasonal faces of the same god. Whether we call them the Oak King and the Holly King, the Stag God and the Bull God, or the Bright Lord and the Dark Lord, Celtic and Germanic mythology in particular is full of stories of two gods, sometimes brothers, who must do battle twice a year. Depending upon the version of the story, these battles can be at the Solstices, the Equinoxes, or at Beltane and Samhain. Often they are rivals for the affections of an earth goddess. Pwyll and Havgan are an example from the Welsh Mabinogion. Havgan is the "bright lord" who must be destroyed by the representative of the Underworld in order for winter to come. Of course, in six months' time, the battle will be re-fought, with a different outcome. The rivalry between King Arthur and Lancelot is, perhaps, an echo of this ancient tale. The Holly and Oak Kings are vegetative gods, each ruling His season. They are both lovers of the Earth Mother, who switches Her allegiance; whichever god has Her favor rules the climate of the Earth.

Yet another dual god is the Red God/Green God duality. Both Holly King and Oak King are vegetative; the Red and Green gods represent the ancient rivalry between the blood red of the hunt and the green of the crops. The Red God is the Stag; he lives in the woods, in secret places, both hunted and a fierce combatant. The Green God is the Bull—domesticated, pastoral. Or, he is no animal at all, he is the grain itself—John Barleycorn. The conflict between these two gods is there in the murder of Abel the shepherd by Cain the farmer; their fight was over the kind of offerings that Jehovah preferred—flesh or crop (in Genesis, God liked flesh). Both the Red and Green gods hang on the fence between life and death, and speak to how we feed ourselves and sustain life by killing, and it is these gods whom we kill—the Red when we eat meat, and the Green when we eat grain.

The Triple Goddess

The idea that the Goddess has a triune nature is one of the best-known Craft beliefs. The triple goddess has a lot of correspondences; let's start with the well-known Maiden, Mother, and Crone.

There are Wiccan teachers that will tell you that *all* goddesses are one of these three; that is simply not so. Maiden, Mother, and Crone correspond to moon phases, to a woman's life cycle, and especially to her *sexual* life cycle, but not all goddesses can be fit into these groups.

The Maiden is the *waxing* (increasing) moon—from just past new to just before full. She is all that is youthful, unrealized, and growing. She is sometimes seen as pre-sexual (pre-adolescent), as virginal, or as voluntarily celibate (like Artemis). In fact, Maiden sexuality *can* be active, but it is playful and uncommitted. Youth, energy, and freedom are Her primary qualities. Her negative qualities are vanity, selfishness and immaturity. In a woman's life cycle, She is seen variously as being a girl before menarche, a girl or young woman who is a virgin, or a girl or woman who has never had a child or been married.

The Mother is the full moon. The roundness of the full moon suggests pregnancy, also fullness and wholeness. The Mother is, of course, maternal. As a mother, she is fully responsible to another, her love is committed and unselfish. Her sexual nature can be lustful and passionate, but oriented toward partnership, whereas the Maiden is oriented toward independence. The Mother's negative aspects are as numerous as her positive aspects, and as complex. She can be devouring, jealous, and cruel. Since whole books have been written about the Mother, it is difficult to cover Her qualities in a paragraph or two. Most people agree that the worship of a Mother Goddess is the oldest worship known to humanity. Our mothers are our original sources of nourishment, comfort and life, and so it is natural for deity to first be imagined as Mother. But, as any Freudian will tell you, the incredible power that Mother has to bring goodness in life is naturally viewed ambivalently. The mother who loves also smothers and devours. The Mother who brings life can also deny life. In a woman's life, she is the central part of life, encompassing the entire period of sexual maturity.

The Crone is the *waning* (decreasing) moon—from just past full to just before new. As the moon shrinks and grows darker, we are reminded of that part of life which is closer to the end than the beginning; we face our own mortality. In a woman's life cycle, the Crone is post-menopausal; as such, she is freed of familial responsibilities. She is wise but removed, a teacher and counselor. The Crone is old age, wisdom, acceptance, and folklore. Her negative aspects are bitterness and illness.

There are goddesses, primarily Greek goddesses, who have three faces that directly correspond to Maiden, Mother, and Crone, though this is by no means universal. Hera was celebrated in three ages: the young Hera was known as "Hebe" or "Green Hera," and at her annual festival, the Heraion, she was said to bathe in a magical spring and thereby renew her virginity. Hera in her womanliness was known as "The Perfect One." Eventually this "wifely" aspect came to be distorted in tales of jealousy and vindictiveness, but those stories were written long after her rituals were no longer popular. Finally, Hera became "Theia" and retreated into widowhood. She abandoned everyone, including her worshippers, and went to live alone in the wilderness. At Argos this was celebrated in a festival that ended in her rebirth as Hebe.[12]

There are also numerous goddesses who are tripled in other ways; sometimes three the same, sometimes not, as well as goddesses with triple "responsibilities" or life phases. Brigid, The Morrigan, and Hecate are examples of triple goddesses of myth.

Honored Guests

The primary metaphor that will carry us through the entire ritual, beginning at preparation, is that you will be welcoming special guests into your home. On Earth, you may be having other Witches come to your home for a circle, but in mythic reality, in Water, you are inviting guests from other realms. The ritual can be seen as a special affair being thrown in honor of the gods.

We can judge a lot of what we do based upon how well we're treating our guests, and it's a metaphor we all understand very well. For example, look at the issue of time once more: Will your honored guests feel utterly welcome if you watch the clock to see if it's time yet for them to leave? Expressing impatience with the proceedings is improper when viewed as the act of a gracious host.

Emotions and Time (Again)

In terms of the emotional goal of the preparation stage, you're aiming for the kind of relaxed calm that will lead to a successful ritual experience. That calm can be playful and light, or serious and anticipatory, but tension, irritation, and distraction should be banished. The goal of the various preparations that eliminate distraction—such as turning off phones, locking doors, and removing clocks—is to maintain the psychological state that readies the mind and heart for a meeting with the gods.

The desired emotional state brings us back a final time to the ban on timepieces. Clock-watching is generally the act of someone who wants to be somewhere else, and that sense of dissatisfaction, if allowed to gain even the slimmest of footing, will begin to permeate the ritual. Noticing the time is the opposite of "be here now," and pulls you out of the mental and spiritual state needed for ritual. Deadlines make people anxious, and ritual is a place for serenity. Have you ever tried to take a nap when you knew that you had to be up again in fifteen (or thirty or forty-five) minutes? Most people can't do it, at least not on their own. You could set an alarm, or ask someone to wake you, but if you count on waking yourself, you'll never relax enough to fall asleep.

Grounding and Centering

"Grounding and Centering" is the first step of the ritual proper, and can be done just before or just after the Declared Opening. Here's why it can go either place: You can argue that *no* part of the ritual should occur before it has officially begun, and I'll grant that you make sense. To 'begin before you begin' is confusing at least. Also, if you do a reversal of this step (which is discussed later), you'll do so just before the ending—the opposite position, just after the opening, is the most balanced. On the other hand, it is the Grounding step that prepares the mind, body, and spirit for *everything* that is about to occur; everything *including* the Declared Opening. Participants are more receptive after Grounding and Centering, and more responsive to the opening cue. For that reason, I prefer to do Grounding and Centering first, and have the Declared Opening serve to end the Grounding and Centering. However, whichever order you choose is fine.

The phrase "Grounding and Centering" is so commonplace that I'm using it to avoid confusion. However, in a group ritual, there is a third part to the process, and the step should more correctly be called "Grounding, Centering, and Merging."

It doesn't make sense to discuss *how* this step is done until we discuss what it means, so we begin with Air.

Air

First, let's break out our step into its component parts:

Grounding—Getting in touch with the Earth.

Centering—Getting in touch with ourselves.

Merging—Getting in touch with each other.

Grounding

Grounding is the name for the process of mentally or psychically linking oneself to the Earth. It involves a connection that can be experienced as physical; we feel our bodies connected to the ground beneath us, almost as though we were rooted to the spot. Grounding is a basic and necessary first step in ritual, meditation, prayer, and psychic work of any kind. It is also useful in many ordinary situations.

A friend who was involved in the New Age movement once remarked to me that she'd observed far too many people who focused on meditations involving the top of their heads. She said these people were only interested in reaching for outer space—so it was no wonder they were such airheads! She had begun teaching people to begin with their feet first, and only then "reach for the clouds." She was talking about grounding.

Grounding helps psychically sensitive people "stay in touch." By setting up a feet-first, physical connection to the Earth, they don't feel painfully buffeted about by their sensitivities. It helps the emotionally sensitive person maintain an even keel, as well.

People who routinely meditate, participate in rituals, or in healings, without first grounding are likely to experience a number of unpleasant side effects. Headaches, exhaustion, and loss of appetite are common. In fact, some people, over long periods of time, can become pale and emaciated, as though they don't inhabit their bodies at all. Healers (whether they practice psychic arts, such as laying on of hands, or more conventional ones, such as massage or psychotherapy) who fail to ground often find themselves acquiring their patients' symptoms—sometimes for mere moments, sometimes for days or longer.

Centering

So many people refer to grounding and centering together that they have come to think of it as one process. In fact, grounding and centering are two different things. Grounding gets you in touch with physical reality and allows you to draw energy from (or drain energy into) the Earth. Centering, on the other hand, gets you in touch with yourself.

Centering is a process of finding out who and where you are. It involves increasing your holistic perception—that you are a whole person, not just a collection of parts. Where grounding is a *connecting* experience, centering is often a *soothing* one. To center is to locate that part of ourselves where we perceive our true and whole self to reside, the center of our spirit, and to function from and with that center. Life is often reactive; to be centered is to behave based on free will at all times, not in response to stimuli.

Grounding and centering are equally necessary—one to connect us with a foundation, the other to connect us with our source. Centering is a process that inherently acknowledges immanent deity; we need to be in touch with *ourselves* in order to do right, to behave well, to be a part of sacred space.

Merging

This step is necessary only in a group ritual—when you are practicing as a solitary Witch, you have connected by centering, but when you are practicing as a coven or other group, you need to connect to the others as well as to your own center. Group magic cannot work properly unless everyone is "on the same wavelength," unless people are united in purpose and intent, and willing to be influenced by one another.

Suppose, for example, that you wished to do a spell to get Marge a new home. You are visualizing Marge in a cozy little suburban Cape Cod, but the guy next to you is picturing Marge in an urban apartment, and the woman next to *him* is picturing Marge in a sprawling ranch house. Get it together, people! Obviously, you should have discussed exactly what kind of home Marge is going for before beginning the spell. But suppose you have discussed it, suppose you've settled on the Cape Cod. Now you're picturing Marge gardening, the man next to you is picturing her working on her home computer in the bedroom of the Cape Cod, and the woman next to him is picturing Marge shaking hands with the realtor while seeing the new home for the first time. This could go on forever; your pictures aren't connecting up, and your energies are scattered into a bunch of individual streams with no meeting place.

If you had merged, you'd be more connected to each other. After you'd discussed the spell enough to know what Marge wants, you'd be better able to make the different pictures of buying and living in a new home connect into a whole. Merging is that which makes the whole greater than the sum of its parts.

Sometimes merging is about tolerance and acceptance. Maybe one person wants to drum, two people want to chant, and one person wants to visualize silently—if you are functioning solely as individuals, this is a conflict. Maybe you'll put it to a vote— drumming, chanting, or meditation? But if you've merged you can see that you can all work together, that these different activities can flow into a single group activity. This is because you're perceiving yourselves as united, and you can perceive that drumming gives chanting a beat, that chanting gives drumming some variety and interest, and that both can be a focusing background music to meditation. Three different activities can be perceived as one because you are open to one another and connected to the concept of each supporting the other.

It's important to know the conditions of merging—what it is that unites this group. If you know each other well, you will be merged in love and trust. But even if you've never met before, you are united in your love of the gods and your intent to worship Them. You can be united by your name ("We are the Puppydog Coven"), by your geographic location, by a cause, or by a ritual tradition.

When you merge you are connecting back to the infinite Web, to the strands of connection that unite us all, and to the knowledge that ultimately we *are* all one thing—the children of Mother Earth—and participants in the energy of creation.

Water

The Emotional Meaning of Grounding, Centering, and Merging

Grounding, centering, and merging are important psychological, emotional processes, as well as ritual ones. A depressed person who remembers to ground is less likely to feel "washed away" by her own sorrow. She uses techniques of grounding the same way sandbags are used during a flood watch—Earth can protect against rivers of dangerous emotion.

Effects of *not* grounding are more subtle, but still noticeable. Phrases such as "space cadet," "airhead," "head in the clouds," and so on, apply to people who have lost a vital connection to the Earth. Such people may be forgetful, disjointed, or have trouble concentrating. Perhaps the saddest trait of all in the ungrounded person is gullibility. Common sense is an Earth-based characteristic. Without common sense, snake oil becomes indistinguishable from penicillin. The New Age movement is filled with people who are willing to pay exorbitant prices for "magical infusions," "healing crystals," and the like. Where is the grounding, the practicality, in such people?

Some people have some of these traits naturally—perhaps you are prone to "airiness" or "wateriness" (emotionality) for astrological reasons. In that case, grounding can help you to become more practical, more earthy, and more connected to the world around you. Grounding is also useful for restoring a lost sex drive or a lost appetite, provided appropriate medical treatment is also sought.

While the ungrounded person is an airhead, the uncentered person is "scattered," or "all over the place"—these metaphors are apt descriptions of someone out of touch with her center. As you move through life, situations will buffet you about, demands will pull you this way and that—it's easy to lose touch with who you are and just respond and react. Psychologically, staying centered is staying *you* no matter how the situation changes. To be centered is to be authentic.

The psychological effects of merging are the easiest to understand. Merging breaks our isolation; it allows us the freedom to drop our barriers to intimacy with the select group of people with whom we do ritual. Merging helps to create interdependency, not dependency; by uniting a group around a common purpose, it forms the beginning of healthy relational bonds.

Mythic Grounding and Centering

While using the basic images of reaching the Earth, remember that this is a religious ritual; this step can and should work mythically as well as psychically and practically. The Earth is not just rock to solidify us, it is the body of the Mother. You're not just reaching roots into the soil and bedrock, you're reaching into the Mother's nurturing embrace. This is the first "prayer" of the ceremony, as you extend yourself down to Her with the (perhaps unspoken) request that She sustain and support you throughout your work.

To balance this, to acknowledge the polarity of God and Goddess, we should include both. As the Goddess is associated with the Earth, the God is associated with Space; mythically, *we* are Their meeting ground. In general, this will be incorporated as (a) Grounding/Goddess, (b) Centering, (c) Reaching up to the God. That way, we can clearly visualize ourselves as a conduit, standing between Them.

Fire

It is perhaps most significant to look at the order in which this process is done. Why do we connect to the Earth before we connect to ourselves? Why do we connect to ourselves before we connect to others? The latter can be seen merely as psychological—we must know ourselves before we can form relationships. But what of the first question? Perhaps it means that our selves *come from* Earth Mother—that we *cannot* find ourselves without Her. Perhaps it is a pattern that teaches humility—that it is wrong to place ourselves before the Earth. As with many mystical questions, it is an answer you must find for yourself, in meditation and ritual.

Earth

How to Ground

Most people find a few simple visualization techniques effectively and quickly connect them to the Earth. For example:

Stand or sit, breathing calmly and slowly. Become aware of your physical self, sparing a brief thought for each part of your body. From your head, to your neck, shoulders, arms, hands, chest, belly, groin, continue down your legs to your feet. Feel your feet touching the ground. If you are indoors, feel the floor beneath you, and imagine the floor's connection to the Earth. Even if you are in a high-rise apartment, continue imagining until you have established a connection from your feet all the way to natural soil. Imagine that your toes are digging in to the soil. Imagine that the soil is responding; caressing your toes, your feet, and supporting your entire body. The Earth is your companion, holding you up, supporting you, encouraging you.

This technique is very simple, and can be done for several minutes, or can be started and finished in thirty seconds—flashing your awareness from the top of your head, through your body, to feet, soil, and back up again in the time it takes to tell.

Another technique involves the spinal cord instead of the feet. In this case, you begin your visualization at the base of your skull; imagine that your spine is alive with a steady glow of life-giving energy. In your mind's eye, follow your spine from your neck down, through upper back, lower back, reaching your tailbone. As you picture this, allow each part of your body to relax—your shoulders as you pass them, then your chest, arms, and so on. When you reach your tailbone, imagine that your spinal cord continues, that you have a tail that is running straight down, into the Earth. Again, continue through any flooring until you've reached soil. Feel this vibrant, glowing tail dig into the Earth. Now feel that it has become a siphon, drawing life-energy from the Earth, being nourished by the Earth's ever-replenishing supply of solid, stable power. Draw that energy back into yourself.

There are innumerable variations that can be used. Both of these examples are direct and physical, and use the body itself. You can use more metaphorical imagery—for example, you can imagine yourself to be a tree, with roots that reach into the earth. Trees are connected to all four elements—their roots are in the soil, their sap is Water, their branches are in the sky (Air), and they are nourished by the rays of the sun (Fire). Connecting our grounding and centering to the elements is useful in ritual, and consistent with everything we do. Some people don't like the fact that trees are rooted to the spot; they say it breaks the visualization when they move. But most people find the "Tree Meditation" very effective.

The meditation that is included in the ritual at the end of the book is one I created myself, called "Pillars of the Temple."

Group work requires a visualization that everyone is a part of and follows along with. It's best to guide the grounding out loud, so that everyone is on the same page at more or less the same time. Choose one person in the group to recite the grounding, or someone with a particularly relaxing voice might record the grounding and then you can play it at each ritual. Some people dislike the artificiality of a recording, but its advantage is that everyone can participate equally, without a "leader."

Another option for grounding is more tactile. Pass a bowl of potting soil or a medium-sized stone around the circle. You'll use just a minimum of words here, something like "As you touch this Earth, connect yourself to Mother Earth." By just holding a physical object in your hands, you can re-experience yourself as a physical being, connected to the ground. You can also combine a guided visualization with holding an object; but in a group, that means everyone needs their own object.

Any meditation or magical technique becomes quicker and easier with time. A long induction may not be necessary after a group has worked with the same grounding for a while. If you're working with an object, the object will become imbued with the grounding, and just touching it will have most or all of the effect you need.

The basics of grounding can be summed up as:

- Connect yourself (your body and your energy) to the earth.
- Draw power (nurturance, support) up from the earth into your body.

How to Center

Find your center, the place in your body where you feel that "you" are located. This might take some experimentation. It varies from person to person, often being the solar plexus, but sometimes the heart or the head.

Centering is simply a matter of locating the center and bringing all of your energy into it. Once you've located your center, simply picture the rest of your energy flowing into and out of that spot; you should immediately notice increased calm and clarity. "Hook up" the energy being drawn from the Earth to your center.

Once you've connected energy from the Earth to your center, you can extend the energy up through the rest of your body, out the top of your head, and to the sky. If you're using a Tree Meditation, this would be the part where you visualize your top branches and leaves and feel the Sun on them.

If you've used a physical grounding, like holding a stone, then you should use a physical centering. Place your hands over your center and breathe, picturing breath coming from and going to the center. Or place the stone itself over your center.

How to Merge

The last part of the process is to form a connection with the others in the circle. Do this by extending the visualization you have used so far. In other words, if you've drawn energy up from the Earth, and then connected it to your center, you should then extend that same energy out toward the others in the circle, and feel the connections.

If you're trees, you should add to the visualization at this point that the trees are in a grove or forest, that the trees are forming a circle and the tips of their branches touch.

Remember that merging works by awakening our knowledge of that which connects us. The verbal instructions should include *at least* one thing that connects this particular group. Several things, for reinforcement, are better.

If your process has been physical so far, then the obvious thing to do is to hold hands. But don't *just* hold hands, which only connects you to the person on either side of you. Instead, once everyone is holding hands, acknowledge that the circle of hands connects everyone in it. You can simply say so, or you can use a joining chant, such as *"We are a circle/Within a circle/With no beginning/And never ending"*[13] or *"We are the weavers/We are the web/We are the flow and/We are the ebb."*[14]

Declared Opening and Stated Purpose

These two steps occur so quickly that they are most simply covered together. In fact, it is often the case that the two steps are performed simultaneously, in a single statement.

Air

Declared Opening

Why must we declare that we're starting? Why not just start? The significance here is twofold; primarily we must address the psychic and psychological needs of the people involved. We must make sure that people step over the threshold from one state of consciousness to another. Throughout the preliminary steps, throughout this chapter, we've been shifting the consciousness of the Witches who will enter ritual space, making sure they are in the most receptive state to meet with the gods and receive their blessings. We prepared the house, we prepared the ritual space, and we prepared ourselves. Then we did a grounding, centering, and merging exercise; a trance induction or a physical enactment, in order to be in touch with the Earth, ourselves, and each other. All of this has brought us to this moment when we enter ritual space. It is vital to know that the time is *now*. Like a checkered flag at an auto race, we must have the signal to move forward.

The second reason has to do with the timelessness of ritual space. If there is no time, we'd better *make* the beginning, as later we'll make the end.

Stated Purpose

Once again, remember how much time you've spent preparing your consciousness for this moment. The best way to take advantage of your receptive and anticipatory state at this moment is to tell yourself (and everyone else) exactly what you're there for.

Many people get together for drum circles or chant circles, raise terrific, powerful energy, and then go home again. They didn't have a stated purpose, so all that happened with all of that juicy power was that people enjoyed the feeling it gave them. It's as if they never realized that there might be more to it.

The beginning of using your power productively and creatively is to state clearly that you will do so. Remember the power of the Word; the very essence of magic is that your say-so has infinite creative potential. To say a thing is to bring it forth—therefore bring forth purpose in your circle by saying so.

Earth

The Declared Opening and Stated Purpose are fairly self-explanatory, and are usually done verbally. A bell or single, strong drumbeat can be used for the Declared Opening instead of a statement. Some groups use a chant, or a chanted syllable, an Aum or an "Aaaah." In my old coven, I was able to "declare" the opening with simple eye contact and a nod—we had all worked together for so long that this was more than enough.

A Declared Opening must always be brief, otherwise it defeats its purpose; it is a threshold and must be stepped over.

The Stated Purpose should include *why* we are here and *what* we are doing. Druids of *Arn Draíocht Féin*[15] use *"We are here to honor the gods"* as their opening statement. This has the strong declaration needed for the opening statement, and also states a clear, specific purpose. The ritual at the end of this book says, *"Welcome all who have come to worship the gods in friendship and in love."* The word "Welcome" is the Declared Opening, it is the signal that something has begun, that you have entered a new place into which you must be welcomed. The rest of the sentence says why you have come "to worship the gods" and the conditions under which you must meet—the ground rules—"in friendship and in love."

Unlike the Declared Opening, the Stated Purpose can be either short or long. The occasion—whatever it is—should certainly be included as part of the purpose. The "Welcome all who . . ." statement is all-occasion; it should be modified according to the holiday, lunar phase, or other purpose.

Examples

- *Welcome all who have come in friendship and in love to witness and celebrate the rite of handfasting for John and Louise.*

- *Welcome all who have come in friendship and in love to worship the gods under the light of the full moon.*

- *Welcome all who have come this Samhain night, to worship the gods and honor the ancestors. We join in friendship and in love on this holy night when the dead walk the Earth.*

These examples show how to modify a standard phrase for various occasions. Standard phrases are incredibly helpful both for memorization and for their psychic and psychological effects.

Whenever possible, rituals should be memorized. Reading from a script is always stiff and weak compared to recitation from memory. As anyone in the theater can tell you, it's only after you've memorized your lines that you can begin to find some depth and meaning in them. It's also terribly awkward to be fumbling with a script by candlelight; sooner or later you lose your place.

Part of the stated purpose can be descriptive and can include actions as well; the actions dramatize the purpose:

If you are lighting candles ceremonially, and also using them for light, work them into this part of the ceremony, because you need to be able to see for the next step!

Priestess: *Welcome to our circle, which honors the Lord and the Lady. Our Lady is the blessed Earth and the triple Moon. We honor Her light.* (Lights the Goddess candle.)

Priest: *Our Lord is Life and Death, He Who Dies and is Reborn. We honor His light.* (Lights the God candle.)

We've already discussed the hypnotic quality of repetition; how doing the same thing the same way has a cumulative effect over time. Standard phrases work well toward this goal, so modifying those phrases for different situations is generally preferable to writing all new scripts.

There are other actions that can be done at this point. You might do a chant that states your purpose or expresses your unity and fellowship (which is part of the purpose). You might all join hands or exchange a kiss of fellowship. Some people use a ceremonial procession into the circle as part of the ritual, but this should only be done if the space accommodates it. If the room is too small or crowded, it can be very awkward to try to have a group walk gracefully and with dignity.

Water

Mythically

Remember that we are entering into a part of the creative dance of the Goddess and the God; that the center of our ritual (Cakes and Wine) will be Their holy union, a fertility rite. It's important in this mythic context that *we* create. The Stated Purpose establishes *what* we will create; what we will give birth to as we emulate the fertility of the gods.

It is said that the Goddess without the God is nothing more than a good idea; she is a fertile womb, she is perfect potentiality, but without His seed, nothing will come forth from Her holy womb. Whereas the God without the Goddess is energy without shape; without Her, his seed can as easily be destructive as it can be creative, but together They bring forth the universe.

The Declared Opening, then, can be seen as the Goddess, the fertile ground. It says, "Here I am, here is the circle" and establishes foundation. The Stated Purpose must follow; it is the seed, the shape the ritual will take; it is the God.

The Circle Story

The entire ritual can be seen as a story, which we'll discuss more in our next chapter. The story begins with a Declared Opening, something like "Once upon a time. . . ."

Metaphorically

We previously referred to treating the gods as honored guests, as if you're holding a special dinner party for them. The Declared Opening is where you open the door, welcome everyone in, and let them know that you're starting. The Stated Purpose establishes the parameters—is it a sit down, a buffet, or a progressive dinner? Together, they say that the party has begun and let everyone know what's happening. Your "guests" will feel more secure and more able to let go and enjoy once they know the basic ground rules.

Fire

These aren't very mystical steps, there's not a lot of Fire to them, but there are a few concepts that could spark meditation. Here are some topics to explore:

- What is the meaning of a beginning? Is it the same as an end? Is it different?

- How can I make something so just by saying so?

- The most important, and most mystical, question to be asked is this: *What is my purpose in doing ritual?*

---

1. I find cigarette lighters to be ugly and incongruous. Wearing robes, working by candlelight, and using knives as tools, we have left the modern world behind. How jarring, then, to be brought back to it by a hot pink Bic. Wooden matches have a nice "feel" to them, and burn better for those times when a candle or incense doesn't light easily.

2. Most occult stores sell them, and some church supply stores as well. Everything magical is easier to come by than it used to be, thanks to the growth of both Wicca and the World Wide Web.

3. In fact, Her forgiveness is easily come by, as She is infinitely compassionate. We'll talk more about the nature of the Goddess and the God in chapter 5, when we are at the point in the ceremony when we invoke Them.

4. "As equal as possible" and "relatively equal" not just because most covens do have leaders and hierarchy, but also because in a larger group, the High Priestess and High Priest will of necessity be the ones in easiest reach. If there are only five people in the circle, everyone can reach, but if there are fifteen, then some people will end up pushed back a bit. I also hasten to add what I said to my own High Priestess many times—that because of the way the statues are placed, only she and the Priest get to see the Goddess' face; the rest of us must settle for Her rear end.

5. The "Witches' Rune" by Doreen Valiente has appeared in many, many published sources. It is here taken from *Eight Sabbats for Witches and Rites for Birth, Marriage and Death* by Janet and Stewart Farrar (London: Robert Hale, 1981) page 45.

6. From The Charge. The Charge is the single most common Wiccan document. It functions as received wisdom from the Goddess. It is quoted in full in chapter 5.

7. There is no general agreement on how to pronounce this word. Most common is probably uh-THAM-ee (that's the one I use), but I have heard uh-THAH-me, AH-thah-may and (most rarely) a-THAME.

8. As far as keeping it with you at all times: *Don't* put it in your carry-on luggage, and *don't* put it under your pillow if you tend to toss around a lot in your sleep. Knives are legally weapons, and they are notoriously sharp.

9. The six-pointed star is a similar symbol, and is used in Tantra to represent the sexual union of Goddess and God. The downward pointed triangle is a symbol of the vulva, and the upward pointed triangle is a stylized phallus. Together they are Goddess and God united.

10. They get "demoted."

11. *The Book of the Law,* chapter 1, verses 29–30.

12. For this concise explanation I am indebted to *Seasons of the Witch,* by Patricia Monaghan (Oak Park, Ill.: Delphi Press, Inc., 1992) pp. 136–145.

13. By Rick Hamouris.

14. By Shekinah Mountainwater.

15. www.adf.org

Chapter Four

MAKING THE RITUAL SPACE

Here are the steps in making a ritual space:

- Sacred Preparations: Consecrations
- Casting the Circle: Making the Space
- Calling the Quarters

Sacred Preparations

Air

After opening the circle, we consecrate the four elements. Since we use them in casting the circle, this must be done before the circle can be cast. The phrases generally used are to *consecrate*, to *purify,* to *bless,* and to *charge.* Let's look at some definitions:[1]

To consecrate is *to declare or set apart as sacred,* also *to dedicate solemnly to a service or goal.* When consecrating the elements, we are setting them apart by declaration (by our Word), so that they are dedicated to a specific purpose.

Consecration goes hand in hand with blessing. To bless is *to make holy by religious rite; sanctify* and *to invoke divine favor upon.* We are saying here that our rite empowers us to perform this consecration, that we do not merely "declare" the elements sacred, but we finish the job—that we *make* them sacred. To bless the elements also means to use the power of the gods (divine favor) to make them sacred. We are using both our own power and their power (in as much as they're separate things).

The purification part is fairly simple. To purify is *to rid of impurities; cleanse* and *to rid of foreign or objectionable elements.* We covered this in the last chapter when we talked about the cleansings that are sometimes done prior to ritual. We are removing the unnecessary, the unwanted, and the inappropriate. With the elements, there is an additional component. We wish to work with the purest form of the element. We don't want our salt to be eighty percent Earth and twenty percent Water. In mundane life, the elements are always intermingled, and in ourselves, they are fully entwined about each other. But in ritual, we want each element to be fully itself, to bring all of its powers to bear. Later we'll combine them, but to start, we want the pure, distilled, perfect form of each element. The purification of the element accomplishes that.

When we *charge* a ritual object, we are using a double meaning. We mean *to impose a duty, responsibility, or obligation on*—which is certainly akin to consecration, in that a duty is similar to a solemn dedication. We also mean *to saturate; impregnate, as an atmosphere charged with tension.* We are filling the elements with power, which they will hold for later use. To charge also means *to cause formation of a net electric charge on or in (a conductor, for example)* and *to energize (a storage battery) by passing current through it in the direction opposite to.* In magic we often use metaphors of electricity or batteries to describe the way in which energy is generated, built up, stored, and then released. When we say that we are *charging* something, we mean, not only that we are imposing a purpose onto it, but more importantly, that we are filling it with magic.

When we talk about consecration, blessing, and purification, it's clearly *theurgic;* it is specifically oriented toward the gods. These words could be used in any religion, and can be seen as conventionally spiritual. That's fine; in many ways, Wicca has much in common with other religions. We all reach toward sacredness, and consecration is a part of that. But Wicca is also, famously, a *thaumaturgic* religion, a religion that practices magic. When we both consecrate and charge, we acknowledge both the religion and the magic. To charge is to fill up with magic, and also to use as a storage battery for magic. We're going to be *using* these elements later. We're going to cense and sprinkle the circle, and perhaps other things as well. So let's fill them now, with the power they'll need and use later. That's what a magical religion is all about!

In sum then, we are taking each element and, by our own declaration, and by the power of the gods, we are making it sacred, and setting it apart for its special and sacred purpose. We are making it pure and perfect, and then filling it with magical power that shall be used later. A tall order indeed, and a good reason to perform this step.

Some people skip this step because it's repetitive. For example, they may get a batch of salt for ritual and consecrate it, and then simply use it each time—it's already consecrated, so there's no reason to repeat the effort. But I think there *are* reasons. For one, divine blessing should be renewed at each ceremony, just as worship is renewed. If once was enough, we wouldn't gather again every full moon. For another, after an element has been used, it's no longer charged up—some of the energy has been expended. Also, as it has existed in the mundane world for some period of time, it may have become adulterated; it may have picked up and absorbed a touch of energy from other elements; it is no longer pure.

It has never made sense to me to consecrate some but not all of the elements, although this isn't uncommon. Some elements are considered more pure than others in some magical systems, and so, in those systems, only the "necessary" consecrations are performed. But let's not forget that a circle is concerned with *balance* and with *pattern*, the balance of elements and of polarity, and the patterns of the lunar cycle, the solar cycle, the life cycle, and the repetitions that induce altered states. To balance the consecrations we must perform all four, and to fulfill our ritual pattern we must do the same. We will use *four* elements, we will call *four* quarters, and so we should maintain that pattern from the beginning.

Not only that, but there should be a pattern in the *order* as well. Since Air is associated with beginnings, since the circle is cast from east to south to west to north, that is the order in which most people will consecrate the elements.

Most but not all. There is one spot in the ritual where that pattern must be broken—in the sprinkling and censing. Whenever we bless, consecrate, or charge an object or person, we will always sprinkle before we cense. This is necessary because water cleanses and purifies, while incense blesses and sweetens. Just as you shower or bathe before you put on your deodorant and cologne, you must cleanse magically before you can add the perfume of incense.

So what should you do? You must decide at this point in the ceremony if you're going to follow the pattern of directions, which is Air-Fire-Water-Earth, or if you're going to follow the practical pattern of how the elements are actually used, the pattern of cleansing and purification, which is Water-Earth-Air-Fire. This decision is entirely up to you, but should be made consciously. You may wish to modify how you perform the consecrations, and what part of the consecrations you wish to emphasize, based on the choice of order you make (or vice versa).

Water

The Circle Story

I alluded earlier to the idea that the entire circle tells a story. Mircea Eliade, the historian of religions, believed that all rituals were re-enactments or retellings of creation stories. The "all" is a bit of an overstatement on his part. Nonetheless, when I first reviewed Wiccan circle casting in light of his theory, I quickly saw that, not only was it very true in this case, but viewing the circle in this way shed light on a great deal of what we do. So, one way we will look at the ritual is as a re-enactment of the creation of the universe.

From the Declared Opening, we have *In the Beginning, There was the Word.* We have the very statement of creation; from here everything else will follow. (The Stated Purpose is a refinement of the original declaration, and will provide some detail on the nature of what is being created.)

From the Consecrations we say this: *These are the building blocks of the universe. This is Air and Fire and Water and Earth. From these, all creation proceeds, and without these, creation cannot be.*

We say more than that, however. We do not merely bring the elements into the circle; we bless them, we consecrate them to a particular purpose, we make them perfect. By doing this, we are starting from a pristine place; creation truly begins at the beginning. Consecration is also that which makes a thing sacred and suitable for sacred work; the creation of the universe is truly sacred work. We have removed from the elements anything acquired by them since creation, so that they are *original;* they are as they were at the moment of creation.

So, in our re-enactment, we have now spoken the original Word that begins creation and gathered for our use the pure and original elements from which all life and matter came forth.

The Honored Guests Metaphor

This entire section of the ceremony—"Making Space"—is about ritually preparing a special place, good enough for the most honored of guests, the gods. Everything has to be perfect before we ask the Goddess and God to join us. The elements are necessary, but not good enough for our honored guests without first being specially consecrated for the occasion.

Fire

There is an irony, a circular reasoning, that will carry throughout our ritual, in that consecrating *for* the gods can only be done *by* the gods. The interdependence of doing for them what is in fact done by them, of receiving back from them what is given to them, and giving it back again, is essentially mystical. It entangles us in an endless circle, like mirrors facing each other and endlessly reflecting, of blessing and being blessed, sacrificing and receiving, consecration without end. We are giving to the gods *what* they give to us, *as* they give it to us. This will strike some people as nonsense, and some people as overly-complex, but it is in the nature of mysticism to be gobbledygook to some, and profound to others.

There is a second mysticism in this, another way of knowing the gods through this moment of the circle. The consecrations of the elements are the first ritual *acts* performed in the circle (the first *doing* rather than *saying*). How is that achieved? To put it in a very different way—where did the first sourdough come from? This used to drive me nuts as a child; when I learned that sourdough was made by starting it from a little bit of sourdough, all I could think of was, how did they make the *first* sourdough? It's almost a chicken-and-egg circle, and sometimes, thinking about it, I could feel my mind spinning back to the dawn of time. What is the *original*? Sourdough was my little-girl introduction to the question.

I'm going to consecrate the elements. Then I'm going to consecrate the circle with the consecrated elements. I'm going to use this first consecration to make a chain of consecration—sprinkling the circle works because I'm doing it with consecrated elements. But the chain isn't complete—how did the *first* consecration happen?

The answer, here and throughout the ritual, is that consecration comes from the immanent God/dess. In that one moment of choosing to consecrate, of beginning the cycle of sacredness that will snowball until it reaches a climax at Cakes and Wine, we are proving, in some essential way, that the ritual isn't really necessary after all. If we have the capacity to make sacred from nothing, then we can know our sacredness, *at any time.* The ritual, indeed, is proven to be mere play-acting; psychodrama that simply informs us of a preexisting truth.

There is mysticism, too, in the play-acting. Somehow, acting as if I have the power to consecrate achieves an effective, even powerful, consecration. How can that be? How is it that my little bit of make-believe has transformed ordinary salt and water into tools of blessing? Is it possible that the line between make-believe and "reality" is not so solid and black as you or I may have thought? Theater came into being in ancient Greece, as a by-product of ritual. Our ancestors knew that to ritually enact was to dramatize—to pretend.

In ritual, one person must of necessity take on the mantle of this enactment. In a solitary ritual, you and you alone must play all roles. In a group ritual, one person must step forward and be that First Cause, that originator of consecration. Someone must act as first among equals, as if she is that tiny bit more sacred, or more in touch with the immanent deity she carries, than the rest. That one person is the High Priestess. In ritual, she enacts the role of the Goddess, and the High Priest enacts the role of the God.[2]

The existence of hierarchy, and its limitations, are controversies within Wicca. A huge range exists, from highly-structured and formal traditions[3] to the most radical and free-flowing of egalitarian anarchy. Most groups fall somewhere in the middle. But despite the formality of the title, what is being discussed here is not authority at all, but the mystical and mythic creative role of the woman who is taking upon herself the functions of the Goddess. Whoever takes this role should be treated, at least for the duration of the ritual, with respect and deference fitting to this extraordinary role. She may enter into the ritual full of self-doubt; she probably doesn't believe she is in any way more worthy than anyone else to take on this special power, but someone must and she does. By deferring to and honoring her, you are empowering her to perform her role effectively. The ability comes from immanence, it comes from the Goddess within, and every human being has that immanent spirit. But someone must reach it, or act as if she's reaching it, long enough to take that first step.

If you think about it, it's a genuinely radical and daring act, to take on this spiritual authority merely by your own say so.[4]

Earth

Some people don't consecrate the elements before using them, some people consecrate them only when fresh (i.e., consecrate a batch of newly-made incense), and some people only consecrate one or two or three of the elements. We've seen, though, that there is plenty of good reason to consecrate the elements each ceremony, and consecrate all four of them.

Some people leave the elements off the altar (to the side), picking them up for the consecration, and then placing them on the altar. This might be done if you want to make sure that only consecrated items touch the altar. It can look very dramatic, and if you do it this way, you could even have a little side table set up to have the elements on before consecration. Another method might be to have each element waiting by the quarter candle of its corresponding element—that is, have the dish of salt in the north, the dish of incense in the east, and so on. Just make sure you've left room on the (main) altar. Before the ceremony begins, put the elements on the altar to be sure that, not only do they fit, but that it isn't too awkward to place them—that your hands don't knock into something else. This may sound silly, but believe me, it happens!

If you're concerned about making sure that everything that touches the altar is consecrated, an alternative is to have each element in a consecrated *container*, which could then touch the altar even before the consecration of the element is performed.

Invoking and Banishing Pentagrams

Some traditional methods of doing these consecrations involves making an appropriate invoking pentagram. In fact, invoking and banishing pentagrams can be used at several different points in the ritual. Since these pentagrams are so very useful, let's take a look at how to make them.

There are invoking and banishing pentagrams for each of the four elements, a total of eight. The difference is the beginning and end point of each. These symbols are

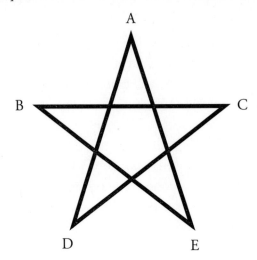

Pentagram for Invoking and Banishing

drawn in the air with the fingers, athame, or other tool. To consecrate an element, you can make the pentagram *in* the element, i.e. by putting the tip of your athame into the salt and drawing, or just *above* the element. Personally, I prefer to touch anything that is safe to touch (not hot coals), but it's not strictly required.

- An *Earth Invoking* pentagram begins at point *A*, then goes to point *D*. You just finish the pentagram from there, so that the whole thing is A-D-C-B-E-A. It's very important to remember to return to your starting point, otherwise the symbol isn't whole.

- Banishing pentagrams reverse the first line drawn. *Earth Banishing* is D-A-E-B-C-D.

When drawing pentagrams, visualize them clearly, seeing each line form as if drawn in neon. After you've finished drawing it, continue to see it in the spot where you placed it.

- *Air Invoking* is C-B-E-A-D-C.

- *Air Banishing* is therefore B-C-D-A-E-B.

- *Fire Invoking:* A-E-B-C-D-A.

- *Fire Banishing:* E-A-D-C-B-E.

- *Water Invoking*: B-C-D-A-E-B (the same as Air Banishing—your *intent* makes the difference).
- *Water Banishing*: C-B-E-A-D-C (the same as Air Invoking).

Now that you know how to draw eight different pentagrams, I will confuse you by telling you that many people (including me) use only two. I use Earth Invoking for *all* invoking, and I use Earth Banishing for *all* banishing.

I believe that all invocation, in a Wiccan circle, is by the power of the Earth Mother, and to use the Earth Invoking pentagram is to invoke Her power. I have also heard it said that to use Earth is to *make real*, i.e., to bring to manifestation, to fulfill, which is what Earth does.

On the other hand, you can't argue with the good sense of using the proper elemental pentagram for the element being consecrated. Certainly Fire Invoking pentagrams are useful for fires that are tough to light, and have been known to make slightly damp wood flare up. The connection between the element and this magical gesture is very old and very real.

Whichever you choose, be consistent with it, and remember that every *banishing* pentagram used must correspond to the one used when you *invoked*.

Words and Music (and Gesture)

The conventional way to perform consecrations is to speak them, but there are actually an awful lot of variations. Remember the principle of *balance;* however you decide to do one is more or less how you should do all four.

The words of the consecration should include:

- What you're doing
- Be specific (name the element)
- How you're doing it
- What it accomplishes; what you want from it
- And it should also sound good

Invocations have a bad habit of getting long and unwieldy. I firmly believe in language that is to the point—it's more likely to get results. You might even make it rhyme, a trick long-associated with Witchcraft.

EXAMPLE 1: WORDS OF CONSECRATION

By the sacred names, by the sacred names, by the sacred names! I charge and consecrate thee, O Air, O Mind, O Inspiration. Bring thy special blessings to this, our sacred rite.

By the sacred names, by the sacred names, by the sacred names!

This is *how* I'm doing it—I'm doing it by the power of the "sacred names," i.e., the gods. The repetition is nicely hypnotic, and "what I say three times is true."

You might also say "by the gods," "by the power of the Lady and Lord," or use specific god-names. You might also choose to use a power other than the power of the gods.

I charge and consecrate thee,

This is *what* I'm doing. I've chosen "charge and consecrate" both for the alliteration and because they cover both the religious and magical functions. (I also like using "thee" but you don't have to.)

O Air, O Mind, O Inspiration.

Note that I'm using another set of three. This is the *specific* part. In magic, the more specific you are, the more specific the result.

The other three consecrations will follow this pattern: O Element, O Part of the Self, O Abstract Quality. Remember that however you do the first consecration should set the pattern for all four.

Bring thy special blessings to this, our sacred rite.

This is what I hope to accomplish. By "special blessings" I'm referring back to the previous line—bring the blessings of Air (in this case). I'm also adding authority to the consecration—not only is it "by the sacred names" but I'm also emphasizing that this rite is sacred, bringing the power of sacredness to bear at this moment.

This example shows how to accomplish a lot with a few well-chosen words. There are obviously any number of ways to accomplish the same thing.

There's a lot you can do with words. They can be spoken, they can be sung if you're musically inclined, or they can be "intoned" (that sonorous sound that falls between speech and song).[6] One person can speak the invocations, lines can be alternated between two people (presumably the Priestess and Priest), or one person can speak and everyone can echo back:

Priestess: *By the sacred names*

Whole group: *By the sacred names*

Priestess: *By the sacred names*

Whole group: *By the sacred names*

Priestess: *By the sacred names*

Whole group: *By the sacred names*

The cumulative effect of this kind of echoing is pretty impressive, although, like anything else, it can be overused.

Words alone can fall flat, but combining the invocation with gesture and/or music is both dramatic and raises additional energy. In addition to using invoking pentagrams over each element, you might find it powerful to move your hands in a way that gathers energy into the process—use your imagination and experiment with different techniques. The following example shows two people working together, using both words and gesture.

Example 2: A Formal Consecration

Priest: Lifts dish of incense into the air, then presents it to the Priestess, holding it before her at about chest level, and nods his head to her.

Priestess: Raises athame into the air, brings it down until she has it just above the dish, pointed into it. She says:
By the sacred names

Priest: *By the sacred names*

Priestess: *By the sacred names*

Priestess: Brings athame down until it touches the incense in the dish. She makes the Air Invoking pentagram as she continues to speak.
I charge and consecrate thee, O Air, O Mind, O Inspiration.

Priest: *Bring thy special blessings to this, our sacred rite.*

Both: *Blessed be.*

Group: *Blessed be.*[7]

Priest: Moves dish of incense into his left hand, lifts censer into the air, then presents it to the Priestess, holding both before her side-by-side, and nods.

Priestess: Takes three pinches of incense, drops them one at a time onto the censer, making sure they begin to smoke (she may poke with her finger or the tip
of her athame to do so). She then raises athame into the air, brings it down until it is in the smoke. She says:
By the sacred names

Priest: *By the sacred names*

Priestess: *By the sacred names*

Priestess: Makes the Fire Invoking pentagram as she continues to speak.
I charge and consecrate thee, O Fire, O Will, O Passion.

Priest: *Bring thy special blessings to this, our sacred rite.*

Both: *Blessed be.*

Group: *Blessed be.*

Priest: Returns incense and censer to the altar, lifts water dish into the air, then presents it to the Priestess, and nods.

Priestess: Lifts athame into the air, brings it down until it is just above the water dish, with the tip just barely wet. She says:
By the sacred names

Priest: *By the sacred names*

Priestess: *By the sacred names*

Priestess: Makes the Water Invoking pentagram as she continues to speak.
I charge and consecrate thee, O Water, O Heart, O Feeling.

Priest: *Bring thy special blessings to this, our sacred rite.*

Both: *Blessed be.*

Group: *Blessed be.*

Priest: Moves dish of water into his left hand, lifts salt dish into the air, then presents it to the Priestess, holding both before her side-by-side, and nods.

Priestess: Raises athame into the air, brings it down until it is just touching the salt. She says:
By the sacred names

Priest: *By the sacred names*

Priestess: *By the sacred names*

Priestess: Makes the Earth Invoking pentagram as she continues to speak.
I charge and consecrate thee, O Earth, O Body, O Constancy.

Priest: *Bring thy special blessings to this, our sacred rite.*

Both: *Blessed be.*

Group: *Blessed be.*

Priestess: Takes three pinches of salt, drops them into the water dish, and stirs with her athame.

This example combines a number of different techniques, for a very traditional and effective result. Note that both gesture and words are used, and that the athame brings that much more additional power. A back-and-forth is established between Priestess and Priest, which, in addition to working well at this moment for this consecration, works to build the polarity between them which should be present throughout the rite. They might even exchange a quick kiss between elements—such as before picking up the censer. Polarity is energizing, and should build from the very beginning toward the peak it will reach at Cakes and Wine.

This example is rather formal, and involves primarily the group's leaders (although everyone joins in for the final *Blessed be*).

The next example uses four different people, for a more egalitarian feel.

EXAMPLE 3: AN INFORMAL CONSECRATION

At a prearranged signal, one person goes to each of the four quarters, where the element is waiting for them. In the east, a person picks up a dish of incense; in the south, a person picks up the censer;[8] in the west, a person picks up the water dish; and in the north, a person picks up a dish of salt. They wait for a moment, making sure everyone is ready.

Eastern Witch: Steps forward toward the altar, lifts dish high.

Lord and Lady, bless this Air!

He brings the dish down to about elbow height.

Southern Witch: Steps forward toward the altar, meeting the Eastern Witch, and holds the censer before the Eastern Witch, who takes a large pinch of incense and drops it into the censer. When the censer is smoking, the Southern Witch lifts it high, saying:

Lord and Lady, bless this Fire!

The Southern and Eastern Witches now place their objects on the altar, and return to the body of the circle.

Western Witch: Steps forward toward the altar, lifts the water dish high.

Lord and Lady, bless this Water!

She brings the dish down to about elbow height.

Northern Witch: Steps forward toward the altar, meeting the Western Witch, and lifts the salt dish high.

Lord and Lady, bless this Earth!

She holds it before the Eastern Witch, who takes a large pinch of salt and drops it into the water, stirring with his athame or fingers.

The Western and Northern Witches now place their objects on the altar, and return to the body of the circle.

This example is very different than the previous one. The language is simple and direct, and the feel is much more relaxed. Yet it accomplishes the same thing, and it follows the same rules. It works with the underlying pattern of the ritual, and it keeps the pattern of four consistent for the elements. Polarity can be used, if you wish, by having each pair of Witches (east/south and west/north) be of the opposite sex, and/or exchange a kiss when they finish their consecrations.

Example 4: A Silent Consecration

Our final example is pretty radical, as it bypasses words entirely, but you'll see that it follows the same basic pattern, and that it is very much informed by an understanding of the nature of the elements.

This can be done by one person, by two, or by four. For simplicity, I am writing it as if it is all being done by a Priestess.

The Priestess lifts the dish of incense, raising it to the gods, either by symbolically lifting it into the air, or by "showing" it to the statues on the altar. She then uses an invoking pentagram over the incense. All her gestures are slow and exaggerated. Finally, she lifts the incense to her forehead, touching it to her third eye. Then she puts the dish back on the altar, takes a large pinch of incense, and places it in the censer.

The Priestess now lifts the censer to the gods, and then uses the invoking pentagram on it. She brings the censer to her face and inhales deeply, waving the smoke toward her nose. Then she places the censer in front of her solar plexus (a traditional location of the will), and again waves the smoke toward herself. She places the censer back on the altar.

Next the water. After presenting it to the gods and invoking over it, she uses her fingers to anoint her heart chakra. The dish is returned to the altar.

Finally, the salt dish is presented to the gods and then invoked over. She holds the dish near her groin, and slowly takes a pinch of salt and rubs it below her belly button, just above the pubic area. The remains of that pinch of salt is placed into the water dish. The salt is returned to the altar and the salt water is stirred.

The Priestess in this example doesn't think much of wordy ceremonies, but she knows what she's doing. The "how" is there, since each presentation to the gods invokes their power onto the consecration. "What you're doing" is expressed by the invoking pentagram; its traditional use in consecrations demonstrates that this is what's going on. Finally, the specific intention is there, in the straightforward interaction with each element—the mind for Air, the will for Fire, the heart for Water, and the body itself for Earth, as represented by the "earthiest" part of the body. In this way, each element is seen to be doing its job; she uses imitative magic here to show the elements what is expected of them.

Casting the Circle: Making the Space

Air

Let's review the logic in our sequence of events.

1. ***Grounding, Centering and Merging.*** First, we prepared the participants to enter ritual space. We couldn't do anything before this because we had to make sure people were ready for a ceremony.

2. ***Declared Opening.*** Once everyone was ready, we were then able to open the rite. Again, we couldn't do anything else until we did this—we have to open the door before we can go in.

3. ***Stated Purpose.*** Technically, we could proceed without this, but this step gives shape and meaning to what follows; it keeps our ritual from being aimless, and in a group setting, it makes sure everyone is joined in purpose. (Since we have merged, we are receptive to this joined purpose.)

4. ***Consecrate the Elements.*** Now we're ready to build the ritual space, but first we need building materials. We consecrate the elements because they are the raw materials of the circle.

5. ***Casting the Circle.*** At last we can create the sacred space of the circle, with our purpose clear, and all participants and ingredients ready.

How Many Times Is the Circle Cast?

I have seen or read about rituals in which the circle is cast any number of times from one to five (the ritual with five castings was unusual, to say the least), using a wide variety of tools. I'll leave it to the Earth section to describe *how* these various multiple castings are performed; for now I want to explain why I think the circle should be cast exactly three times.

THE MAGIC OF THREES

There are certain numbers that are used repeatedly in the circle for their magical and symbolic properties. *Two*'s significance is primarily found in polarity, as already discussed. Two is Yin/Yang, Lord/Lady, Day/Night, Is/Is Not. Two is balanced by dynamic tension—each side holding the other in place. Two is also the dual God.

Four has also been discussed. The four elements are the building blocks of nature, they are a description of reality, they are everything. Four is foundational, it is the square of a pedestal, a solid base. Four doesn't move easily, it is very stable.

Three is the triple goddess, and the triangle is the symbol of many goddesses, not least because it resembles a *yoni*—a woman's pubic triangle.

Three is also the *flux* of nature. Three is in constant motion, as seen in the many *cycles* of three. Birth-Death-Rebirth, Youth-Maturity-Age, Beginning-Middle-End; three is seen in states that are shifting. Think of three juggling balls—the juggler can hold no more than two at once; one is always in the air.

In magic and in folklore, it is said that everything comes in threes. Even today, we can easily think of many stories in which three is the significant number. A genie grants *three* wishes. Hansel and Gretel got lost on their *third* trip into the woods. Psyche was given *three* tasks to fulfill by Aphrodite. Puss-in-Boots helped the youngest of *three* brothers. Cinderella was the youngest of *three* sisters, and also had *three* adversaries—

her step-mother and two step-sisters. (Psyche was also the youngest of three sisters.) Jack planted *three* magic beans. "What I tell you three times is true." "Third time's the charm." How about nursery rhymes? *Three* blind mice, *three* men in a tub, the black sheep has *three* bags of wool, and the *three* characters of Wynken, Blynken, and Nod go on a magical journey. (I could go on.)

Folklore completes things with three, and magic sees three as changeable—is this a paradox? Not really—three completes *cycles*, and as we know, every time a cycle is ended, it begins again. It is the importance of three as a fulfiller of cycles and a bringer of wishes (third time's the charm) that makes us use repetitions of three so often in magic and ritual.

While we're on the topic of numerology, what of other magical numbers? *Five* has many meanings, but is often seen simply as the combination of two and three—Lord (two) and Lady (three), balance and flux. Five is also four fulfilled; we'll see this when we call the quarters—east, then south, then west, then north, then *return to east*, so that the total is five. The squared circle is finished only by the fifth point, the return.

Seven is four-plus-three, and *nine* is three-times-three—numerology relies heavily on taking numbers apart and recombining them.

Casting the Circle Three Times

Although we recognize meaning in two, three, four, five, seven, and nine, three is the number most appropriate for circle casting. Three is the number of repetitions for good fortune, and three is the number of cycles. We've already brought four into the circle with the elements, and will do so again when we call the quarters. Two is a *tension*, its polarity is powerful, but we can't create a *whole* thing, not to mention a peaceful thing, from two. Three is also the right number because we have three important ingredients with which to cast the circle; three important things to do in order to make the circle sacred and whole.

The Components of Circle Casting

The three *ingredients* of circle casting are these:

- Earth and Water—combined in salt water, the "female" elements
- Air and Fire—combined in the incense, the "male" elements
- The will of the Witch.

It is absolutely vital to understand that, although the elements are the raw materials of circle casting, someone must *choose* to cast a circle, and make that choice manifest in word and deed. Circles aren't just there, like churches and synagogues—they have to be *made*.

There are three things that must be *done* to cast a circle, *in this order*:

- The circle must be drawn,
- The circle must be sprinkled,
- The circle must be censed.

The circle must be drawn. It amazes me how many people leave this step out! I have seen plenty of rituals in which the sprinkling and censing are done, but the actual drawing, the tracing out of the circle's perimeter, is omitted. To draw the circle is the act of creating the circle. I cannot possibly explain why it's ever skipped; it's like painting a house and hanging the curtains without putting up the walls!

What Is the Circle?

The circle is a universe unto itself, a microcosm of the real, macrocosmic universe. It is a place-that-is-not-a-place, existing in timeless time, between the world of human beings and the realm of the gods. When we cast a circle, we are creating this timeless, placeless place, so that anything is possible within it. We can cast our spells to distant places, be-

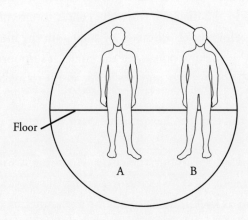

The Circle

cause there is no far or near in our non-place. We can cast our spells into the future, because there is no time. We can have direct contact with gods and other entities, because we are not in our own, mundane world. We can safely do inner work, transformational work, in the circle—work that might not feel safe in the mundane world.

The circle is a container. It is a sealed place that keeps magical energy in, the way that a greenhouse keeps humidity in. Our energies build and build in this mystic greenhouse until we choose to release them by "sending" a spell. Secondarily, the sealed circle keeps unwanted energies out. I say that this protective function is secondary because the Witch's basic attitude toward the world is welcoming; the world is good and we don't fear the things in it—including noncorporeal entities. I've encountered all manner of things and experienced some strange, and some upsetting, moments in my many years as a Witch, but I've never seen or felt anything that fits the description of a demon. In general, the occult is something I have found to be dangerous only in the way that driving a car is dangerous—you have to know what you're doing, be respectful of the rules of the road, and wear your safety belt. There simply aren't hordes of evil demons waiting at the perimeters to gobble you up, although there are some things that aren't pleasant, and some mistakes that have serious consequences. The protective nature of a circle is important, it's helpful, but Wiccans don't believe, the way other magicians in the past have believed, that it's life-or-death.

The circle is mis-named. In fact, it is not a two-dimensional circle, but a three-dimensional egg. The circle is an egg, *not* a sphere. If it was, and we drew the diameter on the floor, then by definition the distance from the center to any point would be the same. A sphere would therefore make too steep an angle—in the illustration, Person A is fine, but Person B's head is sticking outside of the circle. It's important to realize this, because you need to visualize the circle, and the image needs to make sense.

The circle is an elongated egg surrounding and enveloping us. The sides rise very gradually, and the point, the top, reaches up into space. (The egg is also a symbol of the Goddess.)

The circle must be sprinkled. Sprinkling the circle—marking it with the consecrated salt water—cleanses and purifies it. This works in part by the magical principle of *contagion*—a concept every bit as important as sympathy and imitation. Contagion means what it sounds like—magical qualities are contagious; they spread from thing to thing. Consecration is seen as a contagious quality—to consecrate something, touch it with a consecrated thing. The circle is consecrated by water and earth when it is sprinkled.

To sprinkle the circle is to *purify* it, because that is the primary quality that salt water is believed to bring. Water, of course, is used to wash, to cleanse people, places, and things. Water washes away unwanted physical things, and so it also washes away unwanted psychic and magical things. As discussed earlier, we have to sprinkle *before* we cense, because we wouldn't want to "wash away" the censing. Salt, in addition to representing Earth, also has purifying qualities. Its ancient use as a food preservative is considered proof of this—just as it prevents contaminants from affecting food, it prevents contaminants from entering the circle.

The circle must be censed. The censing of the circle brings blessings and attracts positive energy. Just as the salt water is primarily a purifier, *removing* the unwanted, the incense *adds*, bringing more to the circle than was there before: more blessings, more beauty, more qualities that are pleasing to the gods and other entities. We've already discussed the ability of aroma and rising smoke to attract the gods, and to surround ourselves with it marks our circle as an especially pleasing and noticeable place. Many people forget that part of the purpose of ritual is to get the god's *attention*. Pagans don't believe that our gods are watching all of us, all the time, with equal concentration. Omniscience is a concept of monotheism, not Paganism. Part of living a life filled with ritual is that it brings us into their awareness. So, we make our circle interesting and attractive to them to further that aim.

These steps are done in this order because they are a logical progression. We can't sprinkle and cense until we have *something* to sprinkle and cense, and so first we must create the circle. Once created, it can be cleansed. After it is pure, it can be blessed.

The magic of three here has an additional quality. In typical numerological fashion, this three is two-plus-one. The two is the dynamic tension of the female elements (salt water) and the male elements (incense) creating a polarity. The one is the circle and the individual Witch who created it. It is one person, one will,[9] binding the elements together to a specific purpose. When fully cast, the circle is bound together with intelligence, energy, feeling, and stability; bound together by human spirit.

Water

The Circle Story

The universe is a *place;* it is bounded. Inside is the universe, outside is not. Since we know that the circle is a symbol of the Goddess, we know that this circular universe we create *is* the Goddess, *created by* the Goddess.

The first thing that happens to the Body of the Goddess is that it is given form; it is shaped by the Word and by the Will. It is pure (salt water) and beautiful (incense). It is balanced. It is composed of everything that is (the four elements, representing all of reality).

Our story so far, then: *In the beginning, there was the Word; the Word that said that creation would happen. The pieces of creation were the Four Elements: Earth, Air, Fire and Water. From them, and from Her own Will, the Goddess created Herself, and bounded Herself about with everything that is real.*

The Mythic Basis of the Circle

It is said in Wicca that the circle is a gift given to us by the Goddess. In *The Legend of the Descent of the Goddess into the Underworld*[10] we are told:

> *And our Goddess ever inclineth to love, and mirth, and happiness; and guardeth and cherisheth her hidden children in life, and in death she teacheth the way to her communion; and even in this world she teacheth them the mystery of the Magic Circle, which is placed between the world of men and of the gods.*

There are two significant points to this passage, which provide a mythic justification for circle casting. First, it is the Goddess Herself who teaches Witches (the "hidden children") to cast the circle, and second, it specifies that the circle is placed "between the world[s]." Since the circle is described in this myth as a *mystery*, and since that's another way of saying it is *mystical*, let's move directly to Fire.

Fire

The *Legend of the Descent* tells us that the Goddess is trying to teach us something. In fact, she's teaching us the most mystical, most elusive quality of religious life, direct communion with the deity: "*in death she teacheth the way to her communion.*" Well, that's nice, but not very helpful: We find communion with Her, but not until we die. But the myth goes on: "*. . . and even in this world she teacheth them the mystery of the Magic Circle.*" I'm especially interested in that word "even." It seems to connect the communion after death with the mystery She teaches. It seems to say, "We reach communion with the Goddess after death, but in life, She gives us a substitute." If true communion with the Goddess can only take place after death, how can the circle provide that experience in life? Again, the legend provides a clue: The circle is *"between the world of men and of the gods."*

Can it be that this placement is important to our relationship with the Goddess? Can it be that it isn't just a convenient way to do magic? The circle is a *mystery* after all; can that mystery have something to do with its placement?

If the circle exists outside the stream of time, if it exists outside the world of men, of mortality, then it exists outside the laws governing life and death. It is *between* the worlds; we are not in the realm of the gods, but neither are we in our own world. In our world, certain things can only happen when you're dead, but between the worlds, possibilities are much greater. This can *only* be understood mystically; it "doesn't make sense," but it may just be that the circle is the place where we can experience what the afterlife is like, while still retaining our mortal bodies.

If that's true, if that's what this story means, then the most beautiful part is this: It's exactly what the Goddess intends. It's a gift She gives to us, something offered because She loves and cherishes us. "Here," She says, "this is the way to be closer to Me."

Finally, remember that the legend says she "teacheth" this to us. That implies that Her mysteries should be *learned*, should be *studied*, and that there are knowledge and techniques to be mastered.

Earth

As mentioned before, I've witnessed a variety of circle castings, and read about even more. Here's a sampling:

- The circle is cast once, by declaration. One Witch (usually the Priestess) walks the perimeter, with or without a tool. Sometimes the Priestess and Priest cast the circle together in this way.

- The circle is cast once, by the group. An announcement is made such as "We will now make the circle," all hold hands and chant, and the circle is said to be cast. There are a number of variations on this; perhaps everyone dances instead of chanting.

- The circle is walked twice, once to sprinkle, once to cense. The circle isn't drawn.

- The circle is cast multiple times with multiple tools. Sprinkling and censing may or may not be done. I think the oddest variation that I've ever seen was this one: Once around with the sword, once around to sprinkle, once to cense, once with the athame, and once with the staff. A total of five castings were done! Not only does this take forever, but it's redundant; as we've learned, the athame and sword are essentially the same tool.

- The circle is cast three-times-three. It is drawn three times, sprinkled three times, and censed three times. The main problem with this one is that it takes too long, unless you *trot* around the circle.

I've mentioned things taking too long a couple of times. It's important to remember pacing, especially in a group. Obviously, working alone, you can suit your own mood, but in a group, you need pacing that keeps everyone together and focused. A long speech that everyone just stands and watches can cause trouble; fidgety people are un-centered people. One or two such speeches can be fine; a dramatic moment might need an explanatory lead-in. But if every step of the circle is drawn out, the beauty and magic are lost in the restlessness. The parts of ritual that can take the longest without being problematic are the parts that everyone participates in; if one person is doing something while others watch, brevity becomes more important. Don't shorten something to the point where it loses its meaning; don't cut corners. But if you keep an eye on a taut structure, your coveners will be grateful and the energy of the rite will flow better, too.

I'm convinced that the best way is this: The circle should be cast three times; it should be drawn, sprinkled, and censed. It can be done by one person, by two people, or by three different people. Drawing is usually done as a single step, by one person or by a couple together, but sprinkling and censing are often done together, by two people side-by-side, or one right after the other.

How to Draw the Circle

What tool should be used to draw the circle? Since this is the step that uses the *will* of the Witch, and of the coven, it makes sense to use the tool assigned to Fire, since will is Fire. In general, to cast the circle is considered an act of authority, and so the sword is used; but if your coven assigns wands to Fire, you might consider using a staff or wand instead. Since the circle is considered female, casting it with a male tool creates and re-inforces polarity.

Drawing the circle also has an important visual component. Everyone in the group should be visualizing the circle, and they'll be maintaining that visualization throughout the rest of the ritual. *This is important*—every time you look around you from here on out, you should see *circle*, not *living room*. You need to know where the circle is in order to respect the circle (which we'll discuss shortly). Therefore, everyone must know where the circle is located. Marking the quarter points helps; everyone should know whether the quarter candles are just inside, or just outside, the perimeter, and that'll give them a good idea of what the entire shape is.

You can mark the circle on the ground in advance, using cord, chalk, pebbles, or a marked rug.[11] Then, when it's time to draw the circle, you're just tracing the line that everyone can see. This isn't required, but it's helpful, and it keeps the circle very precise.

You can also make sure that whatever tool you're using touches, or comes close to touching, the floor or ground. The tip of a sword or knife makes a clear mark on pile carpet that doesn't harm the carpet, and will stay there until you vacuum. Hard wood floors, on the other hand, should not be actually touched with the sword unless you *want* scratches. Even without marking the floor, though, touching it or coming close to touching it will create a connection, a sense of reality, for the circle. Everyone will see exactly where it is.

Some people are rather indistinct with their drawing, the circle is "out there" someplace, and some people specify that the circle includes the entire room, in order to allow freedom of movement. This isn't a great idea. We already know that magic works best when it's specific, and that our minds focus best when they have something to focus *on*. If there's nothing around me to cue me that there's a circle, I could easily forget. Better a little awkwardness—like not being allowed to touch a wall—than a loss of your ability to visualize. On occasions when I've had so many people in my circle that I *had* to include some wall, I lifted my sword and "touched" the exact spot on the wall out of which the circle extended, so that I remained as specific as could be.

When you draw the circle, start in the east. I pick up my sword from the altar and lift it with both hands, showing it to everyone present; this gets everyone's attention, and therefore everyone's *will*, involved with the process. All eyes gather onto the sword, held above the altar—it can be a riveting moment. Then I carry the sword, still two-handed, to the east, walking clockwise around the circle—*not* crossing quickly from south to east, but going all the way around. In the east I again lift the sword, drawing attention this time to my starting point and pulling everyone into the exact moment when I begin to make the circle. Only then do I point the sword down to the floor and begin. I go all the way around, *clockwise*, making certain that I return to the exact spot where I began. When I say "So mote it be!"[12] I lift the sword two-handed a final time, so that we all know that we've finished where we began.

As with consecrations, drawing the circle can be silent, or you can speak. Everyone can recite something together, or sing, or you can use back and forth echoing. Something wordless, like an Aum or a drumbeat, might be used.

How to Sprinkle the Circle

Sprinkling and censing can be done by one person or by two. The person sprinkling should go before the person censing, but it can be just one or two steps ahead, if you wish to create the impression of a joint effort. If you're working the polarity of the elements, you might have a man do the sprinkling and a woman doing the censing, so that each person's gender is opposite the tool they're using.

You can match all three castings, saying something similar (as with the four consecrations), singing three different verses of one song, or what have you. This will bring the circle casting together, reinforcing the notion that it adds up to one thing.

When sprinkling, carry the water to the east, just as you carried the sword. If you're not using an aspergillum, just dip your fingertips in the water and spray the drops along the circle where it's been drawn, as you walk around clockwise. If you've drawn outside the walls, then spray the walls and visualize the water reaching the circle's outer location.

Some people also spray droplets on the members of the coven, going back and forth, with the circle on your left and the other people on your right. If you've done any kind of ceremonial anointing, you can probably skip this. At the quarters, you should be careful not to get water on the candles. Instead, pause at each quarter and *drop* a bit of water at the base of the candle holder. Return to the exact spot in the east where you started, and spray again at the spot where you started.

How to Cense the Circle

The important thing to remember about censing is that smoke *rises* and *moves*. *Don't* bring the censer to the exact spot to be censed. For example, if you were censing a small object, you wouldn't put it *in* the censer, you'd hold it *above* the censer and pass it through the smoke. When using smudge on a person, you hold the smudge near to the person and wave the smoke toward them with your hand or a fan. So, when censing the circle, don't go out to the drawn circle like you did with the salt water. Instead, stay a few inches inside the circle; if you're using the kind of censer that swings from a chain, then swing it in a light deosil (clockwise) circle so that the smoke moves in the desired direction. Otherwise, you can wave your hand through the smoke so that you're directing the smoke outward, toward the circle's perimeter. Walk around clockwise, pausing at each quarter and giving it a bit of extra smoke. If you sprayed the people, you must cense them as well, but remember to keep the smoke *below* and a few inches *away from* your intended target. For example, to cense the heart, the censer should be held at about navel height and lifted slightly to bring the smoke up.

When you finish drawing, you lift the sword up. When you finish sprinkling, you stop spraying droplets of water. But when you finish censing, there will still be smoke coming out of the censer. So it's important to shift your body language to indicate that you're done. Lift the censer the way you did the sword, and then drop it down as low as you can comfortably hold it, about to your hip. Relax your shoulders and your stance so that "I'm done" is communicated even though you're still holding the censer. Then return to the altar.

EXAMPLE 1: A STRUCTURED CASTING

Priestess: Lifts sword as described. Begins speaking in the east.
        By my True Will

Group: (repeating) *By my True Will*

Priestess: *I circle once*

Group: *I circle once*

Priestess: *I draw this circle*

Group: *I draw this circle*

Priestess: *To contain and protect.*

Group: *To contain and protect.*

Priestess: *O holy place,*

Group: *O holy place,*

Priestess: *be filled with peace.*

Group: *be filled with peace.*

Priestess: *In the Sacred Names*

Group: *In the Sacred Names*

Priestess: *So mote it be!*

Group: *So mote it be!*

The Priestess draws the circle while she speaks. With practice, she'll be able to time it so that she finishes speaking as she finishes drawing. If at any time that doesn't work out, she must still wait until she's finished to say the final *So mote it be!*

The Priestess returns to the altar and places the sword back on the altar. She lifts the censer. The Priest lifts the water dish. They face each other and exchange a quick kiss. They walk together to the east.

Priest: *By Water and Earth*

Priestess: *By Fire and Air*

Priest: *I circle twice*

Priestess: *I circle thrice*

Priest: *I sprinkle this circle*

Priestess: *I cense this circle*

Priest: *To be clean and pure.*

Priestess: *To be blessed and sweet.*

Priest: *O holy place,*

Priestess: *O holy place,*

Priest: *be filled with love.*

Priestess: *be filled with trust.*

Priest: *In the Sacred Names*

Priestess: *In the Sacred Names*

Both: *So mote it be!*

Group: *So mote it be!*

Again, the Priestess and Priest should both have finished, and be at the east, before saying *So mote it be!* together. Since the Priest is a step or two ahead, he should stop at the east, turn, and face the Priestess as she finishes. They'll make eye contact before saying *So mote it be!* and then the entire group will repeat the phrase. Only then will they return to the altar together.

Example 2: A Rhythmic Casting

I learned this one from a tradition of Wicca known as NROOGD,[13] which originated (and is still mainly found) in California. Its beauty is in its simplicity. The same phrase is repeated over and over, without stopping, during the drawing, sprinkling, and censing. In order to work, it should be said rhythmically, with a strong beat. You should keep saying it while putting down one tool and picking up the next, so have someone at the altar waiting, to take the sword and hand you the water dish, and then to take the water dish and hand you the censer. Or, have three different people do the three parts, in relay fashion.

Starting at the east, begin drawing the circle and say:

> *Tout and tout. Around and about.*
> *Power stay in. World stay out.*

Have everyone join in so that the whole coven is chanting rhythmically, perhaps clapping their hands in time. (Don't use drums for this, they drown out the words, but rattles and other small percussion instruments are great.) It's natural for a chant like this to get pretty loud, so by the time you're ready to say *So mote it be* at the end, you should SHOUT it. (Don't say *So mote it be* after drawing or after sprinkling, as it's important not to break the tempo with a chant like this. Save it all for the end.)

After building to a peak and then SHOUTING, you should pause for a moment of silence and re-grouping. Everyone should breath a bit and re-connect to the Earth and their center before proceeding.

Remember that when you pare the words down to a minimum, as we do here, you're depending even more than usual on *visualization* and *intention*. It's up to you to *know* that you're drawing, then cleansing, then blessing; otherwise it's not going to happen.

Respecting the Circle

We've gone to a great deal of effort to make this circle, and we want to make sure it works. One of the most important ways of doing that is to treat the circle as a real thing. You're between the worlds, remember, so you're creating your own reality. The most vital bit of reality to create is the circle itself. The rules for respecting the circle may seem strict and elaborate, but *they work*. By maintaining the circle imaginatively and behaviorally, you maintain it magically.

- The circle is cast by clockwise movement, and the energy in the circle is constantly flowing clockwise. Counter-clockwise movement breaks the flow and harms the circle. Don't do it!

- The circle is a container. A room is a container. If you leave a room without using the door, you damage the room. If you leave a circle without cutting a magical doorway, you damage the circle. Use your athame to cut a rectangular doorway, using the spot where it was drawn as a threshold. Step through, just like a mime. Then close the door behind you by re-drawing the circle with a stroke of your athame, and using two more strokes to symbolize the censing and sprinkling. Now you've sealed it three times to match the casting. (The three strokes form a "Z" and in my group, we used to joke that the circle was sealed by the Mark of Zorro.)

- Even if you use a magical doorway, a little power "leaks" out every time you breach the circle. Keep it to a minimum. One of the reasons we double- and triple-checked everything before we started the ritual was so that we wouldn't have to leave the circle once it was cast.

- Watch your hands and feet! I have seen many incidents of people letting their hands or feet stick out of the circle as they carelessly shifted about trying to get comfortable while seated on the floor. There's no excuse for this! Even if you're uncomfortable, it is the responsibility of everyone in the circle to maintain the circle. If it *does* happen, repair the circle with your athame in the same way you closed the door.

- Animals, and children below the age of reason, are always a little bit between the worlds—it's their nature. So, they can move in and out of the circle freely without harming the energy.

Calling the Quarters

Air

"Calling the Quarters" is one of the most easily recognized parts of Wiccan ritual. It seems that everyone knows that you're supposed to go to each quarter and call . . . what? A guardian? An element? A "watchtower"? The idea that you're supposed to do *something* at the cardinal points is a lot more widespread than any understanding of what it means.

There are basically two parts to quarter invocations; in part, you are recognizing a *direction*, and in part, you are recognizing some kind of *being* in that direction. Let's take these one at a time.

Marking a Direction

We've just finished creating a space between the worlds—about as middle-of-nowhere as you can get. It floats freely in spaceless space and timeless time. It isn't anywhere; it's just where we are. In order to proceed, we need orientation; we need to have a firmer sense of location, and so we must have direction.

Theologically, this has a lot to do with Wiccans seeing ourselves as a part of the natural world. When we place ourselves, we place ourselves in relation to nature, to Mother Earth; Her geography and Her poles. We don't just have a ritual, we have a ritual that is oriented around its place in nature.

How many directions are called? I have seen four, five, six, and seven, which is quite a range. Here are all the possible directions:[14]

1. East
2. South
3. West
4. North
5. Center
6. Up
7. Down

In the system I am teaching, of four elements, four directions are called. In a system of five elements, including Spirit, the center is invoked as the direction of Spirit. Once again, consistency is your watchword—why invoke five now when you've been doing four all along? On the other hand, if you've thought it over and decided to work with five elements, it would probably be a mistake to leave out the direction that corresponds to one of them.

A six-direction system is the four cardinal points plus up and down, and seven adds back the center as a direction. The use of both six and seven directions originates in Native American tradition and should only be used if your ritual is heavily influenced by Native American ways throughout—in other words, don't work a fully European system (Wicca) with Native American directions. Remember that the ritual should work as a cohesive whole.[15]

Who or What Are We Calling?

When we "call the quarters" we are calling something or someone; we are *summoning*. It is vital, then, to know who or what we are summoning—otherwise we have no business issuing the invitation. There are basically three possibilities, or at least three terms that are bandied about:

- We are calling elements.
- We are calling elementals.
- We are calling guardians.

Many people simply call the *elements*, i.e., they call Air in the east, Fire in the south, and so on. If you examine the ritual, however, you'll see that you have already "called" the elements when you consecrated them. Not only are they already present in the ritual, but they've already been *used* in the ritual, so it's really too late to call them.

You might still wish to greet the elements in their directions. You might want a very naturalistic ritual, one that doesn't call on any "otherworldly" or magical entities. Maybe you don't even believe in other kinds of beings; in which case, summoning them would probably make you feel kind of silly. If you want to use just the elements, though, you shouldn't *call* them. If you're calling another entity, someone or something not already in the circle, then a summoning or an invitation is appropriate. But if you're talking about something already present—as the elements are—then an acknowledgment, a placement, or a connection is more appropriate. In other words, you're not saying "O Air, come to our circle!" Instead you're saying "O East, be in our circle. You are the direction of Air!" What you're calling is the *direction itself*, and the element is being placed there; its connection with the direction is being used and reinforced.

Whenever we invoke anything or anyone, we use as many different images, associations, and connections as possible to create a powerful and effective call. For example, suppose you were invoking me. You might just say "Deborah," and I might answer. Or not—it's a common name. You've got a better chance with "Deborah Lipp." But if you said "Deborah Lipp with the dark curly hair, Deborah Lipp mother of Arthur, Deborah Lipp the writer," you have definitely gotten my attention, and made one hundred percent certain that I know I am definitely the one you want. If you threw in a bit of flattery, and a sense of urgency and purpose, I would be even more inclined to come. These factors—specificity, descriptiveness, praise, and need—are the makings of excellent and powerful invocations.

Elementals, unlike elements, are specific beings, beings who have not previously been summoned, who could certainly be summoned now.

It takes a bit of an imaginative leap to understand what an elemental is. There are four kinds of elemental beings, as mentioned in chapter 2. They are the *sylphs* of Air, the *salamanders* of Fire, the *undines* of Water, and the *gnomes* of Earth. Each elemental is made up entirely and exclusively of its own elemental nature. They don't have Spirit, in the sense that Spirit is the combination of the four elements, and so they cannot change themselves. We are so used to seeing our own elemental attributes in combination that it is hard for us to picture beings of just one element.

Sylphs are Air. They think and they float. They are rarified and elusive. They do not respond to feeling, and they do not feel. They cannot be praised, fed, or excited. They are exclusively beings of wind, thought, and flight. You cannot persuade a sylph to care about your ritual, because caring is emotion—Water. Do not expect deep connections with sylphs, because depth is not in the nature of Air.

Salamanders are Fire. They burn and explode; they smolder and burst and consume. They have no caution, no concern, no restraint; none of those are in the nature of Fire. When calling Fire elementals, *you* must always be careful and cautious, because salamanders are incapable of these qualities.

Undines are Water. They feel and flow. They fulfill themselves in desire, intuition, and love. Do not expect them to be sensible, nor to hold still for very long. Sense is for Air, stillness is for Earth, and undines have none of either. You can't reason with an undine, although you can *attract* her.

Gnomes[16] are Earth. Because we live on the Earth, and we are solid, we can often relate to gnomes, but we can also be mistaken about their nature. Remember that gnomes are slow, if they move at all, and are immensely stubborn. They cannot be persuaded or enticed, although they do respond to sensory stimulation and to respect.

Elementals are often called lesser beings. I think this is true, but I don't think this means they are *inferior* beings. They have fewer components than we, are less complex, and are more basic. To call an elemental, you would have to be rather forceful; you would *summon* or *command* rather than *invite*. This is not because you're ill-mannered, but because they are simpler beings who need to be spoken to very clearly, and niceties will confuse the issue. You are calling across a considerable psychic distance—from the world of Spirit to worlds of only one element—and a call across such an expanse had best be clear and strong.

But do you really want to call the elementals? As the personal embodiments of their respective elements, they are powerful beings and can certainly be made welcome in your circle. They are very *natural* beings, partaking in a basic nature that we, complicated and confused as we are, can only imagine—and learn from. However, they can also be difficult to handle. If called at this point in the ritual, they should be thoroughly and specifically dismissed when the ritual is coming to an end. None of them have any regard for humanity, except as we happen to coincide with what they're up to anyway. Many Wiccans choose to call elementals, but many others prefer to call *Guardians* instead.

The *Guardians* are sometimes called the Guardians of the Watchtowers, although no one seems to know exactly what a "Watchtower" is in this context. It is simpler to say they are Guardians of the Elements; from there, you can assume they live somewhere. Maybe they live in towers, but maybe they don't; since the towers have no impact on their function, let's just leave them out.

Like elementals, there is one Guardian for each element, and they share the basic nature of the element. The Guardians, however, are considered "higher" than elementals, in that their functions are more sophisticated. They have been compared to Archangels; some Witches have said that these are different words for the same thing.[17] (Other Witches don't care for Biblical creatures like Archangels to be included in a Pagan ceremony.) The comparison is apt, in that the Guardians are not gods, but they are beings who are otherworldly, and who protect and support human beings. Although I have worked with them in rituals for years, I know little about them, because the nature of the Guardians is elusive. I have come to understand them as beings roughly equal to ourselves, as sophisticated and complex as humans, as spiritually evolved as we, and with a similar relationship to the gods—sharing in their essence but still distant from them in practical terms.[18] Their existence is very different from ours, of course, but so is the existence of a dolphin, another creature which many people have begun to view as roughly equal to human beings.

The primary purpose of the Guardians is to serve the gods; they protect humans and guard us primarily as an adjunct to protecting and guarding rituals devoted to, and sacred to the gods. Outside of ritual, they have little interest in our lives, and don't seem to watch over people in their day-to-day lives. The Guardians protect the circle from danger from their direction and from their element (i.e. the Guardian of the South prevents fire from breaking out in the circle), and they use the power of their element to do so. Their nature is heavily influenced by their element, but the Guardians aren't made up exclusively of their element, the way that elementals are.

Most of the more "old-fashioned" and "traditional" Wiccan traditions will call Guardians in the quarters, rather than elements or elementals. The advantages are that Guardians are protective, intelligent (after their nature), and devoted to the gods. One disadvantage is that they are not easy to know or understand, and many magicians feel (wisely) that it can be dangerous and foolish to summon something without knowing what it is. The other problem with the Guardians is not a disadvantage so much as a matter of belief; many Wiccans do not hold to the idea of a hierarchy of otherworldly beings; it smacks too much of medieval sorcery, with its angels and demons and rankings of each.

As usual, then, we are left with you making a choice as to what is best for *your* worship, based upon what you (and not I) believe.

Water

Gatekeepers

There is a being in many mythologies known, for lack of a better word, as a *gatekeeper.*[19] This deity serves the special function of safeguarding access to the gods. He both keeps intruders away from the gods and lets worshippers in. In Norse myth, Heimdall stands upon Bifrost, the rainbow bridge, which connects Midgard, the world of men, to Asgard, the world of the gods. It is Heimdall who protects this pathway to the gods from being used by an invading army, and he guards it ceaselessly, sleeping with one eye open. In Irish mythology, a nameless deity guarded the hill of Tara, where lived the Tuatha Dé Danaan, the gods of Ireland. This gatekeeper prevented anyone unworthy from entering into the hill of Tara, as recorded in detail in the tale of how Lugh ultimately gained admittance.

In Yoruba traditions (from west Africa), Eshu (also known as Legba) must be invoked before any other gods, because he is the translator for the gods; only he can translate the wishes of humans into the language that his brother and sister gods understand. In Hinduism, Ganesha is the gatekeeper. He is invoked at the beginning of all ceremonies, no matter who the god or goddess being worshiped may be. Because Ganesha is the Lord of Obstacles, his intercession is needed to remove the obstacles to contact with the other gods and goddesses.

It is perhaps a remnant of these gatekeeper tales that places St. Peter at the Gates of Heaven, admitting only the worthy into the presence of God.

It's almost always a mistake to refer to a god or god function as "universal"—somewhere, sometime, there is an exception. But the gatekeeper function is widespread and significant. It suggests even more than it shows; that is, there is plenty of indication of more gatekeepers, in both myth and ritual, than we have record of.

It seems to me that in Wicca, the Guardians act jointly as gatekeepers, holding and protecting the circle, which is the gate between gods and mortals. Wicca is unique in that the worshippers stand *within* the gate, giving us a direct and vital contact with our gods—in most traditions, the worshippers stand *outside* the gate, surrounding, rather than surrounded by, the gatekeeper. Maybe that's why we need four gatekeepers in Wicca, whereas everyone else seems to have just one.

The Circle Story

The Goddess has created Herself, She has made the circle, and she has filled Herself with reality, the elements. She has form but no place. By creating the directions, She creates geography itself. In Her yin/yang dance with the God, She is place and He is time; She is geography and He is history; it is up to Her to create direction.

Having created four directions, Our Lady places a Guardian at each, a being who will embody the essence of its direction and also protect the Lady's place. They stand ever watchful between Her and the mortal world.

Earth

How to Call a Quarter

Anyone can call a quarter—the High Priestess, High Priest, or any member of the circle. There's no particular tradition associated with any one person doing it. It can be done by one person, by two people, or by four. When working a polarity system, you may wish to have the quarter-calling be balanced in gender—having a couple do each, or men do two and women do two.

As with the elemental consecrations, the use of invoking pentagrams is traditional. You should use the same pentagrams now as you did then. In other words, if you used four different ones before, do so now; if you used Earth Invoking for each element earlier, do the same in each quarter.

The person doing the invocation will be the one to draw the invoking pentagram. In some groups, everyone draws the pentagrams together, but the person invoking will start it off or give the signal to start.

Whoever is calling a quarter walks to it clockwise, meaning that even if she's standing in the southeast, she goes *all the way around* to get to the east. Some people just stand at the altar and turn to face the direction. I think circumambulating adds drama and keeps the clockwise energy flow going. It also reinforces the *meaning*, that the quarter calling is part of creating orientation, because you're orienting yourself by walking. In a large circle—twenty or more people—the walk can be too slow and cumbersome. In that case, have the person who will call the quarter stand near it, so they need only take a step or two, or just turn around.

A second person can walk to the direction, or stay at the altar, and strike a bell at the beginning, end, or both (appropriate points for a bell are noted in the examples).

If you lit the quarter candles at the beginning of the circle, either before it began or as part of the Declared Opening ("We are here, we are surrounded by light") you're in business. Otherwise, you'll light them now. This can be awkward; if you're walking to the quarter, carrying your athame, you will probably not feel comfortable also carrying a lit taper. This is a situation in which it's best to have a separate person carrying the taper and lighting the candle, or have the candle lighting and the invoking done in steps ("I light the candle of . . . and now I invoke . . .").

It's important to return to the east for a fifth and final salute after calling the quarters. If you start at the east and end at the east, you've created a complete circle. Otherwise, you've left your circle incomplete, as illustrated. The Priestess who trained me referred to the incomplete circle as a pizza with a piece eaten, but I have always thought of it as a Pac-Man. It looks as silly as it sounds, and magically, it's as senseless. You don't need to "call" or invoke at the return, because that's already been done. Just walk back to the quarter and face it, physically and psychically completing the circular movement that has helped create the geography of the ritual.

When finished, whether you've called just one quarter or all four, you must walk clockwise back to your place, even if it's all the way around. I've already mentioned that, in a large ritual in which you're trying not to have the timing drag, quarter-callers should stand *at* the quarter they'll invoke. If you can't stand exactly at a quarter under these circumstances, stand slightly to the *left* of it instead of the right. If you walk all the way around to call a quarter, everyone has to wait for you, but if you walk all the way around after you're done, the rest of the ceremony can continue while you're returning to your place.

When creating your own invocations, remember the factors we discussed before, as being most powerful: Be *specific*, be *descriptive*, give *praise* to beings who are invited (it's only polite!) and say *why* you need whoever or whatever to come.

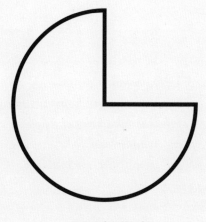

Incomplete Circle

EXAMPLE 1: GREETING THE ELEMENTS

Although you are saluting but not invoking the elements, there is no harm in using the invoking pentagrams if you wish, and they certainly lend drama. (Arguably, you *are* invoking, but the direction, not the element.)

Caller: Walk to the east. All face the east.

O Eastern Realm I call you! (Strike bell, draw invoking pentagram)
Place of Air, place of mighty winds and gentle breezes
You are the cool breath of inspiration and relief
You are the whispered voice of logic and lore
Eastern Realm I call you!
Keep safe your quarter of this sacred circle![20]
Blessed be!

All: *Blessed be!*

Caller: Walk to the south. All face the south.

O Southern Realm I call you! (Strike bell, draw invoking pentagram)
Place of Fire, place of raging flame and soothing heat
You are burning passion and searing lust
You are heated anger and the will to live
Southern Realm I call you!
Keep safe your quarter of this sacred circle!
Blessed be!

All: *Blessed be!*

Caller: Walk to the west. All face the west.

O Western Realm I call you! (Strike bell, draw invoking pentagram)
Place of Water, place of thunderous storms and flowing streams
You are the passage to the Summerland
You are the human heart, the purifier, the initiator
Western Realm I call you!
Keep safe your quarter of this sacred circle!
Blessed be!

All: *Blessed be!*

Caller: Walk to the north. All face the north.

> *O Northern Realm I call you!* (Strike bell, draw invoking pentagram)
> *Place of Earth, place of towering peaks and sloping fields*
> *You are steadfast calm, you are the hearth and home*
> *You are union and contentment and the body of the Mother of us all*
> *Northern Realm I call you!*
> *Keep safe your quarter of this sacred circle!*
> *Blessed be!*

All: *Blessed be!*

All face east for final salute, Caller(s) return to place(s).

EXAMPLE 2: CALLING THE ELEMENTALS

The procedure is the same as before; bells, candle-lighting, and invoking pentagrams are at your discretion. I've put in a little extra use of the bell this time, just so you can see another option.

Caller: Walk to the east. All face the east.

> *Greetings Wise Sylphs* (Draw invoking pentagram)
> *I call you in the east!* (Strike bell)
> *O flying ones, O thoughtful ones*
> *Bring your inspiration to our sacred circle!*
> *In the names of the Lady and the Lord come to us* [21]
> *Guard and balance our holy rite!* [22] (Strike bell)
> *Blessed be!*

All: *Blessed be!*

Caller: Walk to the south. All face the south.

> *Greetings Passionate Salamanders* (Draw invoking pentagram)
> *I call you in the south!* (Strike bell)
> *O fiery ones, O brilliant ones*
> *Bring your willpower to our sacred circle!*
> *In the names of the Lady and the Lord come to us*

Guard and balance our holy rite! (Strike bell)
Blessed be!

All: *Blessed be!*

Caller: Walk to the west. All face the west.
Greetings Lovely Undines (Draw invoking pentagram)
I call you in the west! (Strike bell)
O loving ones, O flowing ones
Bring your intuition to our sacred circle!
In the names of the Lady and the Lord come to us
Guard and balance our holy rite! (Strike bell)
Blessed be!

All: *Blessed be!*

Caller: Walk to the north. All face the north.
Greetings Mighty Gnomes (Draw invoking pentagram)
I call you in the north! (Strike bell)
O supportive ones, O constant ones
Bring your stability to our sacred circle!
In the names of the Lady and the Lord come to us
Guard and balance our holy rite! (Strike bell)
Blessed be!

All: *Blessed be!*

All face east for final salute and final strike of the bell. Caller(s) return to place(s).

EXAMPLE 3: CALLING THE GUARDIANS

Since calling the Guardians is the most traditional (read: "old-fashioned") way of invoking the directions, and since Guardians are considered "more important" than elementals, invocations of them tend to be the most formal. In fact, it's in a traditional invocation of the Guardians that you're likely to encounter a lot of "thee's" and "thou's" and very fancy, medieval-sounding language. I confess to thoroughly enjoying that sort of ritual language; when I write ritual for my own use, that's how I tend to sound.

But that's not the only way to write an invocation, and in a book like this, it's important to see the full range of appropriate styles. Informal language can be just as powerful, and as long as it is well-written, using effective invocative technique, it'll work. It can also be a lot of fun, lending a gutsy immediacy to your ritual. It's especially fun to turn something you expect to be formal on its head, and that's what we're doing with the Guardian Invocations. It wakes people up and makes them pay attention, and when done in moderation, that's a good thing.

You're still following the same rules—walking clockwise to each quarter. A bell might be too "proper" an instrument for these calls, perhaps a tambourine or a drum roll would be more suitable.

Caller: Walk to the east. All face the east.

Guardians of the east!
I, Deborah,[23] am calling you NOW! (Bell or other musical sound)
We want and need you here
You're wise, Air Lord, and we need wisdom
So come to this circle[24] for the Lady and Lord[25]
Enjoy yourself while you're here
Please keep your eye on us.
Blessed be!

All: *Blessed be!*

Caller: Walk to the south. All face the south.

Guardians of the south!
I, Deborah, am calling you NOW! (Bell or other musical sound)
We want and need you here
You're passionate, Fire Lord, and we need passion
So come to this circle for the Lady and Lord
Enjoy yourself while you're here
Please keep your eye on us.
Blessed be!

All: *Blessed be!*

Caller: Walk to the west. All face the west.

        Guardians of the west!

        I, Deborah, am calling you NOW! (Bell or other musical sound)

        We want and need you here

        You're compassionate, Water Lord, and we need compassion

        So come to this circle for the Lady and Lord

        Enjoy yourself while you're here

        Please keep your eye on us.

        Blessed be!

All: *Blessed be!*

Caller: Walk to the north. All face the north.

        Guardians of the north!

        I, Deborah, am calling you NOW! (Bell or other musical sound)

        We want and need you here

        You're firm, Earth Lord, and we need firmness

        So come to this circle for the Lady and Lord

        Enjoy yourself while you're here

        Please keep your eye on us.

        Blessed be!

All: *Blessed be!*

All face east for final salute and final strike of the bell/other musical sound. Caller(s) return to place(s).

Body Language

In learning how to consecrate the elements, we saw that gesture and body language can be as much a part of an invocation as the words used. We spent a good deal of time learning the specific magical gestures known as invoking and banishing pentagrams. We also saw an entire set of consecrations done *only* with body language. Use of our bodies will be important throughout the ritual.

When using invoking pentagrams for the consecrations, they were necessarily small, to fit the size of the dishes and the altar. Now you're standing in open space and facing

Pentagon

out; use big, broad movements. An Earth Invoking pentagram can begin at the highest point your hand can reach and come down below your left shoulder. *Slice* each line into the air, picturing the element emerging in the pentagon you create. Picture a wind blowing through a pentagon-shaped window in the east, a flame bursting from the pentagon in the south, a sea or rainstorm in the west, and solid rock or green, rolling hills in the north.

There's more to gesture than just pentagrams, of course. You can develop your own gestures instead of, or in addition to, the traditional ones. To draw something to your circle, why not try using a pulling in gesture, as if you were gathering energy into your arms? Or perhaps you could use a welcoming gesture, as if you'd opened your door and were gesturing someone into your home. Something as simple but as communicative as that has a lot of impact, especially when repeated four times.

Another way of using gesture is to match each gesture to the element being evoked or invoked. You can use your body, as well as your words, to be Airy, or Fiery, or Watery, or Earthy.

EXAMPLE 4: AN INVOCATION IN GESTURE AND SOUND

This example, and the other examples in this section, can be done by a different person or persons at each quarter, or by the same person or persons throughout. I have seen invocations like this performed by one person, by a couple, or by four or five people all going to the quarter together (this last at a very large ritual held at a festival). Instead of assigning the roles to particular people, I am scripting it for the role "Sound" and the role "Movement." It's up to you to decide who will play what role.

Sound and Movement walk together to the east.

Movement: Walks to the east on tiptoe, swaying side-to-side, with her arms held high above her and her fingers splayed apart. Her body forms a kind of "X" shape, with both arms and legs split apart, and waving back and forth.

Sound: Plays a single, fluttery, high note on a recorder or tin whistle, very airy and light. Finishes the invocation by ending the note sharply, a bit louder than before.

Sound and Movement walk together to the south.

Movement: Jumps or hops, crouching down and leaping up several times. Crouch and then go straight up; crouch and then go to the right; crouch and then go to the left, moving like a flame, ending with a 360-degree spin.

Sound: Strikes a cymbal or gong. The sound is loud and fiery and reverberates while Movement is invoking. Sound may continue a soft beat to keep the vibration of the gong or cymbal going. Finishes the invocation by stopping the vibration of the gong or cymbal with his hand, so that as Movement ceases, there is silence.

Sound and Movement walk together to the west.

Movement: Undulates, moving like a hula dancer or belly dancer, moving arms and hips in a flowing, continuous movement, perhaps circling slowly around Sound.

Sound: Sings wordlessly, warbling a note in and out in a liquid sound. The invocation again ends when Sound becomes silent.

Sound and Movement walk together to the north.

Movement: Walks heavily, stomping her feet. Her shoulders are hunched over; she is like a behemoth or a great ape, hanging her arms low and swinging them, moving hips back and forth as she lifts each foot and SLAMS it to the ground before taking the next step. Ends by bending down and POUND-ING the floor/ground.

Sound: Using a large drum, strikes a slow, steady, deep bass note. Ends with one sharp, much louder beat.

Sound and Movement walk together to the east, simply walking and then standing without invocation, acknowledging their return and the completion of the circle.

This example shows how incredibly evocative body language can be; it doesn't require the skill of a professional dancer, but it does require a certain lack of inhibition and a sense of performance; and to do this successfully, it certainly requires a bit of rehearsal. The two or more people doing each quarter must rehearse together prior to the ceremony, so that they can begin and end in concert, and so that they don't surprise each other. With a little practice, they can work it together, Movement responding to Sound.

If one couple is doing all four quarters, have the instruments waiting in each quarter.

You may not like the idea of singing in the west, either because you don't have a good voice, or because it is unbalanced (only three instruments are used). A xylophone or a rain stick can be used as the Water instrument if you prefer.

You may not want to use something this dramatic at all; however, you might enjoy taking pieces of this kind of invocation and mixing it with one of the verbal styles in the previous examples. Picture performing those invocations using *some* of these techniques.

You'll also notice that this "Sound and Movement" calling necessarily omits naming who or what is being called. As with any nonverbal magic, you must have the idea clearly in your mind since you won't have words to reinforce it.

Fire

I started this section by saying that everyone talks about the quarters, but no one says much. Our relationship with the elements, and with whatever beings may reside in the quarters, is mysterious.

The elements are all around us, and they are also within us: Our bodies are solid—flesh, bone, and muscle (Earth); liquid—blood, sexual fluids, glandular fluids, and sometimes mother's milk and amniotic fluid (Water); Air—in our lungs and bronchia; and Fire—heat and "living spirit," the fire of life that sustains. Our selves have elemental qualities—we have minds, hearts, wills, and bodies. It behooves us to know the elements well, to delve deeply into them.

The meditations in this section are sensory and experiential—instead of asking questions, you'll be going deep within and reaching out your senses, exploring the inner realms. Instead of asking yourself if you "believe in" beings who exist on other planes, use trance to see if you can find out. Reach out your awareness while asking yourself if there is anyone or anything you might encounter, and be open to surprise.

The Four Elements

Meditating on the elements is, in my view, one of the most important components of a magical life because the elements permeate everything we do as Witches and magicians. They truly *are* the building blocks, and everything we know can be enriched by the knowledge of Air, Fire, Water, and Earth.

You should enter into a "course of study" that will allow you to directly and deeply experience each element in turn. It isn't strictly necessary to start with Air and go in order. If you have a weakness, it might be most beneficial to start there. In other words, if you tend to have difficulty grounding, begin your work with Earth; if you tend to be forgetful, begin with Air.

Plenty of people do this work on their own, and it's fine to do so. However, it can be a bit rattling, a bit *weird*, to be totally absorbed in one element. Coming out of the meditation can be disconcerting. If you can, do the work in a group, with one person guiding the group in and then back out. That way the leader can re-establish everyone as beings of all four elements at the end of the meditation, which is a much gentler way to "come back."

End your elemental meditation with something that will counter the effect of the particular element. For Air, Fire, and Water, something to eat works very well. Food is of Earth and helps "shake off" the grip of the other elements. For an Earth meditation, try ice water after it's over, to shock you out of Earth and into the balanced world of four elements.

An elemental meditation can begin within yourself, with pure physical experience.

AIR

Begin with the air in your lungs. Focus on your breathing; feel it fill you and depart from you. Allow your consciousness to follow the air as it awakens and nourishes your entire body, down to the molecular level. Now move your consciousness out, following the air as it flows from your lungs and joins a world of air. Move with the air through the sky, through the wind and clouds. Travel in the realm of Air, and see everything around you from Air's point of view.

As you move through air, as you partake of air, allow yourself to *become* Air, and picture every part of you, inner and outer, as airy.

A fascinating experiment is to speak or write while "under the influence" of each element. Use "I" statements to communicate your experience. Begin with "I am Air" and continue speaking; don't plan or edit what you say.

Eventually, you'll have to bring yourself out. Pull back from Air. You no longer *are* Air, but you're still *in* it. From there, pull back further, being surrounded by, touched by air, but not in flight. Then start adding back the other elements; add Earth and feel the solid ground beneath you. Add Water and feel the flow of blood through your veins, and picture the water around you (anything from an ocean to a faucet). Then add Fire and feel enlivened, so that you see yourself at last as balanced in all four elements. Only now should you end the meditation.

FIRE

Fire is the hardest of the meditations; it is not a "world" that creatures live in—there are birds and fish, but no fire-dwellers. Your Fire meditation, then, will be the most imaginative of the four, the least reliant on day-to-day scenes.

Feel the heat in your body. Feel physical heat at first—simple temperature. Then feel the pulsing fire of your center. Feel how you are made alive by fire. Picture that same fire all around you, as if everyone near you, or everyone you know, is glowing.

Get comfortable with that picture of having a glowing, fiery center. Raise the temperature in your imagination, making it hotter and hotter, while experiencing yourself as comfortable with that heat. After it's fairly hot, you can picture yourself surrounded by flames. The flames are closer and closer, but you remain comfortable, and you become aware that the flames have the very same nature as you do. They surround you closer and closer until you are *in* the fire and *of* the fire.

Now allow yourself to *become* Fire, and picture every part of you, inner and outer, as fiery. See the world as if viewed by Fire. You can begin your speaking or writing experiment, starting with "I am Fire."

When it's time to come back, allow the flames to recede, so that you're surrounded by, but not actually *in*, fire. You're sitting in a circle of flames, which is backing further away until it's gone. Pull your awareness back from heat, lowering your perception of temperature until you don't feel so fiery. Then include the other elements. Add Earth and feel the solid ground beneath you. Add Air and breathe deeply, filling and refreshing your lungs. Add Water and feel the flow of blood through your veins, and picture the water around you. Now you're balanced in all four elements, and you can end the meditation.

WATER

Feel the moisture in your body, feel the saliva in your mouth, feel your sweat; then go deeper within, to the moisture coursing through your entire system. From there, let yourself think of the water that surrounds you in your day-to-day life; you drink water, you cook and wash with water. You are rained on from time to time. Maybe you live near a body of water, even a small one.

Start picturing yourself *in* and *of* that water. Allow yourself to *become* Water, and picture every part of you, inner and outer, as watery. You are droplets, not held together in a single unit, flowing in and around everything else that is Water, with no clear boundaries between. If you're a body of water, rain added to you also *is* you. If you are rain, you dissipate into the lake or river you land in, yet you're still you. You evaporate and disappear, and yet you're still there. Everything is flow, and nothing is still.

As you *are* Water, speak *as* Water, beginning with "I am Water" and allowing speech to flow freely, without censorship.

Eventually, you'll have to bring yourself out. Pull back from Water; you no longer *are* Water, but you're still *in* it. From there, pull back further, being near Water but not in it. Notice that the water in your life and in your body is just a part of who you are. Notice that you're also Earth, and feel your solid body. Notice that you're also Air, and feel your breathing, and recognize that you are a thinking being. Then add Fire and feel the heat of life. Now you're ready to end the meditation.

EARTH

Feel how solid you are. Notice how much of you is made up of solid mass, how still it is, how rooted. You are surrounded everywhere by solidity: floors, earth, rocks, concrete. As you picture more and more of the world as solid, you start to feel more and more rock-like. Soon you *become* Earth. Notice the timelessness of Earth, the longevity. Minerals and soil last a long, long time, watching more ephemeral forms of being come and go. You are a mountain, a canyon, you are geology itself, unmoved by the passage of time except in its furthest reaches. It can be hard to speak as Earth, because Earth's nature is silent. See if you can.

When you begin to come back, begin shifting your weight about as soon as you feel able. The easiest way to regain balance from Earth is through movement; even slight movement will help. You are no longer Earth now, although still solid. Wiggle your fingers and notice that they're touched by air. Lick your lips and feel the water in your body. Feel the Fire that brings the will to live. When you're ready to end the meditation, you should move your *whole* body; get up, jump or wiggle or dance. Shake off the immobility of Earth to regain the balance of four elements.

Elementals

Is there such a thing as an elemental? Once you've developed a bit of comfort with your element meditation, you can use it to see if you encounter any "presence" or personality within the element. When you reach the point of being almost completely immersed in the element, instead of becoming the element, *interact* with it. Instead of speaking *as* the element, speak *to* it. Is there anyone there to "talk" to—anyone or anything you can recognize as sentient? If so, what does it have to say to you? What can you learn from them? Be sure to be gracious to any being you encounter. Thank them and take specific leave of them; when it's time to end your meeting, be clear that you are leaving, and say goodbye. It'll be that much easier to then return to the balanced world.

I don't question the reality of elementals—I've encountered them too often. They can be like over-eager pets, following you home when you haven't a place for them. A loose salamander in the house is downright dangerous (I speak from personal experience). A loose undine is less life-threatening, but water damage is expensive and so is plumbing repair. Gnomes are the least dangerous—you probably *already* have some in your home if it's a pleasant, homey, and welcoming place—those earthy qualities attract gnomes. But in each case, elementals act after their nature. It's not a question of good or bad; it's a question of understanding that these beings are very different from you and me. That's why, whenever you call an elemental, whether in ritual or in meditation, you must *dismiss* the elemental with equal force.

Direction—The Inner Realms

In your mundane life, all four directions are probably characterized more by asphalt and road signs than by Earth, Air, Fire, or Water. Even if that's not true for you, the directions change drastically as geography changes. For example, there is more water in the east than in the west if you live in Boston or New York. Are there enduring qualities to the directions on the *inner* planes? Is there an "Eastern Realm" within? Begin your meditation in any "spot" you choose, and then travel east, to see what that's like. Explore whatever you find in that realm, and then return to your starting point. You'll end up doing at least four meditations—one for each direction, but perhaps many more, exploring each realm thoroughly and looking for consistency (if it's there). Start each exploration from the same spot, so that you begin to learn the general geography of this inner region.

The question of whether directions have elemental qualities on the inner planes is one that many magicians and Witches disagree on, so your personal, mystical experience is the best guide for what you will believe, and therefore what you will do in ritual. If you become convinced that there is no such thing as "inner geography," that the directions only exist in the corporeal world, then you may prefer to set up your ritual in accordance to the actual geography where you live—placing Water in the direction of the nearest natural body of water, Earth in the direction where it is either cold or mountainous, Fire in the hottest direction, and Air in the direction from where most of your strong winds come. On the other hand, you may find no inner geography that you can perceive, and still wish to keep traditional occult attributions. Setting the ritual up in the same way no matter where you are is an advantage, as is drawing on the accumulated power of occult tradition. If you *do* find an inner geography, then you'll wish to use its elemental attributes as your guide.

Guardians

The Guardians are elusive beings, not easy to reach in meditation. I hesitate to call them "lofty," but "preoccupied" seems a fair assessment. If we imagine them as great rulers, overseeing all the activity of their particular element and direction, then we can begin to imagine that they are less accessible than undines, sylphs, salamanders, and gnomes.

To try to reach the Guardians in meditation, begin by visualizing yourself fully as a Witch. This is best done in a cast circle, but at least hold your athame, wear your ritual jewelry and robes, and see yourself as this person who worships the Old Gods. This is how the Guardians know you, and this is something they respect.

Then go into either a direction or element meditation. From the inner direction, or when surrounded by, but not fully immersed in, the element, begin to send out an inner call for the Guardian of that direction/element. In your mind's eye, make the invoking pentagram that you normally use in the quarters (you can make it physically as well). Picture a benevolent and powerful force, at one with the element but not controlled by its nature. Most of all, Guardians are *watchers*; allow yourself to notice the feeling of being watched, and you will be that much closer to these beings. Don't push too hard in this meditation; just let it happen, like a request.

If you reach a Guardian, or even if you're not sure, thank it politely and take your leave. Re-integrate yourself in the four elements, or in your central spot if you used a directional meditation.

Another method is to invoke the Guardians as usual, as part of your circle casting. Then, during the *Using the Blessings* section of the ritual, take your athame, and seat yourself in a quarter, next to the quarter candle. *Now* close your eyes and meditate on the Guardian, who is, after all, already there.

Pace yourself with this technique—don't try to do all four in one night. When you're finished, return to the altar and *touch* the altar, receiving its balanced spirit energy.

A Guardian meditation is challenging; any success at it should be taken as an indication of real progress on your spiritual path.

1. The following definitions are from *The American Heritage Dictionary of the English Language, Third Edition,* copyright 1996, 1992, Houghton Mifflin Company.

2. This could as logically be discussed under Water, since it is a mythic role, or under Air, since it is informed by theology. It is discussed here, under Fire, because I believe the heart of the justification for it is in this particular bit of mysticism—that of the first cause and original consecration.

3. Such as my own.

4. In many traditions, High Priestesses and High Priests train for years before earning that title; they didn't get there "merely by say so." But the act of *assuming* the power is still a radical act.

5. See example 2.

6. Discussed at length in chapter 5.

7. In most Wiccan groups, the phrases "Blessed be" and "So mote it be" are always echoed by all present.

8. If the censer has pre-lit charcoals in it, which I recommend, then be sure that it is resting on a tile, trivet, or other fire-safe surface.

9. Or the unified will of the coven.

10. This Wiccan myth has been published in more places than I can keep track of. I am quoting here from Stewart Farrar, *What Witches Do: A Modern Coven Revealed* (Custer, Wash.: Phoenix Publishing Co., 1971 and 1983) pp. 170–171.

11. It's a simple matter to get a carpet scrap of the desired size, measure out a nice even circle on it, and use fabric paint once you're ready to make it permanent. If you hold rituals of varying sizes—sometimes two or three people, sometimes a dozen—then you might wish to mark concentric circles so that you can select "cozy," "medium," or "holiday" size.

12. "So mote it be" is Wiccan for "So be it" or "Amen."

13. New Reformed Orthodox Order of the Golden Dawn.

14. Hindu ritual uses ten directions: north, east, south, west, northeast, northwest, southeast, southwest, up, and down. I have never seen this done in any Western system, Wiccan or otherwise.

15. There are many wonderful teachers of Native American ways. I'm not one of them. If you choose to do a ritual with a lot of Native influence, you'll have to seek elsewhere for more information.

16. Contrary to Victorian illustration, they don't have pointy red hats.

17. *What Witches Do,* pp. 138–139

18. I don't mean that the gods are distant from us. I mean that our lives tend to *feel like* and *be lived like* the gods are distant from us—that there is a chasm between our inner, godlike nature and our lived experience.

19. A gatekeeper is a type, or category, of god, found in many pantheons throughout the world, just as an *earth mother* or a *dying vegetation god* or a *psychopomp* is a type of god, not someone in specific.

20. For "sacred circle" you can substitute the occasion, i.e., "Keep safe your quarter at this sacred Full Moon circle."

21. Remember that elementals can be mischievous and hard to handle. Invoke by the power of the gods to bring a bit more strength, credibility and control.

22. "Holy rite" is the phrase that can be substituted for the specific occasion, i.e., "Guard and balance this handfasting."

23. Use your own circle name (obviously).

24. Use the special occasion for "circle" as needed.

25. Guardians serve the gods, so doing this in their names makes sense. Of course, you can substitute specific god-names.

Chapter Five

THE CENTER

Here are the steps for the center of a ritual:

- Invoking the Gods
- Giving Offerings to the Gods
- Cakes and Wine (Receiving the Blessings of the Gods)
- Using the Blessings

These steps are the heart of the ritual, the climax, the reason for the ritual to be. They are an intricate give-and-take between humans and deities, complex and mystical. They are also the most misunderstood steps of Wiccan ritual. Get a dozen books on Wicca, and you'll be likely to find a dozen different versions of the timing for when Cakes and Wine (for example) is performed. Yet, you'll get fewer than a dozen explanations for *why* it's performed, because most books seem to leave that out entirely. You'll find rituals where some of these steps are left out, or presented in a different order, in virtually every book on the shelf. Even during my training, when I was learning how to cast a circle and what it all means, there was considerable confusion about where to place spellwork in the ritual, and whether Cakes and Wine should be performed before or after a seasonal rite, and so on. Neither book learning nor traditional lore really covers these questions.

What I'm presenting here is unique and original. It is the conclusion I've reached after learning from many Pagan and Wiccan teachers, reading many books, casting innumerable circles, studying and meditating. I am utterly convinced that this order is the proper and best way for a Wiccan to worship the gods, and the most in keeping with the goals of worship and magic. It is this structure that aligns Wiccan ritual with the underlying structure of *all* religious ritual.[1] It is this structure which makes the energy flow best in the circle, giving Witches what we need, empowering the magic, and truly and deeply reaching the gods.

This is one of those rare occasions in which I'll step away from the "do-it-yourself" belief that underlies much of Wicca, and say that the order shown above is *the* right way to do it. You hardly ever hear that in a religion in which there are multiple truths, and multiple ways of being correct, but just because we believe in a plurality of right answers doesn't mean there aren't any *wrong* answers. It turns out that there are lots and lots of ways of performing ritual that dissipates your energy, disempowers your magic, and fails to make the vital connection to sacredness. There is, however, a structure that years of practice and study have convinced me *works*.

The Steps

1. *Invoking the Gods.* We ask the gods to join us.
2. *Giving Offerings to the Gods.* Immediately upon their arrival, we worship them. We give to them.
3. *Cakes and Wine.* This is communion. We consume food and drink imbued with their blessings. We receive from them.
4. *Using the Blessings.* Now that we have received their blessings, we can use those blessings. What better time to perform magic or other works than when we are filled with the blessings of the gods?

Invoking the Gods

Air

Who are the gods we invoke? What is their nature? These questions recall our earlier discussion of oneness, duality, the two-faced god and the triple goddess.

Oneness

Pagans are often met with disbelief about our polytheism. "But don't you *really* believe in one God?" Many polytheists (not all) do acknowledge that all gods are ultimately one; it is common among Hindus, for example, to say that it doesn't matter which god you worship, that all are faces of the One. It seems to me that monotheists react with relief to these assurances, a sort of "Phew, these Pagans aren't crazy after all." But the "one" that Pagans believe in is very different from the One God of Judaism, Christianity, and Islam.

The easiest way to understand what gods are is to compare them to human beings. Although the comparison is imperfect, it is illuminating and draws on something we understand fairly well—ourselves. Scientists are beginning to understand that all humanity, in fact all life, is connected at the level of DNA. Not only do we all seem to have evolved from a single human ancestor—the genetic Eve—but *all* life seems to have evolved from a single cell.

Setting aside the biological, at the level of spirit, it seems we are one as well. This is something that spiritual teachers have been telling us for millennia and something that many people have fleetingly experienced. In a romance, it is often the case that the couple feels a oneness between them, they feel as if they share the same spirit, and they may have moments of knowing each other's thoughts and feelings with a kind of absolute certainty. This is one of the most beautiful examples of oneness—when we understand that the distance between "I love you" and "I *am* you" is not so very great. A group united in a purpose, or a crowd overcome by the will of the mob, is also experiencing, in a lesser way, a kind of single self.

If we can postulate that all human spirits are ultimately one, and then extend it to the understanding that all biological life on Earth is ultimately one, we can eventually reach the point of knowing that *all that exists* is ultimately a single thing.

This is obviously nothing like saying there is only one God, and all others are "false gods" (whatever *that* means), or that there is only one God, and all other gods are lesser. It *is* saying that all gods partake of the nature of oneness, and are perhaps closer to that nature than mortals. Gods *know* they are ultimately one, just as they know *we* are, whereas we humans drift from day to day feeling separate and alone.

Duotheism

Beyond the oneness of god-nature is "two-ness"—polarity. Many Wiccans are "duotheists"; they worship *one* Goddess and *one* God, and believe that all goddesses are merely names or faces of Her, and all gods are names or faces of Him. *"All gods are one god, and all goddesses are one goddess."*

In this belief, individual deities are *aspects*, they are facets of the whole. Many Wiccans believe that each individual deity is akin to the perceptions of one of the blind men who thought he understood the elephant. Deena Metzger's famous chant "*Isis, Astarte, Diana, Hecate, Demeter, Kali, Inanna*" seems to be saying this—that Isis is no more than the elephant's trunk, that Astarte is no more than its tusks, and so on—that they are all one Goddess in truth.

There is a certain merit to this theory. It's been said before that Catholic nuns don't see visions of Kali, and Hindu brahmins don't see visions of the Virgin Mary. Somehow, the individuality of the Goddess is shaped by the mind of whoever perceives Her. If all goddesses are one Goddess, then it explains how She can appear in whatever form suits the occasion.

Polytheism

Here is the truth: No one *really* knows what gods are. An awful lot of people will *say* they know, but they're making educated (or uneducated) guesses. *My* guess, based on worshiping them, visiting them in trance, and reading untold numbers of books about them, is that gods are parts of the collective unconscious, or the web of oneness—powerful, loving parts, that have separated themselves into individual shapes. They seem to originate as vast archetypes, and then narrow themselves down somewhat—from Great Mother down to Grain Mother, for example. They seem to arise interactively—humans seeking out to an archetypal form, and gods shaping themselves in response, in a deep spiritual synergy. If humans reach out to Grain Mother, they will naturally shape Her, in their minds, based upon what they know of grain in their corner of the world. Hence, deities develop traits consistent with the culture that worships them, and yet retain a strong energetic connection to the original spark in the consciousness that gave birth to them.

In other words, all the answers are true—gods are individuals, fully separate and themselves; gods are faces of the One; gods arise by divine will (their own); and gods are created by humans. Now that we've got that out of the way, let's talk about what this means in terms of the *experience* of worship.

Let's go back to comparing this to human beings. I am a woman. I can be perceived as an individual, Deborah Lipp, utterly unique. You can completely ignore my feminine nature when you perceive me. If you do this, though, you'll be disregarding a wealth of information you probably have about women and about what women are potentially like. You can go to the opposite extreme, though, and see me *just* as a woman. In fact, you can see me as Woman: archetypal, sacred, planted firmly on a pedestal. If you do so, you'll miss a lot about me that isn't the same as other women, and you'll probably offend me as well. Like most people, I like to be acknowledged as an individual and seen as more than a representative of my gender.

In worship, that means that you can invoke the Goddess and the God *as such*, but the minute you call a particular goddess or god by name, you'd better treat Her or Him as an individual, and not merely as a reflection. I don't personally want to be the one to tell Kali that She is "just an aspect," and I advise you not to, either.

We've already talked about multiple realities and multiple truths. We can believe in oneness *and* believe in duotheism *and* be polytheists. But we mustn't mix up these concepts, and we must treat whichever concept we're using in ritual as if it is one hundred percent true.

As humans, we can come to know our oneness with all life without in any way invalidating or diminishing our individuality. We can come to know our sisterhood with all women, or our brotherhood with all men, without thinking we are nothing more than that commonality. And we can also perceive the gods in this way—as a complex combination of one, two, and many.

Knowing the Gods

When we invoke polytheistically, that is to say, when we invoke gods as specific individuals, it is important to *know* who we are invoking. Far too many Wiccans simply toss out names that they found in a book, or that they think would be helpful in the ritual, without truly understanding who they are naming. This is not only insulting to the deity, but does not make for effective invocation.

Drawing Down the Moon

In some traditions, the invocation is done "onto" the Priestess or Priest, rather than to-ward the heavens or Earth. This is called Drawing Down the Moon for a Priestess, and Drawing Down the Sun for a Priest (these are traditional phrases and do not necessar-ily mean that a Lunar or Solar deity is invoked).

This is possible because we believe that the Goddess and God are within us, and so the ritual brings to the surface a reality we already accept. It keeps our religion alive and vital, as our gods can be with us *now*. This is in sharp contrast to Bible-based religions, in which God spoke once, long ago, to people such as Moses. Modern believers can only read about God's presence in these faiths, but Wiccans can experience it for themselves.

Drawing Down is done with a variety of intentions—as theater, as inspired trance, or as actual possession (not unlike Yoruban traditions such as Voodoo, in which the deities "ride" the Priests and Priestesses). Theologically, these aren't that different. There are *practical* differences, and there are differences in how the ritual affects the partici-pants and observers, but in terms of theology, it doesn't really matter if you're "really" speaking as a deity, or if you're "just pretending." The rite is an acknowledgment of an underlying reality, whether expressed through a dramatic reading or through a trance.

Water

The Honored Guests Metaphor

The house is ready, everything is in place, it's time to (a) invite and (b) welcome in our Guests of Honor. Our invitation must be sincere, it must be specific enough so that it reaches the correct "address," and our welcome must be heartfelt.

Relationships with Deities

Since we are invoking the gods, we should examine our relationships with them—rela-tionships informed by mythology and filled with emotion.

There are many potential ways of perceiving our relationship with our gods. Many people talk about the "worship bargain," a kind of tit-for-tat wherein I'll worship you if you give me the blessings I need. Others talk about worship as a kind of marriage: nuns are "Brides of Christ," or as a familial relationship: worship of the Holy Father or of Mother Earth. Other spiritual relationships seem more like a voluntary enslavement—worshippers are servants of a deity to whom they give everything and anything, without asking anything in return (but grateful when they receive anything, be it miracles or crumbs). What is a Wiccan relationship with deity like? Once again, understanding of our relationship with the gods is deepened if we examine our relationships with each other.

The ***worship bargain*** is a venerable concept in Paganism and in Wicca. It is found in many cultures in our Pagan past, and is referred to in many early Wiccan documents. Monotheists think of God as omnipotent, but in polytheism, that isn't necessarily true. Once you understand that gods aren't all-powerful, you begin to understand that there might be something they need. This was inherent in many ancient sacrificial rites; the gods *consumed* sacrifices, which they needed just as we need food and drink. Similarly, there is an understanding that the gods need worship itself, and especially ritual, to sustain Themselves. Humans came to understand that the gods were a kind of captive audience; since the gods needed ritual, the times when they showed up for ritual created an opportunity to ask for something in exchange: blessings, prosperity, good fortune, fertility.

The Greek mythology we all learned in school is full of these bargains, as well as the complex and tragic results of bargains that contradicted one another. Pretty much the entire *Iliad* can be described as a series of bargains gone wrong. But we have to remember that Homer didn't much worship the gods about whom he wrote. He lived in a time when the worship of most of the Greek gods was a thing of the past (Demeter, Dionysus, and Orpheus were exceptions), a rather quaint remnant of a "less sophisticated" time (in the view of Homer and his contemporaries). Most literate people no longer believed in most of the gods of Greek mythology. Perhaps when worship was active and heartfelt, it was not so cut-and-dried.

The worship bargain is parallel to the human relationship of hired help. I pay you, you work for me. It's fine as far as it goes, but most people want more from their religion than that, and that's where it gets tricky. If you start to develop depth and meaning in an "employment" relationship, then the bargain changes.

I think the bargain can be viewed in a different way; the worship bargain can be seen as ***friendship***. In friendship, there is an exchange, but that exchange is freely given on both sides. In other words, my friend and I are generous with each other. I pick up groceries for her when she's sick and don't ask to be repaid. She babysits when I need to go out and doesn't ask for anything in exchange. We do this out of affection and a genuine desire to give. From time to time, though, it's likely we also do it out of oblig- ation; we may drag ourselves out of a cozy chair in order to do a last-minute and much- needed favor, without wanting to do it at all. Such inconveniences are the price of friendship, because if we don't inconvenience ourselves from time to time, the giving takes on an imbalance. If one friend does all the giving and the other does all the re- ceiving, after a while, the giving friend begins to feel taken advantage of. That's no way to treat a friend!

Just so, it's no way to treat a god. We will probably ask far more of our gods than we will give to them—at least it will seem that way to us. Over the course of a lifetime, we'll ask for health, love, safety, good fortune, peace, wisdom—who knows? And what will we give in exchange? Some flowers, some incense, some drumming—it sure doesn't seem fair, does it? All the more reason, then, that we *must* give. In that context, it's not a "bargain," it's *love*.

The ***familial*** relationship most familiar in the West is that of children worshiping a father, although other cultures have other models. At Christmastime, there's a trace of parents worshiping a baby (the baby Jesus) that is far more explicit in the Hindu wor- ship of the baby Krishna, for example. Hindus consider the love that parents have for their children an excellent model of the love that worshippers should have for their God. In fact, *bhakti yoga* (the yoga of love) teaches us that *any* love is a proper model for the love of the gods, as long as it is deeply felt. The idea is to get in touch with the feeling, and then give that to the deity.

Having grown up with a Father God who can be stern and punitive, most Wiccans are deeply attracted to the Mother Goddess, who is an infinite ocean of compassion and unconditional love. She has Her stern and terrible side as well, of course, but even at Her darkest, there is still that well of love issuing forth. To be embraced by the Mother is to be embraced infinitely. To know that the Mother holds you is to know that the universe itself holds you; there is no way to fall, there is nothing that *isn't* hold- ing you, nothing to fall onto.

Beyond the Universal Mother, there are ***patron*** and ***matron*** deities; your *personal* Father or Mother. This is something that "just happens"—there comes a moment when you simply know (or are *told*) that someone is your mother or your father. However, you can further the process of finding a matron or patron. I have often said to my students that you cannot have a spiritual experience with a deity of whom you've never heard. Studying myth extensively, knowing *about* many gods and goddesses, is a vital part of finding the One (or Ones) who call you.

There are other personal deities besides parental ones. One of the most common is the **professional** deity. Brigid is the goddess of bards, smiths, and healers. I know several musicians and nurses who have taken Brigid as their matron. Apollo is another patron of medicine, and Hermes is the god of communications and sales. Sarasvati is the goddess of education and is worshiped by both students and teachers.

Similar to the idea of a professional patron, you might form a relationship with a deity for a particular purpose or period of time. Probably the most common example of this is to call on Aphrodite when seeking a lover. She is worshiped for a period of time, and to fulfill a particular need, but not necessarily at other times. Since this isn't a long-term relationship—like a friend or a mother—it is more of a worship bargain. It is important to be respectful in such a bargain, to give generously both when asking for what you want, and as thanksgiving when your desire has been fulfilled.

It is possible, in such a bargain, to draw on an existing relationship. As it happens, Kali is my Mother, and has been for many years. Some years ago, I had a painful back injury and I was being treated by a chiropractor. Normally, I would deal with pain by going into a light trance, distancing myself from my body's sensations and floating above the pain. But during my treatments, the doctor would ask detailed questions: "Does this hurt more than that? Does this pain radiate or does it stay local?" These questions forced me to stay in my body and pay attention to my feelings, and this was excruciating. During one such session, it occurred to me that Shiva is the Lord of Yoga, and as such, He undergoes extreme deprivation and pain as part of His austerities. I had no relationship with Shiva at all at the time, but I called on Him anyway, visualizing Him while I lay on the table and calling to Him as the husband of Kali. At once, my pain became more bearable. Through the rest of the months of treatment, Shiva was with me, giving me strength and easing my pain. Ultimately, I formed a relationship with Him in His own right, and I have come to worship Him for His own sake. But at the time, I drew on my relationship with my matron, in much the same way I might ask the husband of a best friend for a favor.

Fire

In the *Air* section, I talked about my theories about what gods are. The truth, though, is that they're just *theories*. The only real knowledge of the gods comes from within, or from the gods themselves. Using ritual and meditation, you can simply *ask*, but that assumes They know. I wonder if that's true? Perhaps the nature of individuality distances you from some of the knowledge of your non-individual nature; perhaps that isn't merely a human trait. Much of what I believe about the gods, and many of my pretty good guesses, come from my mystical experience. In vision I have come to know that which theology alone cannot teach. Nor can I teach you how to have a vision—such moments simply come, although attention to the Air, Earth, and Water of religious life definitely helps.

I tend to think that mystical access to the gods—vision and other forms of direct contact—is more available to Neopagans than to many others, because we believe in immanence. If the gods are within us, that makes a direct experience of them more likely.

Immanence

What is meant, in Wicca, when we say the gods are within? Many people suppose it means merely that the gods are metaphors—psychological constructs—as if we were not a religion but a ritualized form of Jungian analysis. In that view, there is no such thing as a god, merely a part of the self best understood, best empowered, by using language *as if* there were gods.

In another view, gods are *only* within—there is no such thing as transcendent deity. Instead, the only gods are immanent, although, in contrast to the previous view, of metaphor, they are understood as truly divine.

I reject both of those views. I believe in gods; not just as parts of my psyche, not just as the divine within, but as *gods*. I also believe that they can be found within as easily as without—that they are as immanent as they are transcendent. The nature of this immanence is mystical.

> *"As above, so below.*
> *As the Universe, so the soul."*

This couplet is based on an ancient magical belief, first written down by the Gnostics around 2,400 years ago. Sympathetic, imitative, and contagious magic are all based on an understanding of the web of connection. These magics all find the connections between one thing and another, and they have been understood for thousands of years before *Six Degrees of Separation* came around. The web extends from its longest strands to its tiniest. The principle of As Above So Below is similar, but a bit more abstract. It says that the microcosm reflects the macrocosm, and that ultimately the two are the same. I imagine that Gnostics and other magical folk were grinning smugly to themselves when it was first discovered that atoms look like microscopic solar systems. The universe in the atom is something that mystics had been postulating for ages.

In fact, science is finding more and more examples of microcosmic reflections of the macrocosm, perhaps most recently in fractals—each of which contains minute repetitions of the macro pattern. But science discovering what magic has long known is nothing new, and science is not our concern here.

Each person is a microcosm of the universe; as Aleister Crowley said, "Every man and woman is a Star." Within ourselves we contain infinite depths, and to explore downward, toward the inner self, is to explore upward, toward the gods. Like following a maze that eventually leads you back to the beginning, like a snake swallowing itself whole, whichever direction you choose leads ultimately to the same place: Self, Spirit, the gods.

The gods are immanent because, at the deepest and most mystical levels, there is no difference between immanence and transcendence. Everything we can find outside of ourselves, we can also find within (and some things we can *only* find within). They are immanent because we are all a part of one another; there is no reason to seek outside. Transcendent gods are real, not metaphorical, but placing them outside of ourselves *is* metaphorical, because, when all is said and done, *nothing* is outside of ourselves.

If the rite of Drawing Down the Moon (and/or Sun) is done, then immanence is enacted before our eyes. Seeing the gods actually arrive in your circle can be a very mystical experience indeed. This rite, at its center, is a merging of transcendent with immanent deity, using the body of the Priestess or Priest as their meeting place. The personality of the individual is always present, but often there is a presence that seems distinctly Other. Only careful meditation can determine which is which, and if you care about the integrity of your trance, you'll never forget that no such rite is "pure"; it is always "tainted" by the person who receives the deity.

Earth

Once you decide *who* you're invoking, you can decide *how* to invoke. Remember the rules for invocations from the last chapter: **specificity, descriptiveness, praise,** and **need**. Also, remember that an invocation should specifically *invoke;* it must include some form of **summons** or invitation. Finally, an invocation should end with an acknowledgment of success, usually in the form of greeting the deity. In other words, don't just call and then stand around and hope. Call and then, assuming success, say "Welcome." Magic is the manifestation of your word into being—once you've called, you've made manifest, so always **greet** the deity you've just brought to your rite.

You should be specific and descriptive of the deity you call. If possible, you should also know what pleases that particular deity. For the invocation, traditional invocations and hymns can be used—Homer is a good resource for Greek invocations, Sir John Woodruff (a.k.a. Arthur Avalon) is a superb resource for English translation of invocations to Hindu goddesses, and Samuel Noah Kramer is the source for Sumerian deities. (There are many other resources, of course.) If whole invocations (some are quite long) don't seem to be appropriate for your ritual, use phrases from them. Traditional invocations are familiar to the gods being called, and so are likely to bring a response.

Nonverbal elements can be added to invocations, and can also lend specificity. Music from the culture where the deity originates can create a pleasing atmosphere, as well as an appropriate psychic environment for the worshipper(s). I often play a CD of sitar music when worshiping Hindu deities, and I find that a sistrum is very evocative when invoking Egyptian and Middle Eastern gods. Steady, slow drumbeats are typical of Native American invocation, and faster, more syncopated beats are associated with certain Yoruban deities. Incenses are often specific to deities, or at least to cultures. Sandalwood, patchouli and camphor are very Indian scents, sage is distinctly Native American, and frankincense and myrrh are Middle Eastern.

Specificity

Specifically who are you invoking, and in what aspect? It is important to focus on the specific aspect when you are invoking deities with long histories. For example, are you invoking Dionysus, God of Theater, or Dionysus, God of Intoxication? If you've been studying a deity and wish to invoke the qualities worshiped at a particular time or place, include that time and place. (This can have the same effect as the "God of . . ."

portion of the name, as each aspect of the deity may have had His or Her own temple site.) If you're invoking the Dual Principal, your invocation will be to The Lady and The Lord, without individual names, although those names could be mentioned in the invocation as manifestations (aspects). But you should still be specific—that you are invoking The Lady as Female Principal, and The Lord as Male Principal.

When you name deities, name them by attributes—which is where names often come from anyway. Kali simply means "Black One," and Isis means "Auspicious One." In fact, don't just give the deity a single name, give Her or Him the titles and attributes that make up an entire name. Call "Thor the Thunderer" or "Hathor, Cow Goddess, Lady of Milk." It is said that no one knows the true name of a deity, and that all deity names are nothing more than these titles—so use them.

Descriptiveness

Descriptiveness has a synergistic effect; it works back and forth between deity, worshipper, and audience (if any). A good, descriptive invocation is almost painterly; you can picture the deity before you, you can allow yourself to truly *know* that the deity is real. The description draws the attention of the deity, and also draws the attention of the worshippers *toward* the deity. The worshippers' attention is an energy that increases the power of the invocation, which then calls more strongly to the deity. As the deity becomes more present, the worshippers become more attentive, and so on.

Description can be physical, as in Brigid's flaming red hair, Odin's one eye, or Aphrodite's extraordinary beauty. It can include attire and other objects—Cernunnos wearing or holding a torque, Hera accompanied by her peacocks, Artemis holding her bow and arrows, Kali's necklace of skulls.

A description can also include mythology. It can include family relationships: Hercules, son of Zeus; Shiva, husband to Parvati, father to Ganesha. It can include place of origin or places of worship, as well as deeds and stories. "Odin, who hung for nine days on the World Tree, Yggdrasil" is evocative and exact, as is "Ra, who rides the Sun Chariot daily."

Praise

This should be obvious, and is a matter of good manners as well as common sense. You *want* the gods to come, so be *nice* to them! Common words and phrases of praise used are:

- Great
- Glorious
- Lovely
- Mighty
- Wise
- Blessed
- Honored
- "We praise thee"
- "Whom we adore"
- "Honor us with your presence"
- "Without whom XYZ bad thing would happen"
- "Without whom XYZ good thing *wouldn't* happen"

Need

You should tell the gods *why* it is that you want them to come; what it is that they're coming to do or see. Reasons you've invited the gods include:

- That we may worship them
- To witness the rite being performed in their honor
- To enjoy the rite
- To guide their children
- To protect their children
- To hear us praise them
- To receive our offerings (to smell the delightful incense, to hear our songs of praise, etc.)
- To bless us (with their presence or otherwise)

You may also have more specific reasons having to do with the purpose of the rite. A holiday, a rite of passage, or a ritual with a magical purpose would have different reasoning behind it, and that could change the invocation.

EXAMPLE 1: WORDS OF INVOCATION

Most Gracious Goddess, Mighty Horned One, Beloved Lord and Lady—hearken unto us!

Great Mother of many aspects. Lady of the Moon, Mother of the Earth, Maiden, Mother and Crone. Glorious bringer of fertility; source of our very lives! Be here among us.

Mighty Horned One of many aspects. Father of the Hunt, Lord of Death and Re-birth, bright and dark, the Two-Faced One. Wondrous bringer of light; He Who fer-tilizes all! Be here among us.

Lord and Lady, we ask Your acceptance of this sacred rite. Be Thou our guide and protection as we, your children, worship you in the ways of old. Welcome and Blessed be.

Specific: *Great Mother of many aspects. Lady of the Moon, Mother of the Earth, Maiden, Mother and Crone.*

Mighty Horned One of many aspects. Father of the Hunt, Lord of Death and Rebirth, bright and dark, the Two-Faced One.

This invocation is a "Lord and Lady" invocation, one that is duotheistic. As such, it is typical of almost all Wicca practiced from the 1930s through the 1970s.

Note that this is spelled out in the invocation; that the Lord and Lady are specifically said to have many aspects. This would allow names to be used, if desired, because those names have already been specified as aspects of the whole. Specific deities or specific aspects could have been named instead.

Note also that the way the invocation is written declares another "aspect" of the Goddess and God, without exactly stating it—that they are equal and balanced. Because everything that is said about Her is exactly balanced by something said about Him, with similar sentence structure, it is implicit that they are equal partners, with neither having power over the other.

Descriptive: *Bringer of fertility; source of our very lives!*
Bringer of light; He Who fertilizes all!

This section is short here because the naming was rather long; the descriptive section can be quite lengthy and flowery, if you're comfortable with that.

Note that this is specific about what the gods do, and is somewhat flattering as well, bringing out those things they do that are absolutely vital to human beings—it all but says "We would die without you."

Praise: *Most Gracious*
Mighty
Beloved
Glorious
Wondrous

This is hardly lavish, it certainly isn't groveling; in Wicca we believe our gods respect and honor us, and so our praise is honest, and not obsequious. Nonetheless, our gods deserve our praise, appreciate it, and respond to it.

Need: *We ask Your acceptance of this sacred rite. Be Thou our guide and protection as we, your children, worship you in the ways of old.*

What do we need? We need the gods to accept the rite. We specify that the rite is *sacred*, meaning it's dedicated to, and belongs to, them—all the more reason for them to accept it.

We need their guidance and protection. We remind them that we are their children, and that we worship "in the ways of old"—meaning that we've been in this relationship for quite some time. What this does is reinforce our right to ask these boons. We have the right (a) because we're their children and (b) because there's historic precedence.

Summons: *Hearken unto us!*
Be here among us.

No amount of florid language can substitute for **asking for what you want!** You want them to come, so you must ask them to come.

Greeting: *Welcome and Blessed be.*

EXAMPLE 2: A FORMAL INVOCATION OF "THE LADY AND LORD" (DUOTHEISTIC)

Priest: Lifts wand,[2] faces Priestess (they can exchange a kiss here).

Priestess: Grasps wand so that they're both holding it, facing each other.

They turn together, face north, and raise the wand into the air.

Priestess: *Most Gracious Goddess, Mighty Horned One,*
Beloved Lord and Lady—hearken unto us!
Great Mother of many aspects. Lady of the Moon,
Mother of the Earth, Maiden, Mother and Crone.
Glorious bringer of fertility; source of our very lives!
Be here among us.

Priest: *Mighty Horned One of many aspects.*
Father of the Hunt, Lord of Death and Rebirth,
bright and dark, the Two-Faced One.
Wondrous bringer of light; He Who fertilizes all!
Be here among us.

Both: *Lord and Lady, we ask Your acceptance of this sacred rite.*

Priestess: *Be Thou our guide and protection as we, your children, worship you in the ways of old. Welcome and Blessed be.*

All: *Blessed be.*

Priest and Priestess turn back to face each other, bring the wand between them, nod to each other and/or exchange a kiss, and put down the wand.

Note how, in this example, the polarity of the deities being invoked is reflected in the polarity between Priest and Priestess. They hold the tool together; they begin and end by facing each other, possibly kissing each other. They are enacting the theology of duotheism—they are equal partners (with the Goddess being First Among Equals), their work flows back and forth between them, and they generate polar energy in their eye contact, nods, and kisses.

Traditional Hymns

For deities with a surviving written liturgy, traditional hymns can be used or excerpted. Such hymns and invocations have an evocative quality—you can almost feel yourself being transported in place and time to an ancient temple in the Pagan world. There are also active, living traditions of course—Hindu, Yoruban, Native American. Invocations taken from living traditions are a touchy thing. Make sure that this portion of ritual is placed *in context*; make sure that the tradition isn't being bastardized.

You might not wish to use a traditional hymn in its entirety. Wicca is a unique religion, with a unique feel; as much as we may worship gods from those traditions, we are *not* India, ancient Greece, or Babylonia. To just pick up a hymn from another religion and drop it into a Wiccan ritual may not work. The aesthetic may be wrong, references to ritual acts you won't be performing may be in the hymn, and theology that is inconsistent with your ritual may be part of the hymn. Simply stated, a Homeric hymn may *belong* in a Homeric context, and a Wiccan circle, for all its beauty, isn't Homer's Greece. For these reasons, you may prefer to "cut and paste" sections of traditional hymns into an invocation such as used in examples 1 and 2.

Here is a hymn to the goddess Inanna:[3]

The Lady of the Evening

At the end of the day, the Radiant Star, the Great Light that fills the sky,
The Lady of the Evening appears in the heavens.
The people in all the lands lift their eyes to her.
The men purify themselves; the women cleanse themselves.
The ox in his yoke lows to her.
The sheep stir up the dust in their fold.
All the living creatures of the steppe,

The four-footed creatures of the high steppe,

The lush gardens and orchards, the green reeds and trees,

The fish of the deep and the birds in the heavens—

My Lady makes them all hurry to their sleeping places.

The living creatures and the numerous people of Sumer kneel before her.

Those chosen by the old women prepare great platters of food and drink for her.

The Lady refreshes herself in the land.

There is great joy in Sumer.

The young man makes love with his beloved.

My Lady looks in sweet wonder from heaven.

The people of Sumer parade before the holy Inanna.

Inanna, the Lady of the Evening, is radiant.

I sing your praises, holy Inanna.

The Lady of the Evening is radiant on the horizon.[4]

You could use this entire hymn as your invocation, or as part of it. You will have to decide if you wish to retain a reference to the "steppe," being as you don't live there, and the references to the people of Sumer, when Sumer no longer exists. You could retain the references because they are the traditional places of Inanna, and they are references to her homeland, or you could remove them because you find them illogical. That decision is largely a matter of taste.

Here's one way of converting a traditional hymn, from an ancient text, into something that will be used in a modern Wiccan rite.

EXAMPLE 3: INVOCATION OF INANNA

By combining the language and style of our modern ritual with the phraseology of ancient Sumer, we can make Inanna welcome and at home in a Wiccan circle. No stage directions are given here; it can be spoken by a single Priestess, or by several people. In a group, you could give each person one or two or several lines, and invoke *around*, each person in turn. You could set it to music, or intone it. A **sistrum** or **hand cymbals** would be appropriate musical accompaniment.

Inanna, Lady of the Evening, come to us![5]

We sing your praises, holy Inanna.

Lady of the Evening, you are radiant on the horizon.

Join our sacred rite, O Radiant Star, O Great Light that fills the sky,

The people lift their eyes to you.

The men purify themselves; the women cleanse themselves.

The ox in his yoke lows to you.

The sheep stir up the dust in their fold.

Bring your radiance to us, Lady of Evening

Bring lushness to our gardens and orchards, to the green reeds and trees,

We have prepared offerings of food and drink for you

Refresh yourself, Lady, in our circle

Look upon us in sweet wonder

We invoke and welcome holy Inanna!

Blessed be!

Sometimes There Isn't a Tradition

There are occasions when you will want to invoke a specific goddess or god, but there is no written liturgy available. This is usually the case because the deity comes from a pre-literate culture. There are ways of constructing an invocation anyway:

- Is there information available about how the deity was worshiped? How she or he was perceived, what her or his attributes were?

- Is there iconography that gives a hint? Do portrayals show ritual objects or offerings?

- What does the deity look like?

- Where is the deity from? What country, region, climate?

- Why are *you* worshiping this deity? What is it that *you* will ask of her or him?

By taking this information, you can begin to construct a rich, descriptive understanding of the deity you intend to worship.

Some people work from a trance experience of a deity. I have done so myself. However, what you've learned in trance should be supported by research if at all possible. First of all, research can actually *improve* the trance; I think that gods treat our heads like filing cabinets—they go rifling through for material. So, if you put material *in*, they're better able to get it out and feed it to you in the form of trance or vision. Secondly, none of us are perfect channels; the subconscious always feeds a bit of its own agenda into any trance experience. If there is primary material that validates the visionary material, you're validating your channel; if they contradict each other, it's probably (although not necessarily) the vision that needs fine-tuning. Use the scholarly material to separate the wheat from the chaff of your vision—guiding you toward what's true, and away from what's merely subconscious static.

The "Venus" of Willendorf

The "Venus" of Willendorf is a Paleolithic goddess figurine, found near Willendorf, Austria, that dates back to about 24,000 B.C.E. There were numerous figurines of the same time period, found in a huge area of Europe, and extending into parts of Asia. They all had similar features—exaggerated breasts and vulva, large belly,[6] indistinct arms (if any), no feet or facial features—and these became known as "Venus" figures. Nowadays, she is often called "Woman of Willendorf" by archeologists, and "The Willendorf Goddess" by Neopagans.

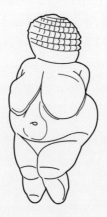

The "Venus" of Willendorf

Because of her great age, anything "known" about Willendorf is conjecture, based on some sketchy facts. It seems clear that she was sculpted from a live model, based on such details as dimpled knees, accurately-shown folds of flesh, and an elaborate hairstyle. However, it doesn't make sense to describe her as a portrait, both because she lacks facial features, and because she is a "type"—the Venus figure—of which there are many other examples. It seems that a live model was used to express a symbolic purpose.

The Willendorf Goddess and others like her are usually thought to be early Mother Goddess idols—fecund, well-fed, nurturing, and sexual (her vulva is clearly exaggerated, and even her labia are detailed). She is variously thought to be a representation of the Great Mother, or a lesser symbol, perhaps a fertility charm or a childbirth aid. Her tiny arms on her breasts are apparently an invitation, presenting to us their obvious fullness, as if offering us to nurse.

One peculiar detail is that the Venus figures all lacked feet. The common thinking is that this was so they could be planted directly into the ground, their little tapered ankles used to quickly dig a small hole, and they were thus made to stand up in the earth.

In four paragraphs, I've summarized pretty much all that is known about this goddess. Her image is hugely popular, appearing on T-shirts, book covers, and sculpted reproductions (I have a small one on my desk right now). Something in her great beauty and generosity has drawn thousands of people to her lovely image, even with only the sketchiest of information.

In choosing to invoke the Willendorf Goddess, I've already made some tacit decisions. Not every scholar thinks she's a goddess, but I'm saying she is by virtue of calling her to my ceremony at this point. I will draw on the scholarly material, and I will also draw on my experience as a Priestess. I have an advantage that most archeologists do not—I actually worship goddesses; I know what that's like, and what *they* are like, and so that knowledge informs my work—a work begun in books, but shaped by love.

Example 4: Invocation of the Goddess of Willendorf

Music, in keeping with the Stone Age feel of the invocation, should be primitive: hand drums, clapping, foot stomping, rattles, and other small, ***simple percussion instruments***. I picture the invocation punctuated by long calls, with low chants, whispers, repetitions, and sudden outbursts being used.

As with the Inanna invocation, the speaking can be done by any one person, by a couple, or by a group.

The invocation should be done with a ***bowl of soil*** on the altar, symbolizing the Goddess. If you have a Willendorf or other figurine, it should be planted in the soil; otherwise, simply use the soil and your imagination.

Willendorf Lady come to us!

Big-belly Mother, hear us!

Full One, Planted One, Feeding-and-holding-and-loving-us One

Great fertile Mother we call!

We call! We call!

Feet in the Earth, arms feeding us

*Feet **are** the Earth, breasts feeding us*

Feel our love for you and Come! Come! Come!

Big-belly Mother, come!

Make fertile our rite! Bring us your gifts

Bring plenty, bring plenty, bring plenty

You are the Earth, and all the Earth's gifts

You are the First Mother, the Great Mother, the Good Mother

O Come to us, Lady, bring good feeling among us

Make us full! Make us full!

Fill us with joy!

Fill us with love for you!

Fill us with love for each other!

Fill our hearts!

Fill our families!

Fill our futures!

Come to us Big-belly Mother

Come to us Ancient One

Come to us First One

Come to us Beautiful One

Come to us Glorious One

Come to us and let us adore you!

Let us worship you!

Let us give gifts to you!

Plant your feet in our earth.

Make this earth here your feet.

Be here in our earth!

Come to us! Come to us! Come to us!

She is here!

She is here!

She is here!

Welcome Lady!

Blessed be.

Sung Invocations

There are a number of ways to invoke without giving a speech. The Willendorf example shows an invocation that, though verbal, is rhythmic, using verbal rhythms and easily accented with percussion.

Invocations can be simpler still, using simply the name, spoken, sung, intoned, or shouted, perhaps with "Come to us" or "Join us" thrown in. A drumbeat could easily be built around such an invocation. This wouldn't be appropriate for a deity like Isis or Apollo, whose worship has historically been more intellectual and verbal—it is unlikely such gods would be pleased by that kind of invocation. The invocation should match the deity; it would probably work very well for Paleolithic goddesses, for ecstatic deities (Dionysus), tricksters, and fertility gods.

Chanted invocations can also be used. The best-known syncretic goddess chant is the one by Deena Metzger that I've already quoted:

Isis, Astarte, Diana, Hecate, Demeter, Kali, Inanna.[7]

For balance, I wrote a god chant in the same scansion so that they can be sung together, perhaps as a round:

Baldar, Coyote, Poseidon, Jupiter, Manannan, Shiva, Osiris.[8]

A chant for the Goddess and God together that I like is:

Mother I feel you under my feet
Mother I feel your heart beat!
Mother I feel you under my feet
Mother I feel your heart beat!
Father I see you when the eagle flies
Spirit's going to carry me higher and higher!
Father I see you when the eagle flies
Spirit's going to carry me higher and higher!

There are many good songs and chants for various specific gods and goddesses. There's a limit to the value of a chant or song printed in a book, but cassettes and CDs are available at New Age and occult stores, and online. There are so many good ones nowadays that you're bound to find a few you like. Use them to add to your repertoire of songs that can be used both as invocation and as offerings, as well as for other parts of ritual, or just for fun.

Nonverbal Invocations

Wordless invocation can be done by pantomiming supplication and invitation before a statue or a picture. Basically, you'd kneel before the statue, and with gesture, indicate your desire to have the deity join you. There are other techniques. You can use sounds, objects, or costume to invoke the deity. You might use a bow and arrow to invoke Diana, a loaf of bread to invoke John Barleycorn, or erotic lotions and lingerie to invoke Aphrodite.

Example 5: A Wordless Invocation to Diana

Since only sounds and props are used, they should be assembled with great care. An invocation this exact should only be performed if you know the deity well, understanding exactly who you are calling. This sample can be mimicked for other deities, using Their specific props and sounds, but with the same care and caution.

An invocation such as this is not simply inserted into a standard Wiccan rite. Rather, it is part of an entire ritual of devotion to a single god or goddess. From opening to closing, the entire ritual would have to be structured around Diana as meticulously as this invocation is.

The altar has a *statue of Diana* and a silver, pewter, or black *bowl filled with water*. If you are outdoors, have the bowl placed so that it reflects moonlight. If indoors, arrange a *silver or white candle* so that it is indirectly reflected in the water in imitation of moonlight. You might need to move the candle around a bit until you have it just right.

You should also have deer *antlers* or another symbol of deer.

Because Diana is renowned as a virgin goddess who eschews the company of men, remove all male symbols (wand, athame, sword) from the altar (except for the antlers). In their place, a *bow and arrows* are on or next to the altar.

Even if you normally practice *skyclad* (nude), you should be dressed for this ritual. Greek and Roman goddesses are generally modest (except for Aphrodite). They prefer to be dressed; Diana's traditional short dress and sandals would be appropriate.

Bow before the altar.

When you are ready, lift your head and howl, like a wolf or dog, at the moon. (For an indoor rite, visualize the moon, or gaze into the bowl and imagine it is moonlight you see.)

Bow again.

Stand. Lift the bow and arrow and "show" them to the statue. Lift them to the moon, or above your head. Then aim them at the antlers or deer symbol. "Stalk" the deer for a bit.

Place the bow and arrow before the statue, either on the altar or at its base—as if placing them at the feet of the goddess.

Gaze into the water and see the moonlight.

Cup your hands into the water, filling them and then letting the water spill back in. "Show" the moon-water to the goddess.

Wet your fingers and anoint the goddess.

Cup your hands again and bathe your face in the moon-water.
Bow again; the goddess has arrived.

Drawing Down the Moon or Sun

In a nutshell, the rite is done by using whatever invocation you choose, but invoking it into a person's body, rather than simply sending it outward or into a statue.

I want to be one hundred percent clear that this is not something you should learn from a book. Most people simply can't learn to do trance channeling without personal training. However, failure is not nearly the problem that success is. If your channel succeeds, you may find it a disturbing experience. The gods do not necessarily behave the way we imagine they will or want them to. They are not always happy and they may choose to express their negative feelings. This can be more than a little uncomfortable.

It can be hard to shake off the feeling of trance, and it can be difficult to get to a place where you feel like you're yourself again. The best way to handle it is to have someone around who understands what's happening, and since I can't provide that to you, I don't feel it's responsible to present the techniques here. Instead, I merely present the information that this type of invocation exists, so that experienced people can see where it fits in the overall ritual pattern, and so that you aren't left wondering about something you've probably heard of elsewhere.

If you have no training available to you, it is perfectly fine to send the invocation outward or into a statue, as normal, and then recite a Charge, as described just below.

Moving from Invocation to Offering

When song, dance, music and drumming are being offered, it is easy to segue directly from invocation to offering. This isn't necessarily a good idea and should be thought about carefully. Suppose you're drumming while invoking the gods—wouldn't it be great to just *keep* drumming, and *offer* the drumming? It seems great, and it keeps the energy flowing, which is often a good idea. But it blurs the distinction between the request and the gift, and there are times when you'll want to make that distinction.

I think a combination of words and music can work. You can have one person say (or shout, if the drumming is really loud): *"Our music has brought the Lord and Lady to us. Now let's give our music **to** Them as a gift!"* In that way, the distinction has been made without the flow being interrupted.

Mostly, though, I think the best thing is to let the invocation end before letting the offering begin, however brief the pause in between turns out to be. You don't need to be afraid of letting the energy slow down for a bit; experience has taught me that it can always be brought back up, sometimes even stronger after a pause for breath and a new focus.

Besides which, not everyone in a group is likely to have nonstop energy. It seems that every group these days has one or more folks who can drum all night, and that's great—but we shouldn't allow that to take over the entire ritual, in a way that is inhospitable to everyone else. Less energetic people, or people with different styles of raising energy, shouldn't be made to feel unwelcome (unless your circle is specifically a drumming circle). If you slow down or stop, you let everyone re-merge, reconnecting to purpose, and to each other. Then you can allow the energy to start up again.

If you're working solitary, then you may not need any pause between invocation and offering. Once you *know* that the gods have arrived, then you can *know* that you are now making an offering to them—you've changed your mental focus, and your words, if you're using words, and so you don't have to stop in between. However, you might choose to stop for a transition even when solitary. It can be good to tell yourself that your invocation has succeeded, and good as well to acknowledge the arrival of the god(s).

EXAMPLES OF TRANSITIONAL STATEMENTS (INVOCATION TO OFFERING)
The statement above, *"Our music has brought the Lord and Lady to us. Now let's give our music **to** them as a gift!"* is an example of a transitional statement, bridging from invocation to offering, and acknowledging that, between the two, the gods have arrived. Here are some other examples:

> *"The Lady Inanna has joined our circle.*
> *Let us thank Her with gifts of incense and song."*

> *"The Lord and Lady are here! Let's sing and dance!*
> *Let's show Them our joy and share it with Them!"*

> *"Pause for a moment, to meditate on the presence of the Goddess and God.*
> *Think upon what you will offer to Them."*

THE CHARGE AS A TRANSITION

If Drawing Down the Moon or Sun is done, the recipient—the Priestess or Priest—then speaks as the deity; the God/dess uses the voice of the Priest/ess. The statement made is known as a Charge, and is meant as instructions to the people, saying how they should live and what the deity wants of us. Once this Charge has been spoken, the offerings are given immediately in response.

There are many, many Charges. Some are delivered spontaneously, some are memorized. Some are derived from traditional sources, and some are written by or for the individual who will recite them. The best know Charge, by Doreen Valiente, is perhaps used or paraphrased by Wiccans more than any other piece of writing:

The Charge of the Goddess[9]

Listen to the words of the Great Mother, who of old was called among men Artemis, Astarte, Dione, Melusine, Aphrodite, Cerridwen, Diana, Arionrhod, Brigid, and by many other names. At mine altar the youth of Lacedemon in Sparta made due sacrifice:

Whenever ye have need of anything, once in the month, and better it be when the moon is full, then shall ye assemble in some secret place and adore the spirit of Me who am Queen of all Witcheries. There shall ye assemble, ye who are feign to learn all sorcery, yet have not won its deepest secrets. To thee I shall teach that which is yet unknown.

And ye shall be free from slavery, and as a sign that ye be really free ye shall be naked in your rites. And you shall dance, sing and feast, make music and love, all in My presence, for Mine is the ecstasy of the spirit and Mine also is joy on earth. For My law is love unto all beings.

Keep pure your highest ideal. Strive ever toward it. Let naught stop you nor turn you aside. For mine is the secret that opens the door of youth, and Mine is the cup of wine of life that is the Cauldron of Cerridwen, which is the holy grail of immortality. I am the Gracious Goddess, who gives the gift of joy unto the hearts of men. Upon earth, I give the knowledge of the spirit eternal, and beyond death I give peace and freedom and reunion with those who have gone before. Nor do I demand aught in sacrifice, for behold, I am the Mother of all living and My love is poured out upon the earth.

Hear ye the words of the Star Goddess, She in the dust of whose feet are the hosts of heaven, whose body encircleth the universe:

I am the beauty of the green earth and the white moon amongst the stars and the mystery of the waters, and the desire of the heart of man. I call unto thy soul, arise and come unto me. For I am the soul of nature who giveth life to the universe. From Me all things proceed and unto Me all things must return. Before My face, beloved of gods and of men, let thine inmost divine self be enfolded in the raptures of the infinite.

Let My worship be in the heart that rejoiceth, for behold—all acts of love and pleasure are My rituals. Therefore, let there be beauty and strength, power and compassion, honor and humility, mirth and reverence within you. And they who seekest to know Me, know that thy seeking and thy yearning will avail thee not, unless thou knowest the Mystery: That if that which thou seekest, thou findest not within thee, thou wilt never find it without thee. For behold, I have been with thee from the beginning, and I am that which is attained at the end of desire.

Giving Offerings to the Gods

Water

The Honored Guests Metaphor

We've invited our guests and now they're here. The first thing we do, before we ask them for anything (like magic or blessings), is to offer them our best. "Hi, how are you? Have a seat. Would you like a drink? So nice of you to come. How can I make you comfortable?" These are the things that a good host says, and these are the things that *we* must say.

In general, there is something we want of the gods, something we'll ask of them. Even if we're not doing a spell, even if we're not asking any particular boon or blessing, at some level, we're fully aware that we are blessed and enriched, merely by being in their presence. So no matter how you frame it, we are inviting them into our circle, our metaphorical home, and then taking something from them. That being the case, shouldn't we first show as much generosity and hospitality as possible?

The Circle Story

Our creation story is complete—the universe has been built. With all of the central steps in this chapter—invocation, offering, receiving blessings, and sending the blessings back into the universe—the gods have entered into an infinite dance of worship: the dance between creator and created, who are in truth One, in their own yin-yang circle—giving and receiving, blessing and being blessed. The story has been told, and now we are living in its Happily Ever After.

The Mythic Basis of Making Offerings

The *Charge of the Goddess* is not typically thought of as a myth, but it is—the myth is unspoken but inherent. The Charge is said to be a statement made by the Goddess to Her children, forming instructions for worship and for living. The myth, then, is implied: once upon a time, the Goddess came to Her children to impart these instructions.[10] The instructions in the Charge form the basis for a true Wiccan creed. They say in part *". . . ye shall dance, sing, feast, make music, and love, all in my praise."* This, then, is the offering to be given at the rites—dancing, singing, feasting, music, and love.

The Charge goes on to say, *"Nor do I demand sacrifice, for behold, I am the Mother of all living, and my love is poured out upon the earth."* Some people take this to mean that there *is* no sacrifice in Wiccan ritual, yet isn't that contradicted by the statement that there is something the people should do in Her praise? I think, rather, that sacrifice is not a *demand*, that the love and joy should be given *freely*. We worship because we want to; we aren't punished for refraining from worship.

Air

In keeping with learning traditional information for invoking, we should also be able to provide traditional offerings, as these will be most pleasing to the gods.

Research on many deities is fairly straightforward; Hindu, Yoruba, and many Native American deities are actively worshiped, and their traditional lore should be respected. Knowledge about ancient Greek, Egyptian, and Babylonian rituals is available in many scholarly books. Other information can be gleaned indirectly, from pictures, statues, and ancient texts, if available. For example, if a deity is always shown wearing or holding a particular item, that is something you know is pleasing to that deity, even though no rituals or invocations survive from ancient times—an example is the torque held by Cernunnos. The kind of things you'll need are listed in detail under *Earth* for ease of reference.

Traditional offerings form a connection to deities; they are strands in the web that connect us to them. The deity recognizes the offerings that have always been given to her or him, and responds to them. Just as Shiva recognizes the traditional image of the Nataraja, so too He recognizes the incenses, ashes, *ghee* lamps and *tabla* drumming that are a part of His rites. That doesn't mean, however, that traditional offerings are the only acceptable offerings—far from it!

The idea here is to give, and give generously. This means more than giving *things*, it means giving intention, effort, and feeling. As discussed earlier, sacrifice is an important notion in Wicca, but so is the notion that sacrifice does not destroy us. We should give what we *can* give, what is within our own limits, and we should *not* give what is destructive to us or others in the giving.

This part of the ceremony might simply be called worship or prayer. In large part, simply praising and giving voice to our love of the gods is an offering. But to *name* the thing, to call it "offering" is to deepen our understanding of what it means to worship.

Earth

Rule Number One is this: *The offering should match the invocation.* If you performed the Diana invocation in example 5, above, you'd better darn well know what kind of offerings to give to *Diana!* You *cannot*, at that point, launch into a generic Wiccan ritual with generic Wiccan offerings. *Don't* invoke a deity unless you're prepared to perform the next step.

Beyond that rule, the rest is this: Give sincerely, and show your sincerity in your effort. Give your best. Give until you're confident you've given enough. If you've scheduled a song as an offering, and after the song is over, you feel unsatisfied, trust your feeling. Do another song, or an incense offering, or a chanted Aum.

There are a number of general groups, or types, of offerings:

• Specific gifts to the deity or deities.

• Joyful energy-raising, such as song, dance, or drumming.

- Somber or contemplative energy-raising, such as resonant chanting or silent prayer.

- Individual offerings, such as incense or spoken prayers.

- Offerings oriented toward immanence, which praise the gods by empowering the individual.

Specific Gifts to the Deity or Deities

There's a huge variety of things that can qualify as "gifts." Any kind of offering at all can be given to a specific god or goddess. Certain gifts are tailor-fitted to particular deities; for example, after the *Invocation to Diana* from the previous section, the bow and arrow could be offered as gifts to the goddess. They could be specially consecrated and dedicated to Her, to only be used for rituals in Her honor. They could be laid at the feet of Her statue or altar, to remain there as a perpetual offering. They could be used in a hunting ritual[11] (Diana is the Huntress, after all), and the meat then given to Her as a "burnt offering."

A gift such as the bow and arrow is emblematic—these tools are Diana's emblems, Her special and particular possessions. There are many such offerings, used only for a specific deity and for no other. Another approach is to take a "generic" offering and adapt it especially for a deity. For example, a libation—an offering of drink—is pretty universal; it's a standard part of Wiccan ritual and can be made for any deity. But if you offered beer, perhaps even home-brew, to Isis, the goddess of beer and brewing, then you've turned a libation into a very specific rite of Isis.

All of the types of offerings on the list above will be described in detail, and examples will be given. *Any or all* of them can be used as specific gifts to one or more gods or goddesses. You might want to do this on any occasion when you've called a particular deity. The deity could have been invited for the occasion—Brigid on Her feast-day of Imbolg (the night of February 1), or for a particular purpose—Bast, the Egyptian goddess of cats, to bless or heal a cat. Or, the deity may simply be one of your patrons or matrons—your personal mother or father, or the mother or father of your group.

How can an offering be adapted, so that it is a gift to one or more deities? Here are some things you should consider:

- What is the deity's favorite color or colors? This is something that can be found in the iconography and folklore. The altar cloth, candles, flowers, and/or other items can be adapted.

- What is the deity's favorite incense or aroma? Descriptions of traditional offerings or rituals can help.

- What are the sacrifices that have traditionally been pleasing to this deity? Once again, even if rituals haven't survived, there might be pictures, stories, or other associations. These foods and drinks should be used during the Cakes and Wine portion of the ceremony in a devotional rite. In fact, in a devotional rite, everything, from beginning to end, should be modified toward the deity's preferences.

- What items are pleasing to the deity? Consider jewelry, hand-held objects, articles of clothing—anything that the deity might need or be attracted by. Diana's bow and arrow is an example. Brigid, as the goddess of smithcraft, welcomes virtually anything made by that art. Articles of clothing might be offered, or worn while making the offering—like a sari being worn when praying to a Hindu deity, or a toga when praying to a Greek deity.

Raising a Joyful Noise

The Charge says, ". . . *ye shall dance, sing, feast, make music and love, all in my praise.*" The gods love our singing and our joy. Moreover, song, music, drumming, and dance are *effective*. Have you ever been to a rock concert and felt what it's like when the crowd goes wild? That's *magic*. People are moved by music, they become exalted and energized, and that energy can be given to the gods as a gift—and come back manifold in their blessings later.

This kind of energy-raising is what has traditionally been called "Raising the cone of power," although, in fact, any power-raising in a circle can be called that, whether it is being raised as an offering or as a spell. The circle works as a container, and the top portion of the egg-shaped circle is conical. "Raising the cone" simply means that, as energy is generated, it stays in the circle, forming a cone of power that surrounds the Witches, moving around deosil (clockwise) and building in strength. When it's time to send the power, it is visualized as shooting out of the top of the circle, like a gigantic arrowhead.

Although any kind of offering can be visualized as building into a cone of energy, the image is traditionally used for a joyous, high-energy dance.

The trick with this kind of joyful power-raising is to let yourself go, to let it build. It's natural for it to start a little slow, and sometimes it can take a while to get the groove. Once in a while, I've stopped the music and started over; if you know the energy and feeling just isn't there, why fake it? Maybe the singing started off-key, maybe the drummers just couldn't catch a beat. The second time has always been better. Don't get impatient; don't think "this is the best we're going to do" and pronounce the offering complete. The best you can do is really terrific, once you let the magic happen.

The other trick is knowing when to stop. Some people just build to a furious peak, and then drum and dance and dance and drum until they're completely spent. Even when doing a spell, there are other ways to build energy, but right now you're doing an offering, and you've still got more ritual to do afterwards. Don't spend yourself. Wait until it feels really great, until it feels joyful and like a gift, and let it go on like that for a bit. Then begin to reel it in.

Your pattern should be like this:

1. *Getting started*—a simple chant, a single drum beat; allow it to falter if need be, to find its own pace. Some nice chants to start with are these:

> *Listen to the Lord and Lady*
> *Call Their children*
> *In the moonlight.*[12]

> *Listen, listen, listen*[13]
> *To my heart song*
> *Listen, listen, listen*
> *To my heart song*
> *I will never forget you*
> *I will never forsake you*
> *I will never forget you*
> *I will never forsake you.*

Fire, Water, Air and Earth
Lord and Lady, Lord and Lady
Lord and Lady, Death, Rebirth
Lord and Lady now![14]

2. *Building*—if you're working in a group, let others get the feel and join in at their own pace. Not everyone sings, not everyone drums, not everyone dances, but as the energy builds, everyone can find their place in it, even if just clapping their hands, or humming, or swaying. If you're working alone, this is the point where you know what you're doing; you've gotten past any uneasiness, and you're allowing yourself to be a little more elaborate, a little more free.

3. *Peaking*—it feels great now; ecstatic. This is a tricky moment. The perfect moment to release the energy, to give it to the gods with a WHOOP, is when you feel absolutely glorious, but also like there's a place just a little bit higher right around the next bend. When you feel you're a tiny moment away from a true peak, you're *there*, you're at the perfect peak, and it's time to let go. That's because the minute you hit the true peak, the top, you'll start coming down again. It's like having an orgasm—in most cases, the top of the roller coaster is followed instantly by the tumble back down to earth. If you wait until you hit the top before giving the energy, you'll be tumbling down by the time you do. There's a delay between deciding to let go and actually letting go, even if that delay is only a nanosecond. If you *decide* at peak, you've passed it.

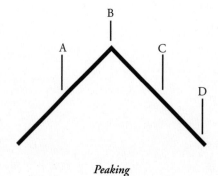

Peaking

Think of it this way: If you decide to let go at A, you'll send energy at B, or near to it. If you decide to let go at B, the energy you send will be at the level of C, and if you miss B by even a moment, you'll be sending at D. This principle applies to all power-raising, whether as offerings or as spells, and understanding it will increase your effectiveness.

You might miss your peak. You might be peaking and feeling great, and the next thing you know, find yourself leveling off, sliding down the slope. When I was younger and less experienced I'd think "Oh no!" and send at once, trying to salvage the situation by sending whatever was left. I learned over time, though, that if I let the energy wane to its lowest ebb, it would start to pick back up again, and head for another peak. It's a tiring and inefficient method if you're doing magic, but for an offering, it can just extend the fun. In other words, there's more where *that* came from!

4. *Letting Go*—Now's the time to release, send it off, let it go. You can whoop and holler and howl, all the time knowing that what you're doing is giving it all to the gods. Every bit of joy and power you just raised is being sent to them as a gift.

SOLITARY CONSIDERATIONS

If you're working solitary, the biggest barrier can be feeling that it's not enough somehow, that one person dancing or drumming doesn't quite hit the ecstasy high-mark. Instead, you can look at it as an excellent opportunity to be really free. When we work in a group, we can hold ourselves back because of our awareness that someone else can see our less-than-Astaire dancing, that someone else can hear our imperfect voices, or notice the occasional skips in the rhythm of our tambourine.

On the other hand, if you're in a group and you lose the beat while drumming, you can usually count on someone else covering for you. As a solitary, "getting the groove" can feel like it's taking *forever* because you're getting there without help. Stay with it; solitary ecstasy is a uniquely satisfying experience.

GROUP CONSIDERATIONS

Some groups form around specific styles or purposes; if you have a drum circle or a choral group you know what kind of sound you'll be making, and you know you're all on the same page. In every other group, the primary consideration is making sure that everyone has space to express themselves in a way that contributes to the offering.

Nowadays, the most common form of drowning out someone's offering is when the drummers get cranked up early, to the point where singers or people with quieter instruments cannot be heard. Another problem is when people spread out on the floor to make music, without paying attention to whether or not people want to dance. It's usually best to leave a certain amount of floor space clear even if no one is dancing, as people often wait until the music and energy are close to peak before jumping up and moving.

It's nice to keep a supply of small, inexpensive percussion instruments around for people to use, the kind that can be bought at educational children's stores—rattles, klava sticks, hand chimes, and the like. This helps everyone to feel that they can participate and gives them a chance to explore.

It's also good if a group can develop a repertoire of songs, chants, and rhythms. You can learn these either at festivals or by buying tapes and CDs, and it's very much worth the effort. Have some rehearsals or music-making time set aside outside of ritual, where you can play, experiment, and learn from each other without feeling that you're "on."

To Summarize

To make an offering of joyful noise, of freeform and joyous music, rhythm, and movement, begin at a low pitch, allowing yourself to get the feel of what you're doing. A knowledge of several different chants and rhythms can help. Allow the energy to build, giving people time to find their own ways of participating. When the energy feels very high, but not quite peaked, release the energy, sending it to the gods as a gift. (Witches often refer to this as "calling the drop," as the person leading the energy-raising "calls," usually by saying "Now!" or "So mote it be!"—then, when everyone sends the energy, they drop to the floor.)

A Quieter Offering

It's a lot of fun to raise a loud and wild cone of power. It's *so* much fun that some people never try any other sort of offering.

There are lots of reasons to make your offering silent or low-key, many of them practical. A late night ritual in an apartment with paper-thin walls is not the best place for drumming and hollering; your neighbors will undoubtedly be grateful if you learned a quieter technique.

You or someone in your group might not have the physical health needed for dancing, or the stamina to tolerate high intensity drumming, chanting, clapping, etc., or the temperament to enjoy it.

In a large group, it is easier to coordinate a quieter offering or power-raising. If you're doing a ritual in a large group, with thirty or more people, it is hard to know if everyone's going to be comfortable with, or able to do, a high-energy offering. It can easily degenerate into chaos.

Although it doesn't often apply to offerings, quiet, low-key energy-raising has additional advantages when working magic. The primary advantage is that you can last longer, and this can be applied to a number of situations.

One reason for needing to last longer is simply that you have a lot to do. If you're making an offering now and plan to work two or more spells later, you don't want to flag too early. Perhaps you're making offerings to several different deities individually. Perhaps you're doing several spells, or perhaps you're doing one spell in several parts. For example, I was once a part of a spell on behalf of an injured child. We worked long and hard on behalf of the child, and our work was broken into several parts. We sent loving energy and prayer, we sent life and vitality, we sent recovery. Finally, after all of these, we sent sustenance to the child's parents, who had been in the hospital with their child for twenty-four hours or more without sleep. The work was exhausting, but one hundred percent successful—the child recovered completely. It could not have succeeded if we'd collapsed in exhaustion after the first few minutes.

If you're doing a multi-group working, it is helpful to work in a way that can last for fifteen minutes or more. There was an incident several years ago in which a well-known member of the Pagan community was seriously ill. Word went out by e-mail and phone. Witches and Pagans all over the U.S. (and probably the world) held healing circles. My then-husband and I helped coordinate the working. Based on the response we received, I estimate there were several hundred, if not over a thousand, groups and solitaries working magic that night.

We decided to work a "coordinating" spell, gathering up all the magics being raised and focusing them; we visualized a giant magnifying glass over the hospital, and we pictured all the healing energies (including our own) flowing into it and becoming intensified, like a beam of light. We wanted to make sure to "catch" as much energy as possible, and so we wanted to keep our magnifying glass in place as long as possible, since we knew that not everyone would send their healing energy at exactly the same time. Obviously, we needed a method that we could sustain for the twenty to thirty minutes required.

The stages of this kind of offering/power-raising are the same as before; the cone is being raised, it is just being done more sedately. You'll begin, you may fumble at first—even in silent meditation you may fumble in your imagination—and then find a focal point or flow. You'll allow the energy to build—resisting the temptation to bring it up too fast. This is the area where it's most different from ecstatic power-raising. You'll stay with the building, slowly adding to it, bit by bit, so that the reaching toward a peak is barely noticeable. As you get closer and closer to peak, you can slow down even more, to sustain the level. Finally, though, you'll release.

RESONANCE AND CHANTING

When most people chant, they simply sing, usually a couplet or two that's easily remembered and can be repeated over and over. However, there are other ways of chanting.

Sound is made from vibration, and vibration moves energy. As a sound moves through your body, it effects a number of physical changes: blood flow, oxygenation, and so on, as well as simply sending a current of movement throughout your system. This movement is also working psychically—just as the broader movement of dance changes consciousness, so does the subtle movement of chanting.

Western mystics often chant vowel sounds—all the vowel sounds, slowly resonated, one after another. These sounds combine to create the full range of possible vibrations, taking you on a psychic and physical journey without ever leaving your seat.

To "resonate" or "tone," start the sound as low as you can (it varies based on the sound). By low, I don't refer to the notes on the scale so much as the place in your body, although lower notes start lower physically. Bring the sound up from your navel if you can. Slowly pull the sound up from the belly, into the lungs and throat, and through the head. Each vowel sound only contains part of the journey. "AH" resides mostly in the chest and throat, while "EH" can be felt in the nose and forehead, and

"UH" begins deep in the belly. Take a deep breath before each sound, and extend the sound the full length of the exhalation, stopping only to inhale again.

When toning the vowel sounds in a group, don't expect each person to take the same length of time per sound—unlike a group song, each individual can begin and end the sections separately. This has an interesting effect as well, as you'll be feeling different vibrations from the outside (others) and from the inside (yourself).

Resonating, or toning, will be something like this:

AAAAAAAAAAAAAAAAAAAAAAAAAAAAAAAAAAAAAAAAAA
(short A as in "cat")

AAAAAAAAAAAAAAAAAAAAAAAAAAAAAAAAAAAAAYYYY
(long A as in "may")

EEEEEEEEEEEEEEEEEEEEEEEEEEEEEEEEEEEEEEEEHHHH
(short E as in "bed")

EEEEEEEEEEEEEEEEEEEEEEEEEEEEEEEEEEEEEEEEEEEE
(long E as in "free")

IIIIIIIIIIIIIIIIIIIIIIIIIIIIIIIIIIIIIIIIIIIIIIIIIIIIIIIIIIIII
(short I as in "hit")

AIIIIIIIIIIIIIIIIIIIIIIIIIIIIIIIIIIIIIIIIIIIIIIIIIIIIIIIIIIII
(long I as in "bite")

AAAAAAAAAAAAAAAAAAAAAAAAAAAAAAAAAAAAHHHH
(short O as in "top")

OOOOOOOOOOOOOOOOOOOOOOOOOOOOOOOOOOOHHHH
(long O as in "go")

UUUUUUUUUUUUUUUUUUUUUUUUUUUUUUUUUUHHHH
(short U as in "up")

OOOOOOOOOOOOOOOOOOOOOOOOOOOOOOOOOOOOOOOO
(long U as in "tune")

To raise energy with vowel toning, simply sit in a comfortable position and begin toning, starting over at the short A when you finish. While toning, visualize the energy of your sound being given as a gift to the gods (if you were doing a spell, you'd visualize the goal and target of your spell instead).

In the beginning was the Word. Sound created the universe. Many mystics believe that it is sound itself that brought about creation, and many have sought after that perfect, original Word. The Hindus believe the original word is Aum. Chanting Aum recapitulates what we've done mythically in casting the circle. Our Circle Myth has been a re-creation of creation; and now we're doing it again, because Aum is the word of creation.

Aum, often spelled "Om," is resonated in the East in a way very similar to the vowel toning described above. Yogis are careful in their chanting to pronounce every sound in the syllable—and there are many, as you'll see. In fact, Aum will take you through every part of the body in vibration, from deep in the belly all the way up to the top of the head, which is reach by making the final MMMMM sound with the tongue on the roof of the mouth, letting the sound vibrate upwards.

A fully intoned[15] Aum is:

AAAAAAAAAAAAAAAAAAAAAAAAAAAAAAAAAAHHHH
(short O as in "top")
OOOOOOOOOOOOOOOOOOOOOOOOOOOOOOOOOHHHH
(long O as in "go")
UUUUUUUUUUUUUUUUUUUUUUUUUUUUUUUUUHHHH
(short U as in "up")
MMMMMMMMMMMMMMMMMMMNNNNNNNNNN
(vibrating the roof of the mouth)

Once you've got the basics down—toning through the full body, controlling your breath and vibration, and sending the energy to the gods—you can use it on other sounds, words, or magical phrases. Appropriate words would be the name(s) of the god(s) that you've invoked in your ritual: "Blessed be," "Lord and Lady," and so on. Remember that the power of the *meaning* is being vibrated, as well as the power of the *sound.*

Silent Prayer

Silence is as legitimate a means of making your offering to the gods as any other. The focused mind and heart, sending the offerings psychically and emotionally, can be potent indeed.[16] It can force the mind to be disciplined in a different way—because we're so dependent upon speech—and this discipline, this re-focusing, can bring forth a depth of spiritual feeling that is your gift to the gods. You might even see silence as a sacrifice—the temporary sacrifice of speech as an offering to the gods.

The simplest thing to do is to make your transitional statement ("*Let us now offer our silent prayers/meditations/thoughts. . .*") and go ahead. However, you may wish to add a little something.

You could use a focal point for prayer—such as the statue(s) of the god(s), a candle, or other symbol. If you're working solitary, you can hold it in your hands, or leave it on the altar. In a group, you might pass the object around, or you might have enough objects for everyone. (The disadvantage of passing one object around to a group is that someone can be deep in meditation and have to be nudged in order to receive the object, while someone else could become impatient waiting for the object.)

For example, you might invoke a god or goddess of the sea, such as Yemaya or Poseidon. You could have a statue or image resting on a plate of seashells, or just the seashells. Then, when the time comes to meditate, you could, with appropriate ceremony, pass a seashell to each person. Then everyone could be holding a shell while sending thoughts to the god or goddess.

If you have a large statue or symbol—perhaps a staff or a cauldron (which is the symbol of several different deities)—it could be placed centrally so that several people could touch it at once. In a small group, say two to five people, placing all hands on an object could be both convenient and empowering—reinforcing group unity while concentrating the prayer.

You could also simply hold hands, and in a group larger than five this might be the most convenient way of reinforcing prayer through touch.

You might also try *nearly* silent prayer. Perhaps recorded music, playing softly, would help to put you in the right state of mind—and this can also work as a kind of timer (like an auditory rosary). You could have one person play a very simple sound— a heartbeat rhythm on the drum, a low rattle, a rain-stick, or a recorder. Perhaps one person could even tone an "Ah" softly. This acts as background music, but is not trivial. It helps to focus the mind and drive away distractions, and in a group, helps maintain unity. It also helps to cover any ambient sounds, giving the mind something to attach to if a car honks its horn or if the heating system kicks in with a whoosh.

Individual Offerings

An individual offering is exactly what it sounds like—each individual offers one thing, whether a pinch of incense, a spoken prayer, a ritualized act, or whatever your imagination comes up with.

For a solitary, this sort of offering will probably seem too lightweight, and is best combined with another offering, such as chanting (you could do either one followed by the other, or chant *while* dropping offerings on the censer). In a group, part of the potency of the offering comes from the act of being together, each of us witnessing the others' gifts. We support one another and lend power to the act by our presence and attention.

EXAMPLE 1: A SIMPLE INCENSE OFFERING

The group stands in a circle around the altar. The invocation has been made, and any transitional statement has already been said.

Priestess: *Let us make our offerings to the Lord and Lady.*

Priest: *As the smoke rises, so rise our thoughts. As the gods enjoy the sweetness of the incense, so They will enjoy our prayers to them.*[17]

Priestess: Lifts censer.

Priest: Lifts dish of incense.

Priestess: Takes a pinch of incense. She holds it for a moment and gathers her thoughts, perhaps holding the incense over her third eye or her heart while she sends her energies into it. When she's ready, she places it on the censer, saying: *To the Lady and Lord.*[18] *Blessed be.*

Priest: *Blessed be.* (Kisses her.)

All: *Blessed be.*

The Priestess and Priest now switch. He hands her the censer; she hands him the incense dish.

Priest: Takes a pinch of incense and gathers his thoughts. When ready, he offers it, saying: *To the Lady and Lord. Blessed be.*

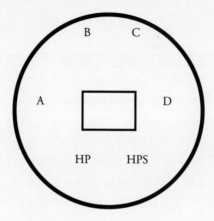

Coven Standing Around the Altar

Priestess: *Blessed be.* (Kisses him.)

All: *Blessed be.*

Now everyone else will make their offerings. There are two ways of doing this, which depends upon how many people you have, and the size of the room.

The illustration shows the coven standing around the altar. The Priestess (HPS) and Priest (HP)[19] are to the south of the altar.

Method 1: People walk around to make their offerings. It has a nice feel to it; everyone gets a chance to move around, and all the movement has its own energy. Since everyone must move deosil, the way to work it is this:

HP and HPS turn around, facing the south. HPS is still holding censer, HP is still holding dish of incense. D steps up to them, takes a pinch of incense and offers it, saying "*To the Lady and Lord. Blessed be,*" or some other statement, or offers in silence, and places the incense on the censer. The HPS and HP say "*Blessed be.*" The entire group echoes. In covens working with polarity, D will kiss the person of the opposite sex—either the HP or HPS. In other groups, D will kiss both or neither.

Now D walks deosil all the way around the circle back to his/her place. While D is walking, C steps forward, walking to the HP and HPS, and offers in the same way. Every time an offering is made, the HPS and HP say "*Blessed be*" and the group echoes. While C is walking back to his/her place, B steps forward, and so on.

Method 2: If there are more than a dozen people, this is really the only practical method.

After the HPS and HP have exchanged offerings, they walk together, deosil, around the circle. They stop in front of A, who makes his/her offering as described in method 1. The HPS and HP say "*Blessed be*" and the group echoes. Kisses are exchanged as described.

The HPS and HP then walk together to B, and so on around the circle. When D has offered, the HPS and HP return to the south of the offer, exchange another kiss, and place the censer and incense dish back on the altar.

These two methods will work for a wide variety of situations, and understanding the way that people should move in the circle will make things flow smoothly, and prevent a lot of awkward shuffling about.

Example 2: An Autumnal Offering

This is an offering made after leaves have begun to fall, connecting the ritual to the season, and the season to our lives. If you live somewhere that doesn't have an autumn, look at this example as a model for the kinds of offerings that can be done that connect us to the gods through nature.

Prior to the ritual, the Priestess sends everyone outside with instructions to pick *one* fall leaf (this is important—I once gave the instruction too vaguely, and people came in with *bags* of leaves). If possible, don't tell people *why* they're getting the leaves. They'll know the leaves are special, of course, and so they'll get a little bit attached to them, and that's part of the purpose of the offering.[20]

You'll have to prepare in advance, though, because the leaves will be burned. I suggest setting up the cauldron (or whatever you're making your fire in) the day before, and burning several leaves in it. You want to make sure that the fire catches and that you have enough material for making the fire *before* adding the leaves (don't count on the leaves as kindling). Be sure that the cauldron is safe—not tippy and not too hot for the surface it's on. Check the amount of smoke generated, especially if there's a smoke alarm in the room.[21] As always in a ritual with a fire, have a fire extinguisher in the ritual room, just in case.

Everyone will bring his or her leaf into the circle when you start. Before making the offering, there will be a short guided meditation. The transition from invocation to offering will be part of that, so there's no need for a "transitional statement."

Leader:[22]   *Close your eyes and think for a moment on the changing of the seasons. The trees have been lush and full of the Goddess'[23] glorious life all through the summer. But summer is over and life is not now lush. The Mother has put on Her fall gown, and the trees understand Her ways. They will shed the beautiful leaves of summer. They will trust that new ways will come. We must learn to do the same. We must obey the will of the seasons. Look inside yourselves. There is much that is beautiful and precious, but not all of it is meant for you to keep. Look inside yourselves, and find something that is ready to be let go of. It could be a habit, or a hobby, a job, or a relationship. Find something that it is time for you to give away, and trust that the Goddess will replace it with something beautiful when the Spring comes. The thing you will let go of, the thing you will give to the Goddess, is like a fall leaf—beautiful but ready to die. Prepare yourself now, to give away that beautiful thing. It is your sacrifice, your offering to the Goddess. As you give, know that you also trust. You have faith that She will make this loss seem like a gain by the time the seasons have turned. When you are ready, open your eyes.*

Pause. Wait until everyone's eyes are open.

Leader: *One by one, we will add our leaves to the fire. As we do so, we will be shedding the fall leaves within, we will be throwing that part of ourselves onto the fire, and letting it go up in smoke to the Goddess. Come around to the fire, now, and make your sacrifice. If you wish to speak, you are free to do so.[24]*

Beginning with the Priestess or leader, everyone will offer up their leaves, exactly as described in Method 1, except that they will be moving around the fire instead of the altar. The Priestess should make the first sacrifice so that everyone else can see how it's done (in case they're unsure). This is her opportunity to set the tone—if she wants offerings done in silence, she'll be silent. If she wants to encourage everyone to say a few words, she'll set an example. She might say something like:

Leader: *As I sacrifice this leaf, I sacrifice my addiction to tobacco. Starting tomorrow, I will no longer smoke.*

After each sacrifice, the entire group says *So mote it be.*[25]

When all the leaves have been placed on the fire, and all the sacrifices have been made, stand and watch the fire for a few minutes. This can be a very emotional moment; the people in the group have made a lot of changes in a short time. It's one thing to say you're quitting smoking, it's entirely another to see your tobacco addiction going up in flames. It can be disconcerting and difficult to be with.

After a few minutes, you may wish to begin a chant. This will help to complete the experience, and lighten the mood. The chanting might even become celebratory. When you're ready to finish, remind everyone of what they've given up, and of their faith in the gods. As you'll see in the next step, there's a second transitional statement that often needs to be made—this time from offering into Cakes and Wine. The transition *out* of this offering should be quite specific:

All: *Our sacrifices have been received by the Goddess. We remind ourselves that in giving to Her, we are never diminished, we always grow.*

Immanence: Offering to Yourself

We've discussed offerings to the "Lord and Lady," to the Goddess, and offerings to specific deities—such as Isis or Diana. We have offered "things," such as incense, emotion, and energy (our joyful noise); and in our Autumnal offering, we gave something of ourselves.

Now we're going to make an immanent offering. We give the offering to the God/dess within; that is, to ourselves. The gift we give is empowerment—we give the knowledge that we are gods and goddesses.

Acknowledging one another's power and supporting each other in that knowledge is one of the best parts about working in a group. We often doubt ourselves; it's easy to forget we have deity within us. Our brothers and sisters of the coven can remind us of our spiritual center, and as we remember that *they* have God/desses within them, we can remember the same about ourselves.

However, this offering can also be a powerful part of a solitary rite. If you're a solitary, you have to remind *yourself* that you carry the God or Goddess within, and performing rites that serve as that reminder is an important part of your Craft.

The construction of a group immanence offering, however, should take full advantage of the group, and so two different examples are provided.

Example 3: Finding the Deity Within Each Other

For this example, refer back to the illustration in example 1. The HPS begins, followed by the HP. It's important that the first two people are familiar with what's expected, so that everyone else can follow along.

HPS: *The God and Goddess are here, not just with us, but within us. It is the Lord and Lady standing on either side of you. It is the Goddess herself wearing that brown robe,[26] the Horned God with his black mustache.[27]*

(The next two paragraphs combine instructions and advice. If this isn't the first time that the group has done this offering, you'll probably want to shorten them.)

HPS: *It is time now to see the Lord and Lady in each of us, one at a time. There are two things to remember about this: First, you'll look into the eyes of the person to your left. Remember to really look, and look deeply. Don't think about your preconceptions about a person you know well; don't think about your ignorance of a person you don't know at all.[28] Second, allow yourself to be truly seen when the person to your right looks at you, and listen to what he or she says. When everyone says "Blessed be" at the end, allow yourself to feel blessed.*

 I will turn to HP[29] and acknowledge the God in him. I will look to him and seek out his godlike nature, and speak what I see. I will praise and bless him. Then we'll all bless him. After that, it will be HP's turn to praise and bless A, and so on around the circle, until D praises and blesses me.

HPS turns to her left and faces HP. She takes his hands in hers and looks directly into his eyes. Her mental attitude is of openness, and she allows herself to feel love.

HPS: *I acknowledge the God in you, HP.*
 In you I see that the God is wise, that He is full of knowledge, and that He will always share His knowledge with His children. Your teaching is of the God.[30]

> *I praise the God in you, HP.*
> *Blessed be, HP.* (Kiss)

All: *Blessed be, HP.*

HP turns to his left and faces A. He takes her hands in his and looks into her eyes.

HP: *I acknowledge the Goddess in you, A.*
> *In you I see that the Goddess is a loving mother,*
> *gentle when needed, and fierce in Her protection*
> *of Her children. In you I see how generous and*
> *open-hearted a truly loving mother can be.*
> *Your motherhood is of the Goddess.*
> *I praise the Goddess in you, A.*
> *Blessed be, A.* (Kiss)

All: *Blessed be, A.*

A will now acknowledge and praise B, and so on around the circle. Note that the structure is formulaic—if someone is at a loss for words, they'll still have the "acknowledge the God/dess in you" part, the "I praise" part, and "Blessed be" with the person's name. This alone can be a rich experience. But the individualized acknowledgments, in which we look into one another and see the particular characteristics that are godlike, is the best part of this offering. Giving and receiving such blessings really changes a person. To receive it is to allow yourself to feel not just good about yourself, but to feel truly exalted. To give it is to free up your ability to love, to move past polite "How are you, I'm fine" inhibitions of speech and be truly generous. Paradoxically, the giver of blessings in each pair will also feel exalted and godlike, because it is godlike to make another person know that he or she is blessed.

Example 4: Offering to Yourself—A Solitary Immanence Offering

If you're a solitary, you don't have the advantage of receiving support from the others in the group. It's entirely up to you to create within yourself the knowledge of the God or Goddess within. Part of the balance of Wicca is the balance between pride and humility. This offering is about pride, but it should also be approached with humility. This isn't the contradiction it sounds like. It simply means understanding that this offering is to you and more-than-you—that it isn't designed as a self-esteem exercise (although it has obvious self-esteem benefits) but as a religious ritual.

The altar is set up with a mirror. The mirror can be your Goddess figure for this ritual, or you can have it in addition to your usual Goddess statue.[31] Find a mirror that is suitable for this purpose—a traditional Witches' mirror is black, which works wonderfully by candlelight, but at least make sure it's reasonably ornate—a plastic make-up mirror just won't do. (Similarly, a magnifying mirror is a bad idea.)

It's important that you be able to see your face in the mirror, so you should experiment beforehand with the altar layout. You might, for example, set the mirror on a stand with suitable decorations all around, and then discover that you can't see directly into it from where you'll be seated, and if you pick it up, you knock over the decorations. Sure, it sounds silly reading about it, but if it happens in the middle of a circle, it's aggravating, not to mention a fire hazard. Once your candles are all lit, you want to be reasonably certain that things won't start falling over.

You don't *have* to set it standing on the altar. You can lay a handheld mirror flat on the altar, or keep it underneath. You just have to make sure that it's easily accessible when it's time to pick it up.

If the mirror is standing on the altar, it is ideal to have the censer in front of it, so that smoke rises in front of the reflection.

You should speak out loud for this offering, *hearing* the praise of the Goddess is as important as saying it.

Gaze into the mirror as you begin to speak:

The Goddess is here, not just with me, but within *me. It's the Lady Herself I see in the mirror. The Lady Herself gazes back at me, with Her brown eyes and curly hair.*[32]

I can see the Goddess within me.

I see the Goddess within me.

I praise the Goddess within me.

I love the Goddess within me.

The Goddess is NAME.[33] *NAME is the Goddess.*

The Goddess is NAME. NAME is the Goddess.

At this point, you'll be looking into the mirror and finding goddess-like attributes. It's important that you allow yourself to *feel* and *believe* each one. In other words, if you say you are beautiful, you must let yourself see and know your own beauty. In the group immanence offering, each person was only praised for one attribute, but the cumulative effect was of hearing and knowing that many attributes of ordinary people are godlike. To achieve the same effect in a solitary rite, you will have to find four or five godlike attributes in yourself.

Each time you name an attribute, you should acknowledge it ritually. I recommend putting a pinch of incense on the censer, but if you don't like the extra smoke, you can also strike a bell or, with a handheld mirror, kiss the mirror.

> *I acknowledge the Goddess in myself, in NAME.*
> *I see in myself that I am beautiful, that my face and body reflect the face and body of the Goddess, and show the world Her beauty and sensuality.[34] My beauty is of the Goddess.*
> *I praise the Goddess in me.*
> *Blessed be. (Add a pinch of incense to the censer.)*

Pause now, and meditate on this blessing and praise. When you are ready, repeat the entire step, with a different quality, like this:

> *I acknowledge the Goddess in myself, in NAME.*
> *I see in myself that I am patient, that I am able to wait for what I want and need. Just as the Goddess endures for millennia, just as Her Earth abides through storms and tribulations, so do I, NAME, abide through the trials and difficulties of my life, remaining patient that all will be well. My patience is of the Goddess.*
> *I praise the Goddess in me.*
> *Blessed be. (Add a pinch of incense to the censer.)*

Again, pause to meditate. You should do at least four "rounds" of praise and blessing.

You might like to finish this offering with chanting and drumming. An excellent chant would be to resonate or sing your own name.

Fire

What is the nature of offering? This is, of course, a subject for lengthy (and lifelong) meditation. In part, the answer can be found in the word *transformation*, a word associated with Fire. An offering is something that is transformed by the act of offering it.

Incense is incense—some herbs, some gums, blended with pestle and mortar. Consecrate it and you distill it to its purified essence. But *offer* it, and you utterly transform its nature. It is no longer incense, it is your offering to the gods; it is a conduit from you to them.

Performance is transformed by offering. One thing I have absolutely forbidden in my circles is applause. Not only does it disrupt the energy flow, but it changes the focus, and not in a good way. A performance is something that draws attention to the performer; the audience is meant to be impressed. But an *offering* draws attention to the *gods*; the performer is merely an agent, and the audience should be exalted. I have seen professional actors and performers ruin rituals by pulling all the focus away from the gods and onto themselves. I have also seen professional performers give their art generously and reverently to the gods. Professionalism is not the point; performance-as-offering can and should be done by *anyone*. I generally avoid singing my offerings, because I wander off-key so badly, but there have been occasions when I wanted to give something that could only be given in song; and it's the *giving* that matters.

Everything that is given is transformed; it becomes something else, it becomes a gift. It ceases to belong to you, it is not to your honor or your credit or your ego-fulfillment. It now belongs to the gods, and the honor is theirs as well.

Offerings to the gods, of course, are more sourdough. We can only give what we receive from them. Only what they have given us is within us, and that is what we give. Since they, themselves, are within us. So we give *of* them in order to give *to* them, on and on in an infinite circle. To raise a joyful noise is magic, and magic comes from the gods. So we give to them what we get from them, and of course, they are within ourselves. A circle. A magic circle—a Witches' circle.

Meditate on the circle, on giving and receiving being two sides of the same coin, on offerings being a salary you draw from yourself to pay yourself so that you benefit. The infinite cycle of giver, recipient, and gift is something that can fill your meditation night after night, always yielding more insight.

Cakes and Wine (Receiving the Blessings of the Gods)

In Cakes and Wine we commune with the gods. We partake of their essence, of their union, and of their gifts to us. The interchange is complex and mystical, layered in meaning. Yet, it is rarely carefully analyzed in Wiccan literature, as we shall do here.

A typical Cakes and Wine rite goes like this:

1. A short statement (a transitional statement from the previous step) is made about what will be done.

2. The HPS holds the cup and the HP holds the athame.[35]

3. A statement is made about love or union, or the Goddess and God, or both.

4. The athame is plunged into the cup (with or without an additional statement).

5. The wine, now consecrated, is sprinkled over the cakes, which consecrates them.

6. A portion of both wine and cakes is set aside for the gods. Some people don't do this until later, after the people have partaken.

7. Everyone drinks and eats.

Water

Mythically, the athame plunging into the cup is the Sacred Marriage. It is the Lord joining with the Lady, an ecstatic union of love, fertility, sensuality, and perfection. In Egyptian myth, Geb, the Earth God, and Nut, the Sky Goddess, make love and fertilize the earth in an ongoing union. They gaze at each other for all eternity.

In Greek myth, Earth Goddess Gaia joined with Sky God Uranus and their love-making conceived the Titans. Thus, the entire pantheon of gods came from this union of Earth and Sky. (Although in the classical story, it ends badly.)

In Sumer, the goddess Inanna was married in an elaborate ceremony with the king. An anointed priestess of the Goddess acted in Her stead to consummate the union. This sacred marriage was what gave the king his sovereignty.

In Hinduism, the union of Goddess and God is venerated in statues known as Yab-Yums. Lord Shiva is seen with a goddess or woman seated in his lap as they make love.

As you can see, the veneration of the sacred union of Goddess and God is quite ancient, and cross-cultural. It can be symbolized in many different ways. There are many instances of it being enacted physically, as in the Sumerian example, but many other instances of it being depicted in a more abstract manner, such as with the athame and cup.

The Honored Guests Metaphor

If we are having a dinner party, then Cakes and Wine is when dinner is served. It is most important to remember who the dinner is being held for, as this will inform what we serve, and how we serve it. We must make sure that everything about the food we serve to the gods honors them.

Although various Wiccan groups differ on this, I was taught to give the gods only the first, best, and freshest foods and drinks. I believe this is the only way to treat the most honored and exalted guests of all. A partly-drunk bottle of wine from the back of the fridge is not a fit drink to serve such guests, nor is it proper to serve something to yourself first, wetting your own whistle before making sure your guests have had their share. Under *Earth*, we'll go over the rules for libations, which is how, exactly, to make sure that the gods are served in the way that honors them best. For now, keep in mind that respect and politeness necessitates such rules.

Our guests have arrived (the invocation), and we have thanked them for coming, and done our best to make them comfortable (the offering). Now it's time to seat them in the place of honor at our table, and wine and dine them with the first servings of the best we have, selected especially for them.

Air

Moving from Offering to Cakes and Wine

Just as you needed a transition from Invocation to Offering, you need one now, from Offering to Cakes and Wine. In this case, the transition is more dramatic; the entire tone and mood of the ritual can change. There's a drama to Cakes and Wine, a sort of "I don't dare breathe" moment of exquisite tension and attention. It is beautiful, erotic, and elevating.

A moment ago, you were making your offerings. This may have been joyous and playful, or it may also have been done in a dramatic fashion; you may have built your offering on the edge of tension and uncertainty. There's a certain kind of humility in an offering; you don't know if it's going to be accepted, and you offer *into* that uncertainty.

In order to be able to receive the blessings of the Goddess and God, then, you'll need a release of that uncertainty. In order to have the faith to receive their blessings, you'll need to acknowledge that your offering was accepted.

On a more mundane level, you simply *need* to change your focus; to shake loose, slightly, the intensity of making offerings; to catch your breath; and to introduce the new intensity of communion.

The transitional statement also tells people what is happening, giving information about the contents of the next step. When we say, *"It is now time to take the blessings of the Mother . . ."* we are imparting important theological information.

The Priestess and Priest Hold the Symbolic Tools

In chapter 3 we discussed the athame as the fully masculine tool (both masculine and male) and the cup as the fully feminine tool. They're polar opposites, drawing polarity's tension apart to its extreme limits. The gender symbolism is doubled when the rite is performed by a male-female couple; but whether you're working the ritual in gender balance, solitary, or in a single-gender group, you're working with polarity—yin and yang, tension and balance, Goddess and God.

A Statement About Union/Athame and Cup are Joined

As with other components of ritual, Cakes and Wine can be done nonverbally—skipping the "statement" step entirely. But just as with a wordless quarter-calling or a silent consecration, the *idea* that would commonly be put into words is there, and it's the idea we're discussing now.

The union of the cup and athame represents the union of the Goddess and the God. There are several different meanings that Wiccans will ascribe to this union: that it represents **procreation,** that it represents **love,** or that it represents the **union of opposites**—a joining of yin and yang into a single whole. Since the union of the Goddess and God is the spiritual core of the ritual, you should think carefully about each of the meanings of that union, the ways in which they differ, and what they have in common, before deciding how to shape your own ritual. It is certainly true that all three meanings can be present simultaneously, but in general, one will need to be in the fore in order for your rite to have clarity of focus.

Whatever the meaning of the symbolism, the symbol itself—the blade plunged into the cup—is clearly a sexual one. Wicca celebrates life in all its earthly pleasures; as it says in *The Charge:* "All acts of love and pleasure are My rituals." People outside of the Craft can find the mixing of the spiritual with the purely physical to be bizarre, if not profane. In truth, to bring these seeming opposites together brings a wholeness to life; to know that the sexy is spiritual, and the spiritual is sexy, is to know that we are all right as is, that it is *possible, attainable,* to have a life that is deeply, richly lived, and lived also in the Ways of the gods.

We should be as frank as we can with this; we should not let the sacredness of sexuality become a coy little secret. It may take a bit of inner work to allow our rituals to feel erotic; we may have to work through some old programming to get there. I'm not talking about orgiastic rites here; I'm talking about the simple and open enjoyment of the erotic energies released when the athame enters the cup. The flow of magical and spiritual energies through our bodies, in general (not just here), can have an arousing quality, and we have to let ourselves know that it's okay. Honestly, it surprised the daylights out of me the first time I felt this. I was in a circle and I felt spiritual, and elevated, and awed, and . . . *hot*. Yow! That certainly startled me. It also awakened in me an understanding of the holiness of my own body, and that when the Goddess says pleasure is sacred to Her, She *means* it.

Procreation

Wicca has often been described as a "fertility religion." The veneration of fertility has roots in the most ancient religious and magical practices. Fertility is probably the earliest characteristic worshiped and sought after in Mother Earth—She is holy because She gives birth.

In the ancient world, fertility was a constant concern, and everyone was well aware that it could not be taken for granted. Not just human procreation, of course, but animal and agricultural fertility were vital. It seems we've come full circle, with upscale couples spending small fortunes at fertility clinics, and geneticists spending their careers tinkering with the reproduction of animals and plants. Now as ever, fertility is recognized as the bottom line of life, and power over fertility the most important power humans can have.

Sympathetic magic tells us that similarity to a thing constitutes a relationship to that thing, and fertility is no exception. Things that have sympathy with procreation are things that arise from seeds and sparks, things that gestate and then are born. Any of the creative arts are fertile—writer's block is a problem with infertility. New projects, new jobs, new ideas—all of these need fecundity. They all are conceived, they all gestate, they all must be born, and at any part of the process, they can whither. A new idea, a book, a painting, a real estate venture—any can fail to conceive, any can be successfully conceived and then whither and die during the gestation period, any can be stillborn.

The magic of procreation is the magic that all of us have in common, since all of us were conceived and born. The miracle of life is something we should all be awakened to from time to time, as it is easy to take for granted. We wake up grumpy and go to work grumbling and complain about our bills, our relationships, and our lives. Rarely do we remember that simply to be alive is extraordinary and unfathomable. For fertility to be the central mystery of our ritual reminds us to be open to the miracle that we wake up to each day.

Love

In *The Charge*, the Goddess says, "My law is Love unto all beings." As quoted earlier, she also instructs us, in our rites, to "dance, sing and feast, make music and love, all in My presence . . ." The Goddess wants us to love each other. She wants us to *enjoy* each other. I emphasize this, lest we take it all too seriously. She groups "make love" with music, dance, and feasting, so love is clearly meant to be a pleasure.

To say that the union of the athame and the cup represents love is a more recent interpretation than to say that it represents fertility. The Craft has been highly influenced by things like the women's movement and the gay rights movement. Modern Wicca arose in England in the 1930s and 1940s, and arrived in the U.S. in the early 1960s. I don't think it occurred to those Witches that the male-to-female "act of love" could be seen as homophobic, but by the 1980s, there was plenty of conversation on the topic in Wiccan circles. The women's movement sensitized people to the issues of rape and sexual abuse, and so venerating the purely physical act, divorced from its emotional connection, was viewed by many as politically incorrect.

Since the emotional and spiritual state of love isn't confined to heterosexuality or heterosexual intercourse, and since the Craft also venerates love, many people made subtle changes to their rituals so that the union of the athame and cup was not the union of sex, but the union of love.

There is no question that love is sacred in Wicca, or that the union of the Goddess and the God is a loving union, and so there is nothing wrong with this interpretation. Fertility is miraculous because it creates something from nothing, because it is life sustaining life. Love is miraculous because it transforms us, it makes us greater than ourselves, and it brings us closer to the gods.

Many early Wiccan groups had strongly anti-homosexual ideas, as did the culture in which these groups arose. Some such groups saw gay and lesbian couples as "imperfect" because their love "couldn't" reflect and enact the perfect love of the Goddess and the God, and some didn't allow gays into their covens for that reason. There is no place for this kind of bigotry in the modern Craft. When the Lord and Lady join They are fertile. When the Lord and Lady join They are Love. *Both* are true. The mistake is in applying the simultaneity of these two things—fertility and love—to our lives. We can love without being fertile. There is fertility without love. And a couple that loves without the possibility of fertility is still reflecting Their love for each other.

Witches who emphasize love over fertility need to look carefully at each part of the ritual that has fertility symbolism, and clearly understand which parts are about love in its abstract and emotional sense, and which parts are about the creation of new life. The Goddess of Love and the Goddess Who Gives Birth are not the same, and if you wish to worship each, you should be careful not to muddle up the two aspects.

The Union of Opposites
When the athame and the cup are brought together, opposites are joined. The tension of poles held apart is released, and a powerful surge of energy rushes into the circle. The wine is imbued with that power, which will then fill the people who drink it. This union is presaged by the dots in the yin-yang symbol—each pole already contains its opposite.

The polarity symbolism has been built step-by-step from the moment the circle began. This is the culmination of every carefully paired set of opposites from the grounding and centering through the offerings. The emotional and magical experience, of finally bringing the polarity together in this holy moment, is intensely satisfying.

The Wine Is Now Consecrated
The joining of athame and cup consecrates the wine. The union of Goddess and God, Their sacred marriage, Their sexual and spiritual joining, is the holiest thing there is in

Craft theology, and whatever is touched by this union is made sacred. This is the procreative and/or loving force that created the universe, and this is the love and life with which any and all blessings are imbued.

The Consecrated Wine Is Used to Consecrate the Cakes

This works on two basic magical principles. The first, the magic of contagion, is one we've already discussed. Touching an unconsecrated thing with a consecrated thing "spreads" the consecration. The second, although very important, is not one we've specifically talked about until now, and it has to do with the magic of consecration itself.

To consecrate something is both a theurgic (religious) and thaumaturgic (magical) act. It is theurgic in that its purpose is to bless and to bring spiritual energy to the object. It's thaumaturgic, though, in that it's an act of will, done to bring about a change. As such, it has to follow basic rules of magic. One of the rules we've already seen in the circle is *completion.*

When we call the quarters, and when we cast the circle, we make sure to return to the east, so that the circle is complete. We don't leave it hanging, we don't leave off the finishing stroke. What would constitute completing a consecration? How can we bring it back, full circle?

A consecration is complete when the consecrated thing is *used.* Since the consecration has purpose, putting the thing to that purpose fulfills it and makes the consecration gel.[36] For this reason, the consecrated thing should be used as soon as possible after completing the consecration. If you look back over the ritual, you'll see we did this at every step. For example, when we consecrated the salt and water, we immediately made salt water and stirred it up, and then used it in the circle casting.

Here we are applying this magical principle to the wine, and using it as soon as it's consecrated—in this case, to bless the cakes.

A Portion of Both Wine and Cakes Is Set Aside for the Gods

As soon as we recognize the gods as something apart from ourselves, we must treat them as first and greatest. We enact this in the giving of libations, making sure that the Lady and Lord receive the first of everything we have.[37]

Dion Fortune, who believed firmly that "all goddesses are one goddess," talked about two faces of the Goddess: Isis Veiled and Isis Unveiled. Isis Unveiled is (according to Fortune) the starry Queen of the universe, and Isis Veiled is Mother Earth. Her "veil" is the verdure of Earth itself—the abundant life is the glorious robe She wears. A more techno-hip description would be that the Earth's rich cornucopia is Her "interface" with us. It is the means through which we interact with Her. It is how She gives to us, and therefore (part of) how we should give back to Her.

To give a portion of the food and drink back to the gods before taking some ourselves is just good manners, as discussed under *Water*. It also acknowledges where the cakes and the wine come from—we are giving *back*. In another cycle of giving-is-receiving-is-giving, we are returning to the gods what we receive from them, in heartfelt thanks and in recognition of our place in their cycles.

We are humble with this gift because we recognize that humans are just one part of the vast array of Nature. Neither sovereigns nor stewards, we are simply participants. We are children of the same Mother as the grapes and the wheat, and so we are active players in our own drama of birth, death, and rebirth. To partake of such a gift without acknowledging its source would be irreverent.

To offer libations is also to demonstrate faith in the gods' generosity. When we set aside a portion of our food *before* eating, we indicate our confidence that there will be enough. Whereas to give only after we've eaten our fill expresses poverty—the fear that there might not be enough, so we'd better make sure. Libating first puts our trust in the gods.

Of the dozens of books on Wicca on the shelves of any bookstore, you'll find a few that skip Cakes and Wine entirely. You'll find those that treat Cakes and Wine as a simple "grounding out" meal that relaxes and centers you after the magical work of circle is over, and not as a theological or magical event in and of itself.

You'll also find those that treat Cakes and Wine with an understanding of its nature, seeing in it the communion with the gods and the exaltation of their sacred marriage, but do not instruct the reader to offer libations to them. Worst, in my opinion, are those that suggest an offering to the gods is proper, but suggest that the Witches eat and drink first, and give the gods the leftovers.

We've already discussed giving our Honored Guests our first and best; to feed ourselves first and give our guests whatever remains (if anything) is unthinkable. From a theological point of view, to feed ourselves first is as if we are not worshiping them, as if their presence is so unimportant to our work that it's an afterthought.

It is also hubris. We know, and our ritual might explicitly state, that the gifts of food and drink come from the Lord and Lady. How then can we partake of those gifts without acknowledging their source? Since the cakes and the wine come *from* the gods, they should be given *to* the gods first.

But let's focus on the positive, and remember that offering libations of food and drink prior to partaking expresses humility, gratitude, honor, and faith.

Everyone Drinks and Eats

For all this talk of the sacred union of Cakes and Wine, we have yet to partake of *communion;* we have yet to take into ourselves the essential and sacred nature of the gods. When we drink the consecrated wine and eat the consecrated cakes, we do just that. As the food and drink go into our bodies, the gods' blessings and holiness enter our spirits.

What exactly is this communion? In the Catholic Church, the flesh and blood of Christ is consumed—to commune is to share the physical life force of the individual God. But in Wicca, we consume the product of the holy union of the Lord and Lady. We consume Their fertility/love/union itself, the product of Their lovemaking. The life force that They give to us is the life force from which Nature was brought into being, whether that force is viewed as fertility, love, or dissolution.

As the High Priestess and High Priest have enacted the roles of the Goddess and God throughout the ritual, after setting aside an offering, they should eat and drink first.

Earth

The steps we discussed under *Air* are:

1. Transitional statement.

2. The HPS holds the cup and the HP holds the athame.

3. A statement about love/union/the Goddess and God.

4. The athame is plunged into the cup.

5. The consecrated wine is sprinkled over the cakes.

6. A portion is set aside for the gods.

7. Everyone drinks and eats.

Transitional Statement

Note that this serves a practical, *Earth* purpose as well as the purposes discussed under *Air*. It cues the stage directions, for one thing. When the offering portion turns into a 45-minute drum-fest, a statement beginning with *"It is now time . . ."* alerts everyone that something is happening. A statement helps when people have closed their eyes during the offerings—whether chanting, singing, or simply visualizing.

Since the cue says "Something is happening," and also *what* is happening, it works like a stage cue in the theater. If you're in a play, and an actor is supposed to say, "I wonder what Anna is thinking," and has forgotten his line, you can effectively cue him by saying, "I bet you're wondering about Anna." He'll remember his line, the play can go on, and the audience probably never noticed the glitch. Building in such cues, and being able to ad lib them, is an important ritual skill. Transitional statements are just such cues.

Examples of Transitional Statements
(From Offerings to Cakes and Wine)

> *"The Lord and Lady have received our offerings and are glad. It is time that we receive Their blessings in return."*

> *"We have been heard! Our song and love have reached the Lady and Lord! Now we shall drink Their blessed wine and eat Their blessed meal."*

> *"It is now time to take the blessings of the Mother. For the Mother has given us the fruits of the Earth, that we may know neither hunger nor thirst."*

Beginning Cakes and Wine

In chapter 3, I warned you to make sure there was enough room on your altar for picking something up without knocking anything over, and you'll have cause to be grateful for that advice now. The two things that can make this awkward are as follows: If you're working in a group, you'll find it convenient to use a fairly large goblet, making picking it up and moving it a two-handed operation; the second thing is that an athame, being a narrow item that lays down on the altar, can easily end up half-buried under something else—perhaps the incense dish was moved when offerings were made.

The best thing to do is to scope out the altar before the transitional statement, so that the Cakes and Wine itself goes smoothly.

If all this warning about knocking things over sounds silly or excessive, remember this: You've just done the offerings, so you're likely to be in an altered state of consciousness. You're at the beginning of a solemn and beautiful part of the ritual, and you don't want it interrupted by a THUD. Most important, athames are sharp and there are lit candles on the altar—two reasons to be especially concerned about safety.

You also should decide whether you're doing the Cakes and Wine seated or standing:

STANDING

- In a group, everyone can see what's happening.
- If you were standing for the offering, the segue is smooth.
- Depending upon the placement of the altar, it can be easier to remove the tools from it if you're above them.
- Two people standing and facing each other over a cup reflects the image on the Two of Cups in the Tarot. If you or your group uses Tarot, this adds more drama and meaning to the rite.
- If people will be walking up to the altar to partake at the appropriate time, it is easier if you're standing to face them (they don't have to bend down to you).

SITTING

- It's more comfortable.
- If you're solitary, you don't have to worry about the visual effect.
- It can be more intimate with a partner.
- Depending upon the placement of the altar, it can be easier to remove the tools if you're level with them.
- If you will be passing people's portions around to them, it can be easier to be seated while serving, especially if additional supplies—such as spare cups—are on the floor.

The Act of Life

The joining of athame and cup is often called "The Act of Life." Theologically, the phrase is really only sensible when the act is oriented around fertility, and so many now use the phrase "The Act of Love."

The four examples that follow will show steps 3, 4, and 5 from the short list of steps just given in the section "Earth":

3. A statement about love/union/the Goddess and God.

4. The athame is plunged into the cup.

5. The consecrated wine is sprinkled over the cakes.

The first three examples are written for a ritual enacted by a male-female couple. A same-sex pair could perform any of them, possibly shifting some of the heterosexual polarity imagery around. A solitary could also perform any of them with some adjustment of the blocking. These three emphasize different theologies; there is one with a fertility focus, one with a love focus, and one with a union-of-opposites focus. A fourth example, written with a solitary in mind, is also given.

Reminders

Before Cakes and Wine begins:

- The wine should be uncorked.
- If anyone doesn't drink alcohol, be sure the nonalcoholic beverage is also in the circle.
- You should have an extra (unopened) bottle of wine or soft drink available, just in case.
- Therefore, you should also have a corkscrew.
- The cakes should not have any wrapping on them.
- The cakes should be spread out on the plate rather than stacked.
- Extra cups should be available if individual cups will be filled. Many groups have everyone bring their own cup, and many people have special cups.
- Everything—cakes, wine, soft drink, and cups—should be in a safe place, under the altar or close enough to it so that they won't get tripped over.

- If needed, a knife for slicing cake or bread should be with the other supplies.
- Napkins are also a good idea.

Example 1: Cakes and Wine as a Fertility Rite

Both because of the erotic feel of this rite, and because the movements are made by people who are seated behind the altar, this version is best suited to a small, intimate group. It can be ideal for a couple alone, or for a solitary, who will modify the movements to play both roles.

After the offering, a transitional statement is made, and the group is seated (if needed, gesture *down* with your hands to get everyone to sit). The HP fills the cup and hands it to the HPS.

The HP and HPS, he with athame in hand, she with cup, raise up on their knees, facing each other very closely; they are only inches apart, making eye contact. Slowly, she lowers herself until she is seated on the floor cross-legged; she doesn't break eye contact while she does this. She lifts her cup to eye level, showing it to the HP (and the group). Still maintaining eye contact, she brings the cup close to herself, so that it's directly in front of her mouth. She lowers it gradually, to her throat, to her breast, and finally resting it in her lap, between her legs.

The HP, already raised up on his knees, straightens his back and brings himself up to full kneeling height. As the HPS begins lowering the cup, he begins raising the athame. He holds it with both hands, point down, and brings it to chest level, then slowly raises it over his head. As the HPS places the cup in her lap, he brings the athame as far over his head as he can.

They hold this pose for a long moment.

HP: *I am the athame, the Horned God, the seed.*

HPS: *I am the cup, the Great Mother, the womb.*

The HP begins to lower his athame, the HPS (slowly)[38] begins to raise the cup to meet him.

Both: *Together . . .*

The athame and cup are almost to the point of meeting . . .

Both: *. . . they bring life. They bring creation. Together, we are all blessed.*

The HP plunges the athame into the cup.

Both: *Behold the act of life!*

Pause for a moment, maintaining eye contact. Cakes and Wine has now reached its theatrical, symbolic, and metaphorical climax. Let the moment sink in; let the people in the circle feel the energy this rite has created—the energy that now fills the cup of wine. The HP removes the athame from the cup.

The HPS now picks up the plate of cakes. She'll hold the cakes in one hand and the cup in the other. If either is too heavy to hold in this position, the cup can be put on the altar, or, if that makes it awkward to reach, she can hold it in her lap or place it on the floor between her and the HP.

The HP is still holding his athame. While they speak the following blessing, he'll be dipping the athame into the cup, and sprinkling droplets of wine onto the cakes, using contagion to confer the wine's blessing onto them. Having the cakes spread out on the plate, rather than piled up, enables him to make sure at least a drop or two falls on each. Continue dipping and sprinkling throughout the blessing.

HP: *Gifts of the gods*

HPS: *Are ever sweet*

HP: *May their taste last.*

HPS: *May they bring us*

Both: *The blessings of life.*

A cake[39] is now immediately placed on the libation plate, and libations are offered, which will be discussed below.

EXAMPLE 2: CAKES AND WINE AS A RITE OF LOVE

This one is a little more theatrical than the previous example, using some dance to enhance the message of love. It uses multiple players to give more of a group feel, and so is especially appropriate for a large-scale ritual, such as might be done for a festival or other public gathering. However, like any of the examples provided, it can be adapted to the people you have available.

After the offering and transitional statement, the group remains standing. A drum beat or other musical accompaniment is appropriate. Refer back to the illustration for making offerings (page 175). B and C are in the north, exactly opposite the HP and HPS. B will be female, acting as a kind of "Maid of Honor," and C will be the "Best Man." (Of course, you can drop the gender assignments if you prefer—it depends upon whether you find this sort of tradition to be enriching or confining—this particular rite can readily be used by a gay couple or couples.)

The HP and HPS face each other and walk around each other in a deosil circle, ending in the same positions in which they began. Then B and C step forward and do the same, except that they end up closer to the altar. B picks up the cup and walks deosil around circle with it raised over her head. When she reaches the south of the altar she fills it, bows to the HPS, and presents the cup to her. Then B takes two or three steps back so that she's slightly behind the HPS in the southeast (D might shift position to allow a little room). The HPS takes one step back, holding the cup raised before her (once it's filled, over her head isn't practical, but she can hold it before her face).

C picks up an athame.[40] He walks deosil to the HP and presents the athame to him, bowing. C takes two or three steps back so that he's in the southwest behind the HP. (A might shift position.)

Now the HP and HPS circle each other again, this time holding the ritual tools. As they circle, they present the tools to each other, enticing. The cup is held out toward the HP, the athame approaching and withdrawing from the cup.

HP: (while circling) *I hold the blade of desire. My desire is for love.*

HPS: (while circling) *I hold the cup of love. My love is unfulfilled.*

The HP and HPS come to a stop, facing each other. The music or drumbeat ends.

HP: (raising athame over cup) *As the athame is to the cup*

HPS: (lifting cup to meet athame) *So we are to each other.*

Both: (as HP plunges athame in) *Behold the Act of Love!*

B and C, who have been standing ready, step forward. B takes the cup and C takes the athame. The HP and HPS embrace. Their loving embrace is the energetic climax, and should be as intense and as sincere as possible.

When the embrace is over, B picks up the plate of cakes. C presents the athame to the HPS and HP, bowing. They take the athame together, each holding it with one hand. C returns to his place. B steps forward with the plate and cup, standing in front of the HPS and HP. (In order for members of the group to see what's going on, the HPS and HP should face the west, with B facing them, all of them south of the altar.)

The HP and HPS will continue to hold the athame together as they dip into the cup and sprinkle the cakes. They continue dipping and sprinkling throughout the blessing. They speak together.

Both: *Blessings of love are for all to share. The love of the gods is our holy food.*
        Blessed be.

All: *Blessed be.*

A cake is placed on the libation plate.

EXAMPLE 3: CAKES AND WINE AS A RITE OF ONENESS AND UNION

This rite can be done small and intimate, or large-scale for a public ritual. If the group is small, the rite might be done seated, with the HP and HPS approaching one another from a kneeling position—in this case, less than a dozen people will be able to clearly see what's happening. For a public rite, the standing HP and HPS might have their torsos farther apart, so that the hand movements are more visible, and those hand movements can also be exaggerated.

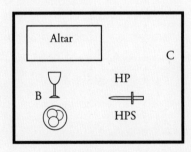

After the offering and transitional statement, the group remains standing (except as above).

The HP spreads his arms straight out to either side, holding the athame in his right hand. The HPS stands in a similar position, facing the HP, her arms spread apart, the (still empty)[41] cup in her right hand. A server stands behind the HPS to the southeast, ready to pour the wine.

HP: *I am the God and the blade, you are the Goddess and the cup. We are apart.*

The HPS and HP take a step closer to each other. Their hands touch. The HP holds the cup in his left hand while the HPS holds it in her right. The HPS holds the blade in her left hand while the HP holds it in his right. They are "nose to nose."

HPS: *I am the Goddess and the blade. I am the God and the cup.*

HP: *I am the God and the cup. I am the Goddess and the blade.*

Both: *We are one.*

They kiss, still holding both tools.

Now they do a little game: The HP feigns taking the cup, then pulls back; the HPS feigns taking the knife, then pulls back. They hand both tools back and forth to each other, as if they can't decide.

Finally, the HP hands the cup over to the HPS. She holds it, but his left hand is still on it (he's also holding the athame in his other hand). While they hold it together like that, the server steps forward and fills the cup (if need be, the HP can signal the server with a nod—the HPS will have her back to the server).

HPS: *I am divided for love's sake, for the change of union.*

HP: *This is the creation of the world, that the pain of division is as nothing.*

Both: *And the joy of dissolution . . . ALL.*

(Yes, it's a favorite quote of mine—poetic, meaningful, and beautiful. If you don't like it, a more traditional wording would be:

HP: *As the athame is to the male*

HPS: *So the cup is to the female*

Both: *For they are one in truth.*

The HP plunges the athame into the cup—the final connection happening at *ALL* (or at *For they are one in truth*). Because this is symbolically a moment of oneness, they should stand close together, maintaining eye contact, possibly touching each other's hands—the effect should be as if they were merging into one another. A Priest wearing a large cloak could use it at this moment to cover both himself and the Priestess; by cloaking them in one garment, they look like one being. Or, an assistant could cloak them together while they hold their pose with athame in cup, then release them.

The server (having already put down the wine bottle), picks up the plate of cakes, holding it before the HPS and HP.

The HP and HPS will do the blessing of the cakes together, holding the athame and cup jointly (each with one hand on each) while they sprinkle the cakes.

Instead of a spoken blessing, a chant should be used. This emphasizes the unity of the entire group, as the blessing is given in one voice. Everyone in the circle (except the three people at the altar) could hold hands, adding to the sense of unity. (Of course, with three people at the altar, there may not be enough people left over to hold hands!)

As I've said before, there are many tapes and CDs of Pagan and New Age music available—a book isn't a good place to learn a tune! The chant should be oriented toward unity, and if it includes a blessing as well, all the better. One that comes to mind is:

We are one/We are one/With the infinite Sun[42]/Forever and ever and ever.

A cake is placed on the libation plate when the chanting is finished, and libations begin.

Example 4: Cakes and Wine for the Solitary

When I first learned to cast a solitary circle, I found Cakes and Wine the least satisfying part—the part where I most missed having other people with whom to work. The rituals that I read seemed to treat a solitary Cakes and Wine rather perfunctorily, as if to say that, without a couple to perform the rite, there's really no point.

This need not be the case; the meaning is as significant to one person as it is to two or to many. Love, fertility, and the union of opposites are deep spiritual currents in each of our lives. If we understand that fertility is where we come from, and how we create, then there's no need to feel inhibited in its veneration just because we're not in a couple. The same is true for love, which is far more than its human expression.

It isn't hard to adapt any of the earlier examples to solitary practice. In the erotic play-acting of example 1, you could play the male role, to a female cup placed on the altar. Or, you could play both roles, bringing the cup to your groin, and then picking up the athame to enter it. Eroticism is a part of every human being, whether coupled or not. In example 2, you couldn't perform the dance, but could use the same words to express the sacredness of love. In example 3, holding the tools simultaneously, and bringing them together side-by-side would express oneness.

For this example, my goal was to create a solitary Cakes and Wine rite that is as engaging and vivid as any performed in a group. In this case, the transitional statement is built in. Begin directly after the offering.

I am thirsty. I am hungry.

Bow before the statues of the Goddess and God.

Great Mother, Horned Father, how can your child eat and drink?

Fill the cup. Alternately, the cup could have been filled in advance and covered with a cloth. Then, you can uncover the cup as if discovering it for the first time.

From Her own essence, the Goddess has given me wine to quench my thirst.

Pick up the athame.

From His own essence, the God brings life to me.

Hold the athame over the cup.

Athame to cup
Lord to Lady
Love to Love
Creation to Created

Plunge the athame into the cup.

Behold the act of life.

Pick up the plate of cakes. If you had covered the cup with a cloth, then the cakes should similarly have been covered and should be uncovered now.

From Their essence, the Goddess and God have given me food to eat.

Sprinkle the cakes with wine from the cup, using the tip of the athame.

Life to Life,
Essence to Essence,
Blessing to Blessing.

It's now time for libations.

Libations: Drinks for the Gods and Drinks for the People

We've already discussed the reasoning behind offering libations before partaking. Here, we'll discuss the practical aspects. In a circle, there are often several cycles of eating and drinking, and several things to eat and drink. My students have often been confused as to what constitutes a proper libation. Here is the simple rule:

The gods get the first of everything.

That's it, that's the whole rule in a nutshell. Here's how to apply it:

- We offer food and drink that is being consumed for the first time.
- We offer the first from a bottle or a plate.
- We offer the first time we drink.
- We offer the first from a fresh cup.

So, a typical ritual might go like this:

1. Cakes and Wine are consecrated in the Act of Life.
2. The first cake from the plate is offered.
3. The first of the newly-consecrated wine is offered by the High Priestess.
4. The altar cup and plate are passed around, deosil.
    a. Each person offers from the altar cup, because it's the first time that person is drinking.

    b. Each person can offer the first few crumbs, or a small bite, of his own cake (or, because this is messy, the group can agree that the first cake is symbolic of all food offerings, and individuals offer drink only).

5. If additional bottles are opened, they are first consecrated (the athame is plunged into the first cup from that bottle) and then an offering is made from that cup.

6. If additional food is brought into the circle, it is also first consecrated, and then offered from.

7. If people bring their own cups to the circle (which is common in groups of more than two or three people), the individual cups are filled and passed to their owners. The owners then make additional offerings, since, even though they made offerings when the altar cup was passed around, these are fresh cups that have not yet been drunk from, and are therefore a first.

How to Make a Libation

Indoors, a bowl is provided, as discussed in chapter 3. Outdoors, an offering can be poured directly onto the Earth. Appropriate offerings can also be placed into a fireplace or outdoor fire pit, i.e., a cookie or a *drop* of wine.

To make a libation, raise your cup, make a spoken or silent statement of offering (more on that shortly), pour into the bowl or onto the Earth, and sip. You can say "Blessed be" either before or after you sip—everyone else responds with "Blessed be!"

A Note on Alcohol in the Cup: In my groups, I have had several teetotalers over the years, both members of A.A. and people who couldn't drink for various health reasons. Many groups simply don't use alcohol in the altar cup under those circumstances. However, it is my tradition to use wine in the altar cup, because of the magical and traditional properties of wine. It is true that whatever the teetotalers are drinking—juice or spring water—will be consecrated, but the first consecration, of the altar cup, is special, and is filled with the blessings of the gods.

Therefore, it's important that even the teetotalers offer libations from the first passing of the cup. My non-drinking people developed a custom of *inhaling* from the first cup, thereby partaking of the blessing, but not the beverage. I think this is a nice idea.

To Whom Do You Libate?

People often mix up a libation with a toast. A *libation* is offered to those in other realms—to gods and to the Honored Dead. A *toast* is offered to the living.

A libation is poured into the bowl. A toast is not. Examples:

(Raise cup) *I offer to the Ancient Gods!* (Pour) *Blessed be!* (Drink)

(Raise cup) *I also offer to my beloved Nana, who has passed into the Summerland.* (Pour) *Blessed be!* (Drink)

(Raise cup) *And I remember our friends Jim and Jane, who wanted to be a part of our circle tonight, but weren't able to attend.* (**Do not** pour) *Blessed be!* (Drink)

(Raise cup) *And to Sally, who just found out she's becoming a grandmother. Congratulations Sally!* (**Do not** pour) *Blessed be!* (Drink)

What to Say When Making a Libation

This time I'm not giving examples or scripts. I feel it is almost always best to make your libations spontaneous and from the heart. This is your moment for communing with the gods in any number of special and personal ways. This is the moment when it's appropriate to give thanks, to honor your ancestors or beloved departed, to look to the future, or just to feel joy. It's one moment when it's okay to name deities not particularly part of the ritual—such as offering to Apollo in a ritual devoted to Isis and Horus. It's a moment to focus your mind on what you want and need; since you're about to ingest the blessings of the gods, you might focus on what you want to use that blessing *for*, and so a little prayer or request is as appropriate as an expression of gratitude.

However, a group leader, or the first person to offer libations, can set the tone for others. If there are new people in the group, people less familiar with ritual, then they'll be watching you to see how it's done. The first libation will let people know if it's okay to be joyous, to be solemn, to be humorous, or to give thanks. A rousing *"Hail to the Old Gods!"* will give a very different impression from a heartfelt *"May the Lord and Lady hear my prayers and accept my love."* Either is fine, and you might not know, yourself, what you wish to say, or in what mood, until the last moment.

You'll also be setting the *pace*, which is just as important. If the group is large, or you have reason to want to keep it brief, then keeping your own libation brief will send a signal to everyone. The best way to keep the libations short (if that's what you need), is to keep them general, such as "*To the Earth Mother and the Horned God.*" A more personal offering, even a short one, opens the door for everyone to come up with personal thoughts to offer, and they may not be as short. If you give thanks for something good that happened to you this month, another person in the circle may be reminded of five or six wonderful things that happened to her, and thank the gods for each, in detail. Sometimes that's fine. In fact, sometimes that's just what you want—but you should realize that it might happen.

As a group leader, I try to be sensitive to the needs and feelings of others when making my libation. If my offering is too personal, they may still be left not knowing what's expected of them. Even if I add something personal, I try to make sure I begin with a straightforward offering to the gods of the occasion (i.e. the specific deities invoked), and/or a mention of the holiday or event being celebrated (*"At this harvest time . . ."*). After pouring, I like to add a toast "*. . . to those gathered in Their names*" and raise my cup to the assembled group before drinking.

Serving Cakes and Wine

There are basically three ways to do this. Which method you choose will be based on the size of the group, the formality of the ritual, and the comfort of the space (i.e. sitting on the floor in a formal hall is probably awkward). They are similar to the methods for making individual offerings. You can do one of the following:

- Have people file around to the south of the altar to drink from the goblet and take a cake,
- Walk with the goblet and plate around the circle, serving each person, or
- Pass the goblet and plate around to everyone (everyone stays in their places).

THE PRIESTESS RECEIVES THE CUP

However the wine is distributed, it is traditional for the HPS, as the representative of the Goddess, to drink first. Sometimes this is made into part of the ritual.

The HP picks up the goblet[43] and presents it to the HPS, saying something like: "*My Lady, it is fitting that this cup of life goes first to you.*"

The HPS bows her head, makes her libation, and drinks. Then she hands the cup to the HP saying something like: *"The Lady makes life only with Her Consort."*

He bows his head to her and makes his libation, then drinks.

The first cake has already been placed in the libation bowl. The HPS now takes the second cake and splits it in half. She eats half and gives half to the HP, who also eats.

Cakes and Wine are now distributed in one of the following ways.

PASSING THE GOBLET AND PLATE

The simplest technique is to simply pass the Cakes and Wine from person to person clockwise. The HPS libates and drinks as above, and passes to the HP, who libates and drinks. The HP passes to the person on his left, who libates and drinks. The goblet and libation bowl continue around the circle until they are returned to the HPS. (If the plate is also passed, people should simply take a cake but not eat yet, so that their mouths aren't full during libations and "Blessed be's." Whether or not the cakes are passed is discussed shortly.)

TAKING THE GOBLET AROUND THE CIRCLE

This is pretty much the same as the method we discussed under the topic of making individual offerings. After the HPS and HP have made libations, they walk together around the circle, starting to the HP's left, one of them carrying the goblet and the other carrying the libation bowl (usually the HPS carries the goblet, since it's considered hers).

This is the best method for distributing Cakes and Wine in a very large group, such as at a public festival. It is best for circumstances where (a) passing the cup will take too long and (b) having everyone shuffle around is too cumbersome. The HPS gives the cup to the first person, who makes a libation, sips, and hands it back to her. The HP will be holding the bowl.

In fact, if the group is *really* large—more than fifty people—then multiple cups can be used. To do this, a pitcher or carafe can be consecrated instead of a goblet. Then the consecrated wine is poured into two or three cups, and the cakes are divided onto two or three plates. A pair of servers takes a cup, plate, and libation bowl, and each server goes to a different part of the circle. The HP and HPS can serve starting in the south (to the HP's left), another couple can start in the northwest, and another couple can start in the northeast (decide in advance how to distribute the serving tasks evenly). Leave one person at the altar with the carafe, so that if any of the goblets run out, that person can step forward and refill them on a signal.

If the group is so large, or the acoustics are such that not everyone can hear what everyone else in the circle is saying—and it doesn't take all that big a circle outdoors for the people 180 degrees from you to be inaudible—then a chant of thanks or blessings can be sung. Everyone will chant except the people distributing the Cakes and Wine and the people actually making offerings. This keeps everyone in the spirit of things, even when they can't hear what's going on.

This tends to become rather informal, as it seems as if there are many private conversations occurring (actually many private libations, but the appearance can be the same). If there are forty people in the circle, by the time twenty-five have made offerings, people are starting to shuffle from foot to foot a bit, and perhaps whisper with the person next to them. For this reason, it's generally best not to plan a very formal or structured "Using the Blessings" after serving in this way.

People Come to the Altar to Be Served

This is the most formal method and is often saved for special occasions, i.e. for Sabbats rather than Esbats. There is a sense of ceremony and courtliness about lining up, approaching the altar, receiving a cup, making a libation, and returning to your place. This can be very beautiful, and will tend to have an elaborate and formal feel no matter how it's done, so it's best to go all out.

If you're going to use this method, do the Cakes and Wine itself standing. The HPS and HP make their libations. The HP hands the cup back to the HPS and holds the libation bowl. The HPS summons the Witches to the altar:

HPS: *Come forward ye all, and partake of these gifts that the Mother has given!*
People come forward one at a time, as described and illustrated under the individual offerings. Everyone can either line up, or in a smaller group, one person at a time can come forward, make libations and drink, and then return to his place before the next person steps forward. There can be a ritualized verbal exchange for each person:

First person comes forward, faces HPS, bows.

HPS bows.

HPS: *Receive these blessings of the gods and be fulfilled.*

Person: (Makes personal offering such as) *To the Ancient Gods. Blessed be.*

HPS (and all): *Blessed be!*

Person now kisses either both of the HPS and HP, or just the one of the opposite gender, bowing to the other, and returns to his place (or moves forward in line).

The statement made by the HPS can be modified for holidays and special occasions. It's a wonderful way to do Cakes and Wine when starting a new group, welcoming members, or celebrating special "family" occasions.

When and How Much to Eat and Drink

There are a number of books and teachers who explain Cakes and Wine as grounding out and relaxation—nothing more than the snack you need after the draining work of worship and magic. This would seem to contradict what *I* teach, and that's because drinking, and especially eating, accomplish two contradictory things.

On the one hand, drinking consecrated wine and eating consecrated cakes serves to bring blessings into our bodies, feeding our spirits as well. This increases magical power and spiritual energy. On the other hand, eating grounds us, connecting us to the earth so strongly that it often breaks more tenuous magical connections. After eating, we often feel satisfied but sleepy, as if the magic had been drained away. We usually feel more ordinary, more ourselves.

We've already established that the best time to *use* the blessings is after we've *received* the blessings. That means that, until we have Cakes and Wine, we haven't yet done our magic or other work for the evening. So we definitely don't want the grounding-out effect. What to do?

The trick is quantity. A sip of wine (or juice) will not break the energetic connection, and probably a small bite of cake, cookie, or bread won't either. A full serving certainly will.

My practice, and what I recommend, is this: Perform the ceremony of Cakes and Wine. Let everyone make a libation and take a symbolic sip—one that fills them with the blessings of the gods, but doesn't fill their tummies. Give out a symbolic nibble of cakes to everyone or just have the HPS and HP offer a cake and take a symbolic bite on everyone's behalf. Then proceed to the next step—*Using the Blessings*. After that step is done, serve out cakes to everyone, and fill each person's individual goblet.

The low-level chaos of figuring out which goblet belongs to whom, and which goblet gets wine and which gets a nonalcoholic beverage, of finding napkins and cleaning up spills, and of suddenly realizing that a bottle is empty and an additional consecration must be performed, all contributes to dissipating the energy and grounding people out. It's another reason why this should be done *after* acts of magic and other uses of blessings are performed.

A final reason is safety. If you're going to be doing anything after the formal Cakes and Wine that involves getting up and dancing or moving about the circle, a bunch of full goblets on the floor makes it hazardous.

In the *Earth* segment of the section on *Using the Blessings*, I'll review whether eating or drinking is appropriate before or during each activity.

Fire
Fertility

Procreation is fraught with an inner mysticism, because procreation is creation, and creation is something from nothing, the original spark, the first cause (and the original sourdough starter). All fertility rites take us to a place before the beginning. In ritual, in our mythic enactment, all fertility is the first fertility—the one, miraculous, inexplicable spark that impregnated everything.

Procreation is mysterious—we never truly know what we're creating. Any parent who ever predicted who her child would be was *de facto* wrong; each child is unique and new. We are all witness to a mystery every time we welcome a new baby into the world, and when we venerate fertility in ritual, we venerate this unknowing, unknowable, and glorious mystery.

Union

The union of opposites in the ceremony of Cakes and Wine is a moment which stands apart from normal life. It exists "before the beginning," in uncreated space and time.

From the moment that reality came into being, it has been divided into pairs of This or That. Everything either *Is* or *Is Not*. To bypass the division of the poles is as if to say that something both can be and cannot be at the same time—the ultimate union of opposites. Obviously, this can't occur in real time. It can only occur in transcendent moments, when space and time are preceded and erased.

The circle is one such moment—between the worlds is a place outside the normal rules of space and time. Yet, we are still bound by and surrounded by our polar nature. We can draw power from it, and celebrate it as a reflection of the Goddess and the God, but we still long to transcend its boundaries and enter into a mystic state of oneness.

I am divided for love's sake, for the chance of union. This is the creation of the world, that the pain of division is as nothing, and the joy of dissolution, all.

To be one is to be like a droplet in the sea, undifferentiated and, perhaps, indifferent to the nature of one's state. But to be divided, to be polar, and then to unite—to dissolve *into* oneness—is an ecstasy that has inspired poets, mystics, and lovers throughout the ages. The ritual of Cakes and Wine celebrates our polarity, our separateness, as well as our dissolution, and celebrates especially one becoming the other.

To have ever been in love is to have known the fleeting moments of being one with another human being; poets have long spoken of the sense of merging with their beloved. Once you know that you *can* experience this oneness, you know something that can awaken you to the cosmos—if it is possible to merge with one other person, the suggestion is there that we are *all* one. The ceremony of Cakes and Wine points to this mystic notion when it characterizes the dissolution into oneness as a sexual and romantic union of the Lady and Lord.

MEDITATION ON ONENESS

This meditation is designed to give you an experience of dissolution, using the image of a drop of water merging into an ocean. The ocean, a symbol of the Goddess and of Her infinite love, is an apt metaphor to use.

Yogis and mystics spend lifetimes meditating with the aim of experiencing dissolution into the infinite. It would be a bit much, then, to expect to achieve nirvana your first time out. However, you can get a sense of it, a chip of the tip of the iceberg, and even at that level it can be a very moving experience.

I've written this as a group meditation, complete with suggestions for pausing while reading aloud and mentions of the other members of the group. However, this can be easily edited to use in private meditation or in a solitary circle. Since it's written to be read aloud in a circle, I've included some induction[44] material for relaxing and getting into a receptive state prior to the meditation proper. If you're working with a less-experienced group, with people who haven't done much of this sort of work, you should expand that section and make sure the induction is really thorough.

I want you all to relax. Find a comfortable, unconstricted position, and relax. Breathe deeply and slowly. As you breathe, you become more relaxed, and feel more like you're floating. You are totally open to my voice and easily able to see everything I say. Each time you exhale takes you deeper into that floating, open state. Inhale deeply now, and when you exhale, feel yourself floating and opening up. Exhale now. You're floating and relaxed. As you become more relaxed, it will be easier and easier to clearly picture and feel what I am saying to you.

I'm going to count to ten. At each number, you'll become more relaxed and more open. With each number, breathe in deeply and breathe out. As you breathe out, you're more relaxed and open than before. One . . . you're so relaxed. Two . . . you're open and receptive. Three . . . very relaxed and open. Four . . . Five . . . Six . . . extremely relaxed now. Seven . . . you feel like you're floating. Eight . . . very open. Nine . . . Ten . . . completely relaxed and open.

Imagine you are a drop of water. Picture yourself being a drop of water. Your consciousness is contained in that little droplet. You know yourself, and you are a droplet.

Now begin to flow. You are a droplet flowing together with other droplets. Now you are a trickle. You still know yourself as a droplet, but you also sense the other droplets. There is an A Droplet, a B Droplet,[45] and as you flow together you know them, and know yourself, and know you are all part of one thing. As the trickle flows and streams, you begin to know that you are A, and yourself, and B, and yourself . . . Allow yourself to experience this flowing self, this person named A-B-C-D.[46] You have thoughts, feelings, images, and knowledge that belong to the entire stream. (Pause)

The stream is still flowing, the trickle that is one-and-many. As you flow, more droplets join. You are beginning to lose your sense of self, but there is no anxiety. You are utterly comfortable; in fact, you are joyous. It is blissful to be you and to be so many, and to forget sometimes which one is you, is as natural and as sweet as falling asleep when you're tired. Flow for a moment in this pleasant and joyful state. (Pause)

Now your stream has reached the ocean, an ocean of infinite droplets with infinite personalities. In such a vast sea, you no longer have any knowledge of which droplet is you, just a sense of flowing as a part of many selves who are all one self. You know things, but you don't know how you know them, or what exactly they are, or what they have to do with you. You feel joy and bliss, and you know that the ocean is Love. You flow in Love and nothing else matters. Like a dream of comfort and happiness, you have merged into the infinite ocean of Love. Flow there a while. (Longish pause—about five minutes)

It's time to return to your individuality. Flow in the ocean a moment more, saying goodbye to this experience and knowing that it will always be a part of you. (Short pause)

Notice the stream of droplets with which you entered the ocean. You've reached a small inlet, and your stream has become separate. You're no longer a part of the infinite sea, you're A-B-C . . . You're flowing with the group consciousness of your circle.

Now as your stream reaches the shore, your droplets separate and become individuals. Your mind gently lets go of the group and becomes one mind. Know yourself. Say your name to yourself. You are one being. You still have a connection to the people in your circle, but you are one droplet, one soul.

It's time to return to the circle. You'll no longer be a drop of water, you'll be a person, yourself, in a circle of Witches. As I count backwards from ten,[47] you'll become more and more aware of your body and your self, and more and more ready to be back in the circle. You'll feel alert and refreshed when you return. Ten . . . become aware of your body and the circle. Nine, Eight . . . more awake and refreshed . . . Seven, Six, Five . . . very refreshed and aware . . . Four . . . connected to your body and your center . . . Three, Two . . . ready to return . . . One! Fully awake and refreshed. You're back in the circle. Stretch a little and when you're ready, open your eyes.

Using the Blessings

Once you have received the blessings into your body by ingesting (literally or symbolically) the Cakes and Wine, you are at your greatest magical potential. Everything you do in the circle afterwards will have a unique spiritual quality available at few other times in life. This is the portion of the circle I refer to when teaching as "freestyle." When training students to perform ritual, I give them the option of following the script exactly, but this entire section is left blank, and I expect the student to come up with her own ideas. I will do much the same to you—with the same suggestions, hints, and guidelines that I give to students in person. Because I will not be walking you through this section in as much detail, the written structure of this section will differ as well. We'll start with *Earth*, giving both Earth activities and practical tips for this part of the circle. Under *Air, Fire,* and *Water*, I will give ideas for activities that can be performed that relate to each element.

It is healthy for a ritual group to vary the element on which their work focuses. Just as each of us should be balanced in the elements, so should a group. By looking at the various activities by their elemental associations, you can see how to schedule a full range of activities that will deepen your experience and make the ritual accessible to all parts of you.

Earth

Transition from Cakes and Wine to the Next Step

Just as with other transitions, it is useful in a group to make a statement here. There is some information that needs to be conveyed:

- What's going to happen next (especially important here, because there's not necessarily an expected routine).

- The *purpose* of the next activity—if a spell, why? If a season, what season? And so on.

- What's happening with the food and drink—will we have individual servings now, later, or not at all? (In very large group rituals, of fifty or more people, individual servings are often skipped.)

- Some additional instructions about the formality of the rest of the circle are usually in order. On many occasions, this will be a time when people will sit, get cozy, and not worry so much about ritual posture or staying focused. So, people need to know if they can do that now, and under what conditions (reminders to watch the perimeters of the circle are useful, especially for beginners).

The "Work" of the Circle

Earth is the down-to-business element, and so under Earth we place the things considered "work" in Wiccan ritual:

- Rites of the Season,
- Rites of Passage,
- Magic.

It's amusing to note that this is the moment in the circle most appropriate for both work and play, and perhaps this bespeaks some of the *joie de vivre* that typifies Wiccan thought. But for now, let's focus on work.

Reviewing the circle's steps again, we see that we've:

- Prepared and created the ritual space.
- Invoked the gods, welcomed and worshiped them.
- Had communion with them and received their blessings.

We're now ready to use those blessings. The gods have done *their* work, and now we're ready to do *ours*.

The work of Wicca has to do with both nature and the community—the community of Witches and the community at large. In nature, our work is to mark the passage of the seasons, celebrate and intensify it. Folklore has it that the seasons only turn if we do the proper rites to make them turn. Most people now are content to give a more rational explanation to the changing of the seasons, but the belief in the necessity of the rites gives a gravity, an urgency, to performing them that we shouldn't forget.

In the community, our work is supportive, healing, helpful, and acknowledging. We perform magic to heal and help. We mark life passages—birth, marriage, death—in order to support and acknowledge. In both rites of passage and rites of seasons, we bring the attention of the gods onto the event we mark, but we also bring the attention of ourselves and our community. This recognition is supportive, encouraging stability in a new marriage, providing counsel and assistance to newborn babies, and helping to give a larger, loving context to bereavement. A rite of passage or season should be interwoven throughout the ritual. This was discussed when the quarters were called, and again when offerings were made. Another example is that, during a handfasting, it is traditional for the bride and groom to perform Cakes and Wine instead of the Priestess and Priest. Finally, though, there will be a portion of the rite that enacts and finalizes the passage, and that is performed here, just after Cakes and Wine. Often, "feasting" is worked into the rite of passage—libations are performed and only a symbolic sip is taken. Then the rite of passage (or season) is performed, and then individual cups and the cake plate are passed as a celebratory feast. The second set of libations (from the individual cups) are traditionally focused around the event that just took place. That is, instead of "To the Gods," an offering would be "To the turning of the Wheel" (any holiday), "To the newborn Sun King" (Yule), or "May the Gods bless the happy couple" (a handfasting). If the rite of passage is somber, such as a funeral, then the meal is honorary rather than celebratory.

An entire book could be written about these rites (and eventually I'll write one). There isn't the room here to explore the topic fully, and this brief overview will have to do for now.

Some Notes on Magic

This is the section of the circle in which spells will be done. Some Witches do spells every time they cast a circle and consider spellcraft an intrinsic and necessary part of Wicca; they would no more do a circle without a spell than most married people would leave the house without their wedding rings. Other people, however, feel that magic and Wicca are two separate things; that Wicca is unique in that Witches believe in and are encouraged to do magic, but that it's not required. They feel that magic is a craft, and Wicca is a religion—not the same thing at all. Some people even feel that to do a spell on an occasion when there isn't pressing need is abusing the gift of the gods that magic is.

Entire books are written on how, when, and why to do magic. This is not that book. Instead, I'm simply laying out for you the options, and since this is a book about ritual, putting magic in a ritual context.

Magic itself is an Earth activity, because it has a practical, earth-based goal. That is, you do magic for a purpose that is measurable in the real world. However, the way that the magic is done can be centered in any one or more of the elements. For example, healing is often associated with Fire, but psychological healing is of Water. Money and job magic are considered Earth, and magic to gain wisdom and insight is of Air, as is magic associated with travel. The goal of the magic and the spell should match.

Some years ago, I got involved in a discussion of whether you actually need to raise power at this point, to do magic, since you're already filled with the blessings and power of the gods. I've come to the conclusion that you definitely do. First of all, the divine power is there, but not at the forefront, it needs to be brought out; that power has already been used a little, in any requests made during libations, and has already "relaxed" a little. Secondly, although filled with divine power, you must also bring your human power to bear. Finally, the power needs to be raised *toward the magical purpose*, and with proper visualization of your magical intention.

After you finish Cakes and Wine, you should state your magical goal. It's probable that you already know what you're planning on doing—it was probably discussed before the circle began. Now that you've had this communion, it's good to restate it, possibly getting last-minute insight. It also serves as another transitional statement. You'll raise power and do the spell. Afterwards, you'll pass the individual goblets and plate of cakes. If you're doing more than one spell, pass the goblets only between spells and the plate after they're all done.

Other Earth Activities

Any practical activities are Earth activities. We've already discussed the primary ones: magic, holiday rites, and rites of passage.

As mentioned earlier, game-playing is also an Earth activity (laughter is very earthy). There are many traditional games associated with various holidays. Chase games of the blind-man's bluff variety, kissing games, "truth or consequences"-style guessing games, among others, are associated with Pagan holidays. The gods want us to be happy and to celebrate, and most Witches are only too pleased to comply. Eating and drinking during games is fine, provided that the food and goblets don't block the play area and aren't at risk of being stepped on.

Another Earth activity is the making of magical objects. There are many arts-and-crafts projects that you'll do outside the circle, but making things inside the circle lends extra magic to the process. You might start a project in secular space, so as to take advantage of modern tools, and then put on the finishing touches in the circle. This allows you to use consecrated tools for making tools that will be consecrated—thereby spreading the contagion. It is natural to eat, drink, and chat while making such projects.

Doing Multiple Workings or Activities

It is not unusual to do more than one activity that draws on the blessings of the gods in a single ritual. As a rule of thumb, do the most difficult and serious work first—spells before divination, divination before discussion. If it's a holiday, always do the holiday first—before any spells, no matter how urgent. The holidays honor the gods and so should be given precedence. You may have more than one spell, of equal seriousness. If so, you may want to rest between them, and that's a good time for a light discussion. Between workings or other activities, pass cups and plates—always remembering not to fill the stomach if you're doing magic or trance (you can eat, just eat light).

Air

Air activities are activities based in thought. Discussion and teaching are Air activities. In circles in which newcomers or guests are present, I almost always set aside time to ask for, and answer, questions about what has happened in the circle thus far. By having people in the circle answer each other, I try to encourage discourse. Air activities aren't just for beginners, however, as there are mysteries to be explored by even the most experienced Witch.

Discussions such as this are generally reserved for the very end of the circle, and are a nice way to "hang out" before closing but after serious work has been done.

Discussions are fine times for eating and drinking, which makes the atmosphere pleasant and less like a classroom.

Air Activities

- Questions and answers; either opening the floor for discussion, or having a prepared list of provocative questions to spark discussion.
- Reviewing class materials; that is, if your group holds classes, lectures, etc., reopening discussion of previously covered material.

- Any verbal exploration of a topic; analyzing the meaning of the current occasion, or discussion of the elemental or other attributes of something, or exploring different ways of approaching the ritual.

Fire

- Meditation of all kinds is a Fire activity. Any of the suggested meditations in previous sections can be done here as a group activity, such as the Guardians meditation or the hypnotic exploration of oneness just above.
- Dancing and drumming are fiery activities. Often dancing and drumming are done *around* a fire, as they are natural companions.
- Chanting, especially toning, is fiery.

Fire work is *theurgic* work—it is done to raise consciousness and expand the mind and spirit, rather than to meet a particular goal. Chanting, dancing, and drumming can be used to raise power for magic (thaumaturgy) or they can be used theurgically, to alter the consciousness and exalt the participants.

Before meditations, everyone should have had enough to drink, both because they'll be uncomfortable if they're thirsty, and because a little more wine (for those who imbibe) can help one move into trance. For chanting and drumming, drinks are equally important; chanting dries the throat and drumming can be exhausting. If there's no dancing, pass food during drumming, but if there *is* dancing, make sure that both food and drink won't get tripped over.

Water

Water activities are those that touch upon myth or the subconscious mind. They include:

- Divination
- Storytelling
- Role Playing
- Psychological and Interpersonal Work

Divination

Divination can be done almost anywhere, at almost any time—it doesn't *have* to be done in the circle. However, there are many appropriate occasions for doing so.

Being between the worlds can often improve one's receptivity. It is an excellent atmosphere to experiment with less familiar forms of divination. For example, I am an accomplished Tarot reader; I have read professionally for almost fifteen years and have given classes on the subject. However, I never did tea leaf reading until my group experimented with it as part of our circle work. The experience was fascinating.

The circle is an excellent place to experiment with divinatory methods that are best done by candlelight, and work in part by altering the vision (both the candlelight and the smoke contribute). Crystal gazing, water and mirror scrying, and candle gazing are examples.

There are ritual occasions that call for divination as well. It is a traditional activity on Samhain (Halloween), because the veil between the worlds is considered thinnest at that time. It is also appropriate to use divination to determine the best course to take for a spell, to find information needed for a spell, or *as* a spell.

Here's an example of determining the best course: A member of your coven is scheduled for surgery, and you want it to go well. Would it be best to cast a spell enhancing the surgeon's skill, or a spell protecting the covener? An example of finding information in order to do a spell comes from real life: My good friend was pregnant and had suddenly stopped calling me or returning my calls. I feared for the pregnancy because I knew my friend wasn't in good health. I was brand new to magic at the time and decided to do a protection/blessing spell for the fetus. It turned out, though, that my spell was too late. My friend was out of touch because medical complications had caused her to miscarry, and very nearly killed her as well. At the time I did the spell, she was feeling too emotional to call. In retrospect, I should have used divination to determine what was wrong, before deciding what to do about it.

Finally, there's divination as a spell. This is most often used for finding someone or something that is lost.

Storytelling

Storytelling is a natural Water activity. The most likely stories are those about the gods being worshiped during this ritual (provided any stories are known), or stories related to the holiday being celebrated. However, fairy tales, parables, and fables should not be excluded. Many of them have Pagan and ritual origins, and are enhanced and deepened by a ritual atmosphere.

It's not a good idea to schedule storytelling without preparing in advance. You need to know a few stories (or have someone in the circle who does). Unlike drumming and dancing, this rarely works spontaneously.

On the other hand, you could have a storytelling game, making up a story line by line around the circle, thereby combining the Earth activity of a game with the Water activity of telling a story.

Role Playing

By this I mean any theatrical/mythic activity in which a story is enacted or members of the group take the roles of the gods. It takes storytelling a step further, so that the Witches *become* the gods.

A rehearsed skit could be performed, in which various members of the circle take the roles of the deities, heroes and so on. This could be the holiday portion of a Sabbat rite or in some other way related to the season. It could be something related to the group or the group's concerns. Or, it could just be a story about gods and goddesses who are of particular interest to the group or are the group's patrons.

Instead of a rehearsed skit, members could simply take on the roles without a script, allowing the interaction to unfold naturally. Perhaps two or three people will prepare in advance and encourage other people to participate, to ask questions, or to interfere. This is somewhat similar to a party game, in which people are given characters to play, with goals they hope to achieve. The goals may be in conflict, so interaction is often surprising. The difference here is the religious content of the "game." As the roles are enacted and people improvise their way through conversations, gods and goddesses unfold themselves before the group. Everyone enjoys the game and gains insight at the same time.

One way I have done role-playing in my groups is as a trance. After a short receptivity induction (relaxing, breathing slowly and deeply), deity names are given out at random (I had people pick from a cauldron, which is witchier than a hat). This only works if everyone is familiar with all the deities they may be asked to "play." It works very well when a group has been studying a pantheon. I gave out names of Olympian gods and goddesses, whom most of us studied in school. I also provided small costume pieces—different colored scarves, jewelry, and the like. After the induction, people read the names assigned to them, and then another short meditation was done, allowing people to "become" the deities. Then they selected their costumes and were allowed to speak freely.

Psychological and Interpersonal Work

If you're a solitary, your psychological work is done outside of circle, or in meditation, or perhaps in a journal. But if you have a group, the possibilities expand. Psychological work is one way of using a group as a support system and a place of healing. It's also a way of building trust and strengthening bonds within the group.

There are myriad factors which determine what you can and should do in this area. How well do you all know one another? How long have you worked magically together? How long do you *intend* to work together? How experienced are the various people with psychological work? Has anyone been in therapy? In support groups? How comfortable are people with sharing personal information? With (nonsexual) touch?

You can use '70s-style self-actualization exercises, such as eyes-closed trust exercises and group hugs. There are many books with dozens of ideas on the topic. You can use group communication exercises. One that I like is to tell each person three positive things and one negative thing about themselves. Hearing positives about yourself is empowering, and hearing negatives can be very helpful. The three-to-one ratio makes it possible to listen to both positive and negative without causing pain. *Speaking* both the positive and the negative is also very freeing—it helps us learn how to communicate in safe space and in a nurturing way even when the information isn't "nice," and we all discover just how much we have to say to each other.

Another exercise I like is to pair people up and simply have them look into the other person's eyes. It's not a stare-down; you're allowed to blink. It's a way of establishing a warm bond while bypassing our constant need for words, words, words.

The exercises above are easy—they don't require a lot of intimacy in the group. As you become closer to one another, you can do more detailed sharing and work, in a safe way, on issues that trouble you. For many Wiccan groups, this is their primary focus.

---

1. I am indebted to Isaac Bonewits for his extensive work in researching that underlying structure, and for teaching it to me.

2. Many people believe that, while the athame is the proper tool for invoking elementals or even the Guardians, it is far too aggressive for calling the gods. The wand, being a gentler tool, issues less of a summons and more of an invitation.

3. Inanna is a multifaceted Sumerian goddess. She is the Goddess of the Morning and Evening Star (the planet Venus), of civilization, of sacred prostitution, of love, war, and sovereignty, among other things. Her stories and hymns are among the oldest writings known. The invocation quoted is to the Evening Star.

4. *Inanna Queen of Heaven and Earth: Her Stories and Hymns from Sumer*, Diane Wolkstein and Samuel Noah Kramer (New York: Harper and Row, 1983) p. 101. Used by permission.

5. If the rite is being performed solitary, substitute "me" and "I" for "us" and "we."

6. Some people say she is pregnant. This is a mistake—she is fat. Pregnant bellies are rounder; they thrust forward, and the skin across the middle is taut. The navel sticks out or disappears. Fat bellies are different— the flesh is less taut, it will hang and form folds. The navel deepens. Fat is evenly placed around the front and sides, sometimes more on the sides. Willendorf Goddess is *large*, not pregnant. Her belly represents the most precious and wonderful possible commodity of the Stone Age—enormously plentiful food.

    Perhaps people think she is pregnant because we have a prejudice against fat. Many texts remark upon the tender affection the sculptor seemed to have for his or her subject; the Willendorf figure is lovely. It seems to me that this fat woman was seen as beautiful in her day, and we are mistaken if we see pregnancy, but not fat, as beautiful.

7. Briefly, Isis is the Egyptian goddess of fertility, auspiciousness, magic, and beer (among other things). Astarte is a Babylonian form of Inanna mentioned in the Bible; Diana is the Roman maiden goddess of the moon; Hecate is the Greek three-faced goddess of crossroads and witchcraft; Demeter is the Greek Mother goddess of grain; Kali is the Hindu Mother goddess of destruction and rebirth, and slayer of demons; and Inanna has already been discussed.

8. Baldar is the beloved Norse god whose death brought on Ragnarok. Coyote is a Native American trickster. Poseidon is the Greek god of the Sea. Jupiter is the Roman ruler of the heavens. Manannan is an Irish sea-god. Shiva is the Hindu god of destruction, yoga, and tantra, and the husband of Kali (in her aspect as Parvati). Osiris is the dying-and-resurrecting Egyptian god of agriculture and husband of Isis.

9. If the Descent is found in innumerable places, The Charge is found in ten times as many; it is the single most commonly known piece of Wiccan lore. Here I quote from Janet and Stewart Farrar, *The Witches' Way: Principles, Rituals and Beliefs of Modern Witchcraft* (London: Robert Hale, 1984) pp. 296–297.

10. The modern Charge was written by Doreen Valiente, but its precursor is found in *Aradia: Gospel of the Witches* by Charles Godfrey Leland, and in *Aradia*, the myth is explicit.

11. I am neither endorsing nor condemning hunting or hunting rituals. That's up to you, not to me; I'm simply placing the idea in a ritual context.

12. I don't know where this one comes from. It's sung as a round.

13. Some people know this one as *Lady, Lady, listen,* but this is the original; it's by Paramahansa Yogananda and is found on the *Love, Serve, Remember* album put out by Ram Das in the 1970s.

14. By Victoria Ganger.

15. This is the full range that can be printed in English. There's a lot of nuance I have to leave out.

16. It'll never be *my* preference, but I suppose it's natural for a writer to prefer words.

17. This can have more or less explanation in it, depending upon the experience of the group. If you've all done this many times before, then a statement as simple as "*Let us now make our offerings of incense*" is plenty. If anyone in the group has *never* done this before, then make an explanation of how it's done part of this statement: "*We shall each place an offering of incense on the censer. As we do so, let us send our thoughts to the gods, silently or aloud.*"

18. Some people will offer in silence, and some people will be inclined to make an individual statement, perhaps a long one. If the Priestess and Priest confine themselves to the same simple, standard phrase, people who don't know what to say will pick it up.

19. These are standard abbreviations in the Craft for High Priestess and High Priest. I have *no idea* who came up with them, or why the *S* in Priestess is capitalized.

20. This offering can be done solitary. Obviously, there is no element of surprise, and you can use more than one leaf to make the fire a bit bigger. Even without the surprise, pick the leaf (leaves) with care; make them special to you. You *should* be letting go of something you find beautiful and special, as you'll see.

21. Smoke alarms in ritual rooms are a good safety precaution, but they can cause problems. For a ritual such as this one, disconnect the alarm, and reconnect it as soon as the circle is over.

22. This can be the Priestess, or the Priest, or whoever is leading this portion of the ritual. The meditation can also be broken up between two people—the Priest taking some lines, the Priestess others, as we've done in other examples. If solitary, read this aloud or in silence, changing pronouns as needed.

23. This entire offering is written to "the Goddess." You can substitute "the Lord and Lady," a specific deity, or a pair of deities.

24. Obviously, if you want silent offerings, you'll change this sentence.

25. "So mote it be" rather than "Blessed be" because this is a magical offering, and "So mote it be" is what we say when we wish to manifest our intentions.

26. This should be personalized, picking up identifying characteristics of the people in the circle.

27. You get the idea.

28. Here again, you'll edit. If everyone knows each other well, leave out the "ignorance" part; if it's a group of strangers, leave out the "know well" part.

29. In all cases, where I have HP, A, B, etc., *say the name.* It is remarkably powerful for a person to hear his name being spoken in ritual.

30. Obviously, this is an example, so that you can see how this blessing and the ones following are individualized.

31. This offering will be written for a solitary woman praising the Goddess, although either gender can choose to praise either the Goddess or the God. The mirror is a traditional symbol of the Goddess. If you're praising the *God* within, you'll want to keep the mirror off to the side of the altar, so as not to mix metaphors.

32. Obviously, you should personalize this.

33. Use your own name.

34. Once again, only an example. Your most important task is to come up with praiseworthy, goddess-like qualities in yourself, and to allow yourself to believe what you say.

35. If the male/fire principal that you've been using previously in the rite is the wand, use the wand instead of the athame for Cakes and Wine.

36. When an object is consecrated for an altar that has no practical function—for example, as a gift to the Goddess—then its purpose is to be that gift, and it is "used" by being presented to the Goddess.

37. Offering a cake as soon as it's consecrated constitutes "using" it, as discussed above.

38. Rehearse this. You'll find that if the cup is raised at the same rate as the athame is lowered, it will seem as if the cup is moving faster. The object moving up just seems to be accelerating somehow. Also, you have to be careful with the cup, since it's full. Let the athame do most of the movement, but move the cup enough so that it is clearly a willing and enthusiastic participant.

39. This assumes that there are separate, individual "cakes," which is traditional. Many people use cookies or biscuits. If you're using a loaf of bread, you can tear off a piece for the libation plate. If you're having cake (i.e., birthday cake), tearing off a piece is messy, so at least a few pieces should be pre-cut.

40. Many people want no one but themselves to touch their athames. No one should *ever* touch someone else's athame without permission. C and the HP should agree in advance if C will pick up the HP's athame (as his "second"). An alternative would be for C to use his own, taken either from the altar or from a belt scabbard. Keep in mind that the HPS will also be touching this athame.

41. This will be too tricky with a full cup—practically a guaranteed spill.

42. These are the original lyrics, but a more Wiccan version might be "*With the Mother and Son.*"

43. If this is done, then it's awkward for the HPS to be holding the cup during consecration of the cakes. After the goblet of wine is consecrated, *switch* tools; the HPS handing the cup to the HP, and the HP either handing his athame to the HPS, or putting his away so she can pick up her own.

    Then the cake consecration is performed with the HPS sprinkling and the HP holding the cup. *Then* the HP hands the cup to the HPS.

44. This is fairly standard hypnotic induction technique; it's safe and effective.

45. Name everyone in the circle, including yourself.

46. Still using everyone's names.

47. A hypnotic induction should be matched with a corresponding release. Just as a ritual is worked backwards through its steps when it ends, so is a trance. Also as with a ritual, it is easier and quicker to come back out than it is to go in.

Chapter Six

CLOSING THE CIRCLE

Here are the steps in closing the circle:

- Thanking the Gods
- Dismissing the Quarters
- Uncasting the Circle (optional)
- Reversing the Grounding and Centering (optional)
- Declaration of Ending/Reconnecting to Earth

Sooner or later, your ritual has to end and you'll have to return to the mundane world, the world of time and space. It is important that the circle be officially ended, just as it was officially begun, to preserve the boundaries between ritual space and ordinary space, and to ease our return to time and space—just as creating the circle eased our entry into the place between the worlds.

Although closing the circle is a mirror image of opening the circle, it is much briefer. It is easier, psychologically and psychically, to exit an altered state than to enter one. The mind rushes towards the familiar with little hesitation when it is told to do so. So, where long invocations were done, short "thank you's" are all that is necessary.

A mirror image reverses direction as well as each step. That is to say, last in, first out. If you look at the steps given, you'll see that the last two steps—Declaration of Ending/

Reconnecting to Earth and Reversing the Grounding and Centering—match the first steps of a ritual, that Uncasting the circle matches the casting which comes next, and so on. (You'll note that there is no reversal for consecrations. Un-consecrating something isn't done; it's neither needed nor a good idea. Blessings that remain on an item are all for the good.)

When to Close the Circle

If *Solitary:* Close when you feel your work is done, when your mind has wandered away from the gods and towards mundane things, when you feel you're just spinning your wheels.

If a *Small Group (a Coven or Grove)*: After your work is done, you'll probably wish to sit and just chat with each other. Not only is that fine, but expressing warmth and friendship, and having fun, is part of what the Goddess wants us to do in the circle (according to *The Charge*). You don't have to end the minute work is done. However, once the conversation or the mood turns to things that don't belong in sacred, between-the-worlds space, it's time to close. People can chat about their jobs and traffic later; that doesn't belong in the circle.

If a *Large or Public Ritual:* Close immediately after work is done. In a large group, casual social time quickly becomes chaotic, and a sense of the circle is lost. It's practically a given that someone will forget themselves and violate the boundaries of the circle, or move widdershins, and with twenty-five or more people, it's impossible to keep your eyes on all of them. Go straight from Using the Blessings to closing, without time for the circle to degenerate into a hang-out.

Thanking the Gods and Dismissing the Quarters

Because closing steps are so brief, we can cover them two at a time.

Air

How these steps are done is dependent upon two things: Our perceived relationship with the various entities who are leaving (deities, Guardians, elementals, and elements), and our occult experience.

In the case of deities, we perceive them in two basic ways: as immanent and as transcendent. Immanent deities are, of course, not leaving; they are in us always. So, we're actually saying goodbye to the transcendent aspect of deity, the part that is outside of us, as separate from us as another human being is separate. The deities to whom we say goodbye are perceived as higher than us; we bow to them, we worship them, we obey them and are humble towards them. When we say our thanks and goodbyes, that attitude should be reflected.

Guardians and elementals are beings whom we respect but do not worship, treating them as relative equals. We communicate with them over a significant distance, and so we should speak firmly and clearly to them.

Elements aren't *entities*, they aren't sentient beings; they are simple forces, parts of nature. Although most Wiccans like to be polite, it isn't strictly necessary to thank them. If you called elements instead of elementals or Guardians, you did so because in some way you didn't wish to invite sentient beings of an occult nature into your circle. You invited a force, a concept, an energy. It is no more necessary to treat an energy with good manners than it is to thank your chair for allowing you to sit. If you thank the elements anyway, you're doing so because you want to use consistent language in closing the circle.

When I speak of occult experience, I mean first-hand knowledge of what happens during and after circles as a result of the presence or absence of various beings. It is important to understand that just because you *like* a being, doesn't mean you want it hanging around unsupervised. Elementals in particular have little understanding of things we consider perfectly obvious. Salamanders don't understand that a burning house is a bad thing. When undines hang around, they can cause us to think in an unclear, watery way, and they don't know that we'd have a problem with that. In a circle, which is contained, balanced, and consecrated, such entities don't usually misbehave, but it's a bad idea indeed to leave them loose after the circle has ended. There is a popular phrase used when thanking the quarter entities: *"Go if you must. Stay if you will."* I do not allow that phrase to be used in my circles. Saying this encourages elemental mischief. *Don't do it!*

Water

Honored Guests

Our "honored guests at a dinner party" metaphor will here be an extension of the ideas presented in *Air*. When you give a party, there's a time for it to end. No matter how much you adore your guests, sooner or later, they've got to *go*. You've got work in the morning, you've got clean-up to do, and eventually you tire of being on good behavior. Often your guests leave when you'd love them to stay, but if they stayed long enough, you'd be dropping hints and yawning as obviously as possible.

When my sister was sixteen and I was twenty (and our Mom was away), we threw a huge party on a Saturday night. It was great, we had a glorious time, and when a couple of guests wanted to sleep on the couch we were happy to let them. But when I got home from work Monday evening and they were still there, I was more than a little uncomfortable, and when they were still there on Tuesday, I was downright annoyed and insisted that they leave. Older and wiser, I've learned that *any* guest can overstay his welcome, and I've learned to set clear boundaries when entertaining.

A ritual is not so different. You must thank your guests for coming as graciously as possible, and you must make absolutely certain they know it's time to go. Being a good hostess now ensures that next time, your party will go equally as well, and your guests will be just as enthusiastic about arriving.

The Gods

When thanking the gods, you must be certain that you say goodbye precisely to whom you greeted, in similar style. If you used the Willendorf invocation from the previous chapter, you certainly shouldn't use a generic "Lord and Lady" farewell. Use similar phrases in your goodbye as in your hello, honoring the same aspects and qualities in a shorter form.

If you invoked an additional deity after the first invocation, say farewell and thank you to that deity before the ones you invoked first. This often happens when a spell was done. The matron and patron deities of the circle may be invoked first, and then a god or goddess of healing is invoked for a healing spell, or Athena is invoked for a spell of justice, etc. In this case, first say thank you and farewell to Athena (or whomever) and then to the matron and patron deities.

In order to be very clear about this, examples of thanking the gods under *Earth* will match the invocation examples from chapter 5.

Earth

The same person or people who did each invocation should do its reversal. Just as words are fewer, movements can be less elaborate, but they should not be omitted. If you walked to a spot to invoke, be in that same spot to say farewell. The style should match as well—silent invocation/silent reversal, sung invocation/sung reversal, and so on.

When saying farewell to the gods and dismissing the quarters, use the same tools as were used during the invocation. The tools don't have to be *used* the same way, though. If you used invoking pentagrams, of course you'll use the corresponding banishing pentagrams. If you used other gestures, you can reverse those—if you mimed opening a door, now you can mime closing it.

In a polarity ritual, you can reverse tools. For example, if the Priestess held the pentacle up while the Priest invoked with the wand, the Priestess can now draw the wand close to her body (pulling the energy back in) while the Priest holds the pentacle.

Thanking the Gods
Example 1: A Formal Farewell of The Lady and Lord (Duotheistic)

Priest: Lifts wand, faces Priestess (they can exchange a kiss here).

Priestess: Faces Priest, grasps wand so that they're both holding it.

They turn together, face north, and raise the wand into the air.

Priestess: *We thank you Great Mother of many aspects. Lady of the Moon, Mother of the Earth, Maiden, Mother and Crone, for attending our rites and blessing us, and now we say: Farewell!*

All: *Farewell!*

Priest: *We thank you Mighty Horned One of many aspects. Father of the Hunt, Lord of Death and Rebirth, bright and dark, the Two-Faced One, for attending our rites and blessing us, and now we say: Farewell!*

All: *Farewell!*

Priest and Priestess turn back to face each other, bring the wand between them, nod to each other and/or exchange a kiss, and put down the wand.

EXAMPLE 2: THANKING INANNA

Remember that in the invocation, you may have used music or intoning. If so, you'll use the same technique, but gentler, with less intensity.

> *Inanna, Lady of the Evening, we thank you![1]*
> *Holy Inanna, Lady of the Evening,*
> *in gratitude we know you have joined our sacred rite.*
> *O Radiant Star, we have been blessed by you,*
> *O Great Light that fills the sky, we thank you!*
> *Farewell, and Blessed be!*

EXAMPLE 3: THANKING THE GODDESS OF WILLENDORF

The invocation for Willendorf was ecstatic and elaborate. Building that energy up again is inappropriate—it draws power *to* the circle, and it's time to let the power go. A short, simple farewell, with a single drumbeat, growing quieter until, at the end, it falls silent, is all that is needed.

> *Willendorf Lady we thank you!*
> *Big-belly Mother, you have heard us!*
> *You have made fertile our rite!*
> *You have brought us your plentiful gifts.*
> *You have filled us. We are blessed by you!*
> *Until next time, great Mother*
> *Thank you and Farewell!*

EXAMPLE 4: A WORDLESS FAREWELL TO DIANA

The Diana invocation was suggested as something that would be used only as part of an entire ritual oriented around the Goddess Diana. It would bear little resemblance to standard Wiccan ritual, because the primary purpose would be to worship and serve a single goddess in a style familiar to her. The closing of that ritual, like the invocation, would only make sense in that larger context.

If you have been using the Goddess' implements in the ritual—Her bow, her antlers— return them to Her, placing them in their proper places and putting your hands over your heart in a gesture of thanks. Standing before the altar, bow your head. Make a gesture of completion and humility: Spread your hands out to either side of you, moving them down from face to chest (an "all finished" sign); bow your head with eyes closed, then lift your eyes to the statue of the Goddess with an adoring gaze.

Cup your hands into the bowl of water, filling them and then letting the water spill back in. Fold your hands to show you're finished with the water, placing them again over your heart.

Bow again; the Goddess has been thanked.

The Quarters

As discussed under *Air*, how you say goodbye depends upon who or what you invited, but the dismissal is generally more forceful than the farewell to the gods (even the word "dismissal" is more forceful than "farewell").

As with saying goodbye to the gods, the following examples match each of the callings presented in chapter 4.

When dismissing the quarters, use the banishing pentagram that corresponds to the invoking one used earlier, and *don't* forget to return to the east to complete the circle you've made. You can also use the bell or other sound in the same spots used during invocation; alternately, you can choose to use a bell as a tool of summoning only.

EXAMPLE 5: RELEASING THE ELEMENTS

Caller: Walk to the east. All face the east.
Hail O Eastern Realm! (Strike bell, draw banishing pentagram)
Place of Air, you have kept safe your quarter of this sacred circle!
Thank you and Farewell!

All: *Farewell!*

Caller: Walk to the south. All face the south.

> *Hail O Southern Realm!* (Strike bell, draw banishing pentagram)
> *Place of Fire, you have kept safe your quarter of this sacred circle!*
> *Thank you and Farewell!*

All: *Farewell!*

Caller: Walk to the west. All face the west.

> *Hail O Western Realm!* (Strike bell, draw banishing pentagram)
> *Place of Water, you have kept safe your quarter of this sacred circle!*
> *Thank you and Farewell!*

All: *Farewell!*

Caller: Walk to the north. All face the north.

> *Hail O Northern Realm!* (Strike bell, draw banishing pentagram)
> *Place of Earth, you have kept safe your quarter of this sacred circle!*
> *Thank you and Farewell!*

All: *Farewell!*

All face east for final salute. Caller(s) return to place(s).

Example 6: Dismissing the Elementals

As discussed above, elementals must be clearly dismissed; they must know that the circle is over. There are Wiccan groups that do not believe in dismissing the elementals—I have seen all sorts of strange "coincidences" happen after their circles were closed. Sudden gusts of wind knocking over the altar, candles toppling and causing small fires even though they were well-anchored, and so on. *Do not* forget to do this step.

Caller: Walk to the east. All face the east.

> *Hail Wise Sylphs of the East!* (Strike bell)
> *Our holy rite is finished.*
> *We thank you for your protection and aid.*
> *Now it is time to go.* (Draw banishing pentagram)
> *Thank you and Farewell!* (Strike bell)

All: *Farewell!*

Caller: Walk to the south. All face the south.

Hail Passionate Salamanders of the South! (Strike bell)

Our holy rite is finished.

We thank you for your protection and aid.

Now it is time to go. (Draw banishing pentagram)

Thank you and Farewell! (Strike bell)

All: *Farewell!*

Caller: Walk to the west. All face the west.

Hail Lovely Undines of the West! (Strike bell)

Our holy rite is finished.

We thank you for your protection and aid.

Now it is time to go. (Draw banishing pentagram)

Thank you and Farewell! (Strike bell)

All: *Farewell!*

Caller: Walk to the north. All face the north.

Hail Mighty Gnomes of the North! (Strike bell)

Our holy rite is finished.

We thank you for your protection and aid.

Now it is time to go. (Draw banishing pentagram)

Thank you and Farewell! (Strike bell)

All: *Farewell!*

All face east for final salute, and final strike of the bell. Caller(s) return to place(s).

Example 7: Farewell to the Guardians

Remember that this is meant as an exact match to *Calling the Guardians* in chapter 4. As you'll recall, that was kind of an unusual calling, so this reversal will only make sense when paired with that calling. If you used a more traditional call, then use a similar reversal.

Caller: Walk to the east. All face the east.

Guardians of the East! (Bell or other musical sound)

I, Deborah,[2] *thank you for your wisdom and help.*

> *Air Lord, it's been our pleasure.*
> *Now we say farewell!*

All: *Farewell!*

Caller: Walk to the south. All face the south.
> *Guardians of the South!* (Bell or other musical sound)
> *I, Deborah, thank you for your passion and help.*
> *Fire Lord, it's been our pleasure.*
> *Now we say farewell!*

All: *Farewell!*

Caller: Walk to the west. All face the west.
> *Guardians of the West!* (Bell or other musical sound)
> *I, Deborah, thank you for your compassion and help.*
> *Water Lord, it's been our pleasure.*
> *Now we say farewell!*

All: *Farewell!*

Caller: Walk to the north. All face the north.
> *Guardians of the North!* (Bell or other musical sound)
> *I, Deborah, thank you for your firmness and help.*
> *Earth Lord, it's been our pleasure.*
> *Now we say farewell!*

All: *Farewell!*

All face east for final salute, and final strike of the bell/other musical sound. Caller(s) return to place(s).

EXAMPLE 8: A DISMISSAL IN GESTURE AND SOUND

The trick here is to use the same technique as was used to invoke, but with much less drama. Drama is powerful; it creates strong feeling that contributes to the magic. Since we're working now to move from magic to mundane, building up more magic is inappropriate. Yet we want to be consistent. So the movements should be more subtle, the music quieter, the feeling that of finishing up rather than of creating.

To achieve this, the players ("Sound" and "Movement") will walk normally to the quarter. Movement will assume her elemental posture for a moment, essentially as a reminder. Sound will play his note briefly.

Sound and Movement walk together to the east.

Movement: Walks to the east normally. When she reaches the quarter, she stands on tiptoe, reaching her arms up as she did to invoke Air. She allows her arms to flutter down to her sides, as if the air had gone out of them, meanwhile coming down off her toes. She exhales audibly while doing so, again creating the impression of Air departing.

Sound: Uses only the finishing note from the invocation.

Sound and Movement walk together to the south.

Movement: Walks to the south normally. Makes one quick spin, imitating the 360 degrees she did when invoking. Then brings her hands to her mouth as if holding a flame close to her, and BLOWS, releasing her fingers quickly, as if she's blown out a candle.

Sound: Strikes the cymbal or gong once, not as hard as earlier, and then stops the sound immediately with his hand so that there is no vibration afterwards.

Sound and Movement walk together to the west.

Movement: Walks to the west normally. Does one undulating movement, then cups her hands to her mouth, as if holding water. Then she releases her hands, as if the water had spilled, and lightly shakes "droplets" away.

Sound: Repeats the warbled note from earlier, but it is shorter.

Sound and Movement walk together to the north.

Movement: Walks normally to the north. When she arrives she stomps her feet once or twice. She hunches down in her Earth posture, then stands suddenly, as if freed, wiping "earth" off of her in a few sweeping motions.

Sound: Strikes one deep bass note on the drum.

Sound and Movement walk together to the east, completing the circle.

Fire

There is little mysticism in closing the circle. The task now is to move out of the Fiery realms and back into mundane life, in which things are more or less what they appear to be. Focusing on the Fire aspects of the circle at this point would be counter-productive.

The Final Steps in Closing the Circle

Air

The Optional Steps

Both uncasting the circle and reversing the grounding and centering (and merging) are optional because in each case, many people see that they are accomplished de facto in the course of closing the circle, and so an official step is redundant:

- The circle itself is broken when it is walked across without a proper door being cut, as described in chapter 4. If everyone walks across it willy-nilly, as they will when the circle is officially declared over, it is essentially trampled out, and so no uncasting is needed.

- As we've mentioned several times, it's much, much easier to come out of a trance than to get into one. By the time we've said goodbye to everyone, our minds have received plenty of cues that it's time to return to a normal state, and the Declaration of Ending will finish the job. Therefore, very few people feel the need to specifically state that they're no longer "trees in a grove" or "pillars of a temple" or whatever your visualization was. If you had no special visualization besides a connection to the Goddess and God, then that's an additional reason not to undo the step—why disconnect from the Mother and Father? We are, in fact, always connected to Earth and Sky; we just don't usually think about it.

As a general rule, more people choose to uncast than choose to reverse grounding and centering. A lot of people think, with considerable justification, that leaving the circle lying around without picking it up when you're done with it is just poor housekeeping. Failing to do so also breaks the feeling of symmetry created when you reverse every step; the mind notices the missing step and feels dissatisfied. Part of your decision can be based in the specific working that was done that evening. In an intense circle, with lots of trance, heavy spell-work, divination, or other arcane work, you might need extra effort to "come out of it." In that case, taking the extra step of reversing the Grounding and Centering can be a good idea. On the other hand, for a group that meets on a regular basis, using the same ritual pattern (although not necessarily the same ritual) every time you meet is very reinforcing. It helps people get in sync with the pattern and allows them to flow more freely with the ritual. You may not want to add or remove steps from the pattern on a case-by-case basis. It's not *wrong* to do so, but it takes a little extra thought and planning, and sometimes it rattles people.

Another thing to consider is mood. Do you want to send people away from your circle in a serene state of calm or in a happily boisterous mood? If you reverse the grounding and centering, you'll calm people down—it'll be a *good* calm, but maybe that's not what you want.

Using the optional steps is an excellent idea for a larger or public ritual; first, because people less familiar with ritual will benefit from the extra guidance, and second, because the calming effect at the end can be very helpful for people not used to ritual, or for when you're in a public place (like a park). Uncasting is useful in this case because it reassures everyone that you've left nothing behind.

If you're working solitary, uncasting is entirely up to you (of course). Reversing the grounding and centering is almost certainly unnecessary, and if you do it, should only take a moment.

If you *do* choose to reverse the grounding and centering, do so before the Declaration of Ending. In chapter 3, we discussed whether to ground and center before or after the Declared Opening. You might think that, if you put the grounding and centering before the Declared Opening, then symmetry demands that its reversal be after the Declared Ending. Although this is true in terms of symmetry, it is nonetheless a bad idea in terms of ritual. Ending the ritual dissipates the energy—and that's as it should be. If you try to keep people in ritual mode long enough to lead them in a reversal meditation, you'll be working counter to your own goal of ending ritual mode and re-entering the "real" world. If anyone has had trouble getting "back to earth," as will be discussed next, having more ritual after the ending is declared will make matters worse. Furthermore, once it's over, it's over—no holding back the tide. It makes no sense at all to say a thing is over and then keep doing it. So, for symmetry, this is the exception that proves the rule.

Declaration of Ending and Reconnecting to Earth

The need to declare an ending parallels the need to declare a beginning. As was said when we discussed the Declared Opening in chapter 3, there are psychological, psychic, and ritual reasons why we cannot simply stop without clearly and formally stating that we are finished.

At the beginning, we gradually altered our state of mind so that we were receptive to entering a magical space. At the end, we've been gradually altering our state *back* so that we will be receptive to returning to ordinary life. Crossing the threshold is important, and so we must make sure we know exactly where the threshold is—we must draw the line that marks the border between here and there.

Ritually, we must also remember that between the worlds there is no time. The only beginnings and ends are the ones we make ourselves, and so we must do so conscientiously.

At this point the ritual as I was taught it is over and, strictly speaking, this is the last step you need. However, experience has taught me differently. Many people are still a little "floaty." It depends on the people, of course, and how each individual is balanced in the elements. People with less Earth within often find it harder to get back to earth. Some people find that magic hits them pretty hard—they have as much trouble getting out of ritual consciousness as my son has getting up in the morning. A splash of ice-cold water works for my son, and that would work here as well . . . but no one will like it much. Under Earth, less offensive techniques are discussed.

Fire

The circle has, well . . . come full circle. There's mysticism in the cyclical nature of the circle, and of all things—beginnings becoming endings, which become beginnings again.

- Meditate on life flowing in cycles. The structure of the ritual reflects the flow of the seasons, which is reflected in our lives. The microcosm is the macrocosm: As Above, So Below.

- Meditate on symmetry. You might use a mandala (a geometric symbol gazed at during meditation) and note the circle's relationship to it.

- Meditate on things that end only to begin again. You might try sitting in a quiet room, taking a few deep breaths, and making a written list of endings in your life—ended jobs, ended relationships, ended phases. Then go back to the top of the list, and next to each ending, write a beginning that came out of it. For example, next to the end of the old job, you could list the new job you got right afterwards. Some people don't consider a writing exercise to be meditative, but I find that you definitely can alter your consciousness with your eyes open and pen in hand.

Water
Mythically
The ritual has been the stage upon which the story of the Goddess and God has been played. We have lived out Their sacred creation, and we have witnessed, and partaken in, Their holy union. In ending this mythic theater, we are respectful, joyful, and anticipatory of next time.

The Circle Story
At the Declared Opening, we said, "Once upon a time . . ." Now it's time to say, "The End."

Earth
Uncasting the Circle
There are a number of different methods to be used to pick up the circle, any of which can be done with or without words.

- You can go around the circle with the sword (or whatever tool you used to cast with), visualizing the glowing circle being drawn back into the tool (sort of like one of those automatic electric cords that vacuum cleaners have, but slower).

- You can walk the circle with a different tool, designed to "seal" it (a traditional example is provided).

- You can walk the circle without any tool, with a statement of closing (an example of this is provided as well).

- You can sweep the circle with the broom, sweeping away the magic.

- If the circle was marked with a cord or with pebbles, you can physically pick up the circle—but if it was marked with sand, salt or chalk, you can't.

WHAT ABOUT WIDDERSHINS?

One of the first questions my students tend to ask when discussing this step is "Shouldn't the circle be uncast widdershins, since moving counterclockwise reverses or undoes things?" Many traditions do use a widdershins circumnavigation of the circle to uncast it. However, I am uncomfortable with it.

Widdershins movement, in Wicca, is associated with black magic and with death. Yes it reverses—in the harshest possible way. I believe that to uncast a holy and positive circle this way is at least overkill, if not irreverent. The energy in a Wiccan circle is constantly flowing deosil in a slow, steady movement, from the time the circle is cast until the closing. To walk the other way is highly disruptive, breaking the circle instead of merely finishing it. Save this movement for when you really need to break something (there are other appropriate uses besides negative ones, but they are all rather serious).

EXAMPLE 1: FIRE SEAL THE CIRCLE

This closing was created by one of the traditions known as "Welsh" in the mid-1970s. It has since been adapted by many others. It is used in those groups in which a candle is used on the altar to represent Fire (and incense represents Air alone).

After the quarters have been dismissed, the Priestess[3] picks up the Fire candle and walks to the east. She walks deosil around the circle carrying the candle, repeating the following:

Fire seal the circle 'round.
Let it pass beneath the ground.
All things as they were before,
Since the beginning of time.

The Priestess says this once alone, and the entire coven joins in for the repetitions. The number of repetitions depends on the size of the circle; you'll keep repeating until the Priestess returns to the east. She probably won't arrive at the east exactly at the end of a cycle, so she'll stand facing east until *since the beginning of time* is said for the last time. She then goes back to the altar and returns the candle to its place.

The effect of this closing is sedate and dramatic. Everyone will be calm and still, standing together waiting for the final step(s). That makes this method particularly handy if you're planning on reversing the Grounding and Centering.

Example 2: Closing with Your Body

Once again, the Priestess goes to the east. She'll be using her body to close the circle in one of two ways:

1. She'll face out, with arms spread out at shoulder height, as if pressed up against the circle. Walking quickly around, she'll "slice" through the circle with her body.

2. She'll start in basically the same position, but facing forward, in the direction she's walking. The hand behind her grabs and pulls in, grabs and pulls in, as if closing heavy draperies. The hand in front makes a smaller movement, pulling inward, but most of the movement is being done by the left hand.

I use this style of closing to flow directly into the Declared Ending. When I reach the east again, I raise my hands up, as if making an important announcement. Walking quickly back to the altar, I shout the closing, and drop my hands dramatically. This is a very enthusiastic and upbeat closing.

Reversing the Grounding and Centering

The trick here is not to take the word "reversing" too literally. Think about it: You neither need nor want to be ungrounded or uncentered, so you don't need or want to undo the grounding and centering work you did when you began. Instead, free the subconscious minds of the participants from the bonds of the imagery created, without breaking the connection to Earth and to their own centers. You do want to reverse the merging, but only insofar as the group was merged toward a single mind and purpose; don't undo the interconnectedness of the group.

EXAMPLE 3: REVERSING A VISUALIZATION

If you "became" something during the initial Grounding and Centering, you'll simply undo that transformation. For example, if your initial meditation was a tree, your meditation should guide people out of "treeness" in reverse order:

> *Close your eyes for a moment and take a deep breath.*
>
> *Remember that you are a grove of trees. Now become aware of yourself as an individual tree. You are not just part of a grove; you are yourself. And now notice your branches. Notice that they are not branches at all—they are arms and hands. And notice that your trunk is a human body. And notice that your roots are feet. Notice the sap you have been drawing up from Mother Earth. It isn't sap at all—it's the love Earth Mother has for all of Her children.*
>
> *And now you are yourself, a human being. You are no longer a tree in a grove, you are a person in a circle, and you may open your eyes.*

EXAMPLE 4: COMING BACK FROM A SIMPLE GROUNDING AND CENTERING

If your meditation at the beginning wasn't based in imagery, but was simply one of relaxation and awareness, your job is even simpler:

> *Close your eyes and relax. You are where you were when we began. Feel your connection with the others in the circle. You retain that connection, but you are ready now for all of us to go our separate ways. Feel your connection to the Earth and the Sky. You retain that connection, but you are ready to leave Their sacred circle. Feel your connection to your center. You never lose that center, it is with you always. It is the place from which all other connections are known.*
>
> *You may open your eyes.*

Declared Ending

Make it short and sweet. A simple *"It is done"* gets the message across. I prefer the widespread and familiar statement:

> *The circle is over and the rites are ended.*
>
> *Merry meet, and merry part, and merry meet again!*

This phrase is so commonly used that I've seen it in Internet chat rooms as MMP-MMA (*M*erry *M*eet, *M*erry *P*art, *M*erry *M*eet *A*gain), or simply MM for hello and MP for goodbye.[4] It conveys the "feel" of Wicca, and conveys important information: The ritual is over (Declared Ending), you have been welcome (Merry Meet), and you are welcome back (Merry Meet Again).

My preferred method is to close the circle with my body as in Example 2. As soon as that statement is finished, I raise my hands into the air and begin *"The circle is over . . ."* That's enough to get people who've circled with me before to join in, and by the time we get to the "Merry's," even newcomers are saying it along, so that we all end in unison, usually in a joyful shout.

Reconnecting to Earth

Like waking my son up in the morning, a splash of cold water in the face will work, but no one seems to want to try it! Instead of water, reconnect to *earth* by making immediate, firm contact with something solid as soon as the ending is declared—slap the floor or a wall or stomp your feet. Although this is a small act, it works psychically to ground the last bits of excess psychic juice. (Excess psychic energy can also be drained into your athame or the altar.)

After the Circle Is Over

Fire

Sacrifice

There is an important mystical function that is carried out after rituals—the sacrifices are completed. If you circled outdoors, you were probably able to pour your liquid offerings directly onto the ground. If you had a large fire in your circle, you may have thrown offerings directly into it. But it's likely that at least some of your sacrifices were merely set aside, to be completed after the circle has closed.

The logistics of doing so is covered under *Earth*. Here in Fire, it is important first to remember the meaning of the sacrifice, the Fiery place in which it resides and to which it is sent. In a way, every sacrifice is a Fire sacrifice. Food may be eaten by an animal, or may decompose, liquid may evaporate, but the spiritual *essence* of the offering is carried to the gods, as these offerings are made, just as incense carries our thoughts and hopes to them.

I know it has often been the case that I have placed my offerings outside hurriedly—concerned about prying neighbors and the cold wind under my robe—but it's important not to do just the physical job of placing a libation onto the ground. It's important to know and remember what you're giving, and why. This is the completion of your evening's intentions; do it with reverence and with love of the gods.

Vision

If there was visionary/trance work done in the circle, it is useful to write down what happened as soon as possible after the circle ends. Like dreams, meditation and trance-derived information fade quickly after the return to normal consciousness. Keeping a diary of everything that happens in the circle—what the ritual was, who attended, spells done, moon phase, and so on—is a good idea, but it is especially important that the Fire experiences be recorded if you wish to refer back to them, because they are the hardest to retain.

Water

Another portion of your ritual journal can be Watery—covering mythic, emotional, and dream experiences. Sometimes dreams the night following a circle can be significant, and you may wish to record them. Mythic journaling is less straightforward.

In circle, we have an experience of who the gods are. That experience can be direct or indirect, visionary or theatrical. But whatever the form, we can gain insight into gods and goddesses far more profound than research can provide. Research—Air-based knowing—is important, and should form a foundation upon which to build other kinds of knowledge. But the mythic knowledge derived in the circle can shape our beliefs and our rituals and should be heeded. Write down what happened, what you felt, and what you believed in the moment.

Finally, there are the stories. Your ritual has been a story in several ways. Every ritual recapitulates creation; you have participated in the creation of the universe, and you have told the story of the creation of the universe, both at the same time. You may have also told the story of the Charge—the story of the Goddess coming to Her children and speaking Her instructions for us. You have told a metaphorical story of welcoming honored guests to your special occasion. After the ritual is over, write the story of the circle, as if you were telling a new story, and see what happens.

Earth

Snuff all the candles and turn on the electric lights immediately if you're indoors—it puts the finishing touch on the sense that you're back to modern, mundane life. When candles get sooty-looking, they can be used as utility tapers to light other candles, or can be burned around the house, and can be thrown away when they become stubs. If you make candles as a hobby, then it's okay to melt down old candles for wax—they don't retain their magical association once they've been substantially changed in that way.

Libations are offered to the Earth. If your ritual was indoors, the bowl of liquid should be poured onto soil afterwards. (The first ritual group I ran met in New York City; it is possible to find earth to accept your offerings even in the most urban environments.) Food offerings can be simply left under a bush or in another discreet outdoor spot as a gift to the fairy folk. Any animal who consumes such food is considered an agent of the Goddess. Flowers can be similarly left on the earth. Although it's acceptable to keep them in the house for their beauty, they must eventually go back to the Goddess and should not be put in the trash.

Compost piles are not "trash"—they become Earth and fertilize Her, and so any offerings can be placed in them.

The salt water can be poured out with the liquid libations. Neither salt nor alcoholic beverages are good for plant life in high concentrations, so don't use the exact same small spot every time.

Ash from the censer can have ritual uses, but otherwise is just waste, like candle stubs, and can be thrown away. However, in a bowl-type censer that uses charcoals, some ash makes a good bed on which to rest the next charcoal (and is nicer to look at than kitty litter).

The consecrated salt can be reused next time. It can also be used for various blessings and purifications—such as a ritual anointing or a house blessing. It *isn't* waste and is still consecrated, so it shouldn't be thrown away. Consecrated salt can be used when cooking ritual foods (such as the cakes for the next ritual).

Put the candle holders and anything else with wax on them right into the freezer—by the next morning, they'll be easy to clean.

Air

One of the ways to improve your ritual on all levels is to have a "debriefing." It shouldn't happen right after the circle, because that would drain away power and good feeling, but the next day is ideal. If you can't meet together again soon, everyone should sit down the next day and take notes, while it's still fresh, about what went wrong and what went right. You'll then meet at a later time to discuss your notes. It can be simple, practical things—like asking the Priest to make sure the censer is good and smoky next time before censing the circle, or it can be complex and even mystical—like questioning the reasoning behind a portion of the ritual. In fact, although analysis itself is an Air activity, what you analyze can be in any of the elements—you can examine the practical, the mythical, the emotional, the mystical, and/or the theological.

These critiques are a large part of how I learned much of what has gone into this book. Circling once or twice a month can be educational, but it can also be routine. But Circling that often and then questioning what went wrong and what went right is positively illuminating.

In a group setting, you'll need to use good interpersonal skills to address problems. Don't get on someone's case without also offering praise for what you liked. But don't ignore problems either. If one person's drumming is so bad that he throws everyone else off, you're impairing your ability to do what you want and need to do. Everyone would benefit if that person was gently told that he needs some practice, and in the meantime, maybe he could use a quieter percussion instrument rather than the loudest drum in the room.

You'll learn what works and doesn't work for the individuals in your group, what kind of spell-casting feels powerful and what doesn't, and what sorts of invocations resonate with people. Your group will become stronger both in its ritual techniques and in its interpersonal bonds as a result of these debriefing sessions.

---

1. If the rite is being performed solitary, substitute "I" for "we."

2. Use your own circle name (obviously).

3. Or whoever cast the circle.

4. The phrase has been traced by various parties to the Masons and/or to Robert Graves' *The White Goddess*.

Chapter Seven

A RITUAL SCRIPT

The following is *one* ritual that can be used—it is very similar to the one I use at home. Throughout the book, decisions were left up to you—here they have been made—with a bias toward polarity and duotheism. The intention is to provide an example of how a fully developed ritual based on these steps will look. For convenience, sections are marked with the same names as given in the previous chapters. To make it easy to read by candlelight, all spoken words are in **bold** type.

Preparation

This ritual begins with a God candle that is already lit; it is gold or green. The Goddess candle is not yet lit; it is white or red. Both are of a matching size and shape—a thick pillar style is preferred. Quarters are set up but unlit.

A seasonal ritual (a Sabbat) or a special occasion might call for extra items on the altar, or decorations.

In addition, the following items are on the altar:

- A God statue.
- A Goddess statue.
- A vase of flowers.
- The censer with a *lit* charcoal in it.

- A wand.

- A sword.

- A goblet.

- A pentacle.

- A salt dish.

- A water dish.

- A dish of loose incense.

- A bell.

- The athames belonging to the HPS and HP.

The following items are under or next to the altar:

- Extra charcoal.

- Tongs or another tool for handling the charcoal.

- Matches.

- A utility taper for lighting quarters.

- The libation bowl.

- The wine (opened) and additional beverages.

- A corkscrew.

- A plate of cakes.

- An ashtray.

- If needed, a knife for cutting cake, and napkins.

Grounding and Centering

Anyone can be selected to read the following; it doesn't need to be a group leader.

Close your eyes and take a deep, cleansing breath. Now another. Now another. Good. I want you to allow the cleansing energy to fill you, relaxing and focusing you, from head to toe. It fills your head, and any tension in your head, jaw, or brow becomes relaxed.

Let the energy fill your neck and shoulders, and your neck and shoulders relax. Now let the breath fill your arms, your upper arms, your forearms, and your wrists, and any tension in your arms relaxes. Your wrists, hands, and fingers are relaxed.

As the cleansing energy fills your chest, your torso and your upper back become relaxed. As the breath fills your stomach, your tummy and your lower back now relax. The energy fills your hips and groin, relaxing all the tensions in that part of your body. Now the energy is flowing down through your legs, relaxing your thighs, knees, calves, and ankles, and finally filling your feet and toes.

Now you feel that your body is flowing with energy, that energy is your life force, it is you—relaxed, aware, and full of life. Send a cord of that energy down through the soles of your feet, down through the floor, down into the Earth.

Your energy reaches deep into the Earth. From your feet, into the soil, where it is embraced by the cool, damp, nurturing soil of the Mother. The energy that extends from you is like a tap root, and from the Mother's soil you draw Her energy up. Her energy, thousands of times greater than yours, reaches up the root, into your feet, filling your body. The Mother's energy nourishes and supports you, providing the power for your magical work. The strength and energy from the Earth rises up, through and around your feet, surrounding you like a cylinder of white light.

Now connect to your center. Find the center of yourself, the place within your body that you feel is you. Connect to your center and feel the energy throbbing there. Feel the pulse of your center's power. Feel the Mother's energy rushing into your center.

Reach that energy up through your body, up from your center, filling your body, until it comes out the top of your head like a burst of light. The light-energy streams from the top of your head, reaching toward the sky, toward the vast, starry sky. Allow your light-energy to touch the Sky Father, connecting to the God and His infinite stellar energy. His energy flows back to you, thousands of times more powerful: brighter, stronger, and infinitely potent. The God energy flows back to you in a return stream, a stream of white light from the heavens, into the crown of your head and reaching your center.

Now you are the meeting place of two cylinders of light. Light from the Mother comes up from your feet, light from the Father comes down from your head, and you are a pillar of light, a strong white pillar where the two energies meet. Picture yourself as a strong, white pillar of light.

Now notice that you are a white pillar surrounded by other white pillars, all in a circle. Notice how you form a circle of pillars like the pillars of an ancient temple, pillars standing in the open air, under the stars. Below you is the Earth, above you is the Sky. Between Earth and Sky are the pillars—the place of Their worship. You are the meeting place between Earth and Sky, and you are part of a temple formed here for Their sacred rites. You are connected to the other pillars by the floor of the temple; you are connected to the other pillars because together you are a temple.

Now stand a moment, knowing you are a pillar of a temple, knowing your brothers and sisters of the circle are pillars of a temple, and that the rite we are about to perform is a rite dedicated to the gods.

And when you are ready, you may open your eyes.

Declared Opening and Stated Purpose

The HPS makes a broad gesture of welcome, encompassing everyone in the circle with her open arms and her gaze.

HPS: Welcome all ye who have come in friendship and in love to perform the holy rites of the Lady and the Lord.
Our God is the Father, the beginning, the source of life, the first light. By Him is all creation sparked.

The HP lights the taper from the God candle. He holds the lit taper and says:

HP: Our Goddess is the Mother, the cauldron. From Her all creation proceeds.

He lights the Goddess candle.

HPS: From these two lights come all light. From the Lord and the Lady come all life.

Sacred Preparations

The HP lifts the dish of incense into the air, then presents it to the HPS, holding it before her at about chest level, and nods his head to her.

The HPS raises her athame into the air, brings it down until she has it just above the dish, pointed into it.

Group:[1]   **By the sacred names, by the sacred names, by the sacred names!**

HPS brings athame down until it touches the incense in the dish. She makes the Air Invoking pentagram and says:

HPS: **I charge and consecrate thee, O Air, O Mind, O Inspiration. Bring thy special blessings to this, our sacred rite. Blessed be.**

Group: **Blessed be.**

HP moves the dish of incense into his left hand, lifts censer into the air, then presents it to the HPS, holding both before her side-by-side, and nods.

HP takes three pinches of incense, drops them one at a time onto the censer, making sure they begin to smoke (she may poke with her finger or the tip of her athame to do so). She then raises athame into the air, brings it down until it is in the smoke.

Group: **By the sacred names, by the sacred names, by the sacred names!**

HPS makes the Fire Invoking pentagram and says:

HPS: **I charge and consecrate thee, O Fire, O Will, O Passion. Bring thy special blessings to this, our sacred rite. Blessed be.**

Group: **Blessed be.**

HP returns incense and censer to the altar, lifts water dish into the air, then presents it to the HPS, and nods.

HPS lifts athame into the air, brings it down until it is just above the water dish, with the tip just barely wet.

Group: **By the sacred names, by the sacred names, by the sacred names!**

HPS makes the Water Invoking pentagram and says:

HPS: **I charge and consecrate thee, O Water, O Heart, O Feeling. Bring thy special blessings to this, our sacred rite. Blessed be.**

Group: **Blessed be.**

HP moves the dish of water into his left hand, lifts salt dish into the air, then presents it to the HPS, holding both before her side-by-side, and nods.

HPS raises athame into the air, brings it down until it is just touching the salt.

Group: **By the sacred names, by the sacred names, by the sacred names!**

HPS makes the Earth Invoking pentagram and says:

HPS: **I charge and consecrate thee, O Earth, O Body, O Constancy. Bring thy special blessings to this, our sacred rite. Blessed be.**

Group: **Blessed be.**

HPS transfers three measures of salt into the water and stirs with her athame.

Casting the Circle: Making the Space

The HPS lifts the sword from the altar with both hands, raising it straight up and showing it to all present. She carries the sword, in this position, to the east, walking clockwise around the circle. She lowers it to waist height, and then lifts it high again. She then points the sword down to the floor, placing her hands on the hilt. She begins speaking in the east.

HPS: **By my True Will,**

Group: **By my True Will,**

HPS: **I circle once.**

Group: **I circle once.**

HPS: **I draw this circle,**

Group: **I draw this circle,**

HPS: **To contain and protect.**

Group: **To contain and protect.**

HPS: **O holy place,**

Group: **O holy place,**

HPS: **Be filled with peace.**

Group: **Be filled with peace.**

HPS: **By the Sacred Names**,

Group: **By the Sacred Names**,

HPS: **So Mote It Be!**

Group: **So Mote It Be!**

The HPS draws the circle while she speaks, walking clockwise. With practice, she'll be able to time it so that she finishes speaking as she finishes drawing. If at any time that doesn't work out, she must still wait until she's finished drawing and has reached the east, to say the final *So mote it be!* She lifts the sword two-handed a final time at the east.

   The HPS returns to the altar, and places the sword back on the altar. She lifts the censer. The HP lifts the water dish. They face each other and exchange a quick kiss. They walk together to the east.

HP: **By Water and Earth**,

HPS: **By Fire and Air,**

HP: **I circle twice.**

HPS: **I circle thrice.**

HP: **I sprinkle this circle**,

HPS: **I cense this circle,**

HP: **To be clean and pure.**

HPS: **To be blessed and sweet.**

HP: **O holy place,**

HPS: **O holy place,**

HP: **Be filled with love.**

HPS: **Be filled with trust.**

HP: **By the Sacred Names,**

HPS: **By the Sacred Names,**

Both: **So Mote It Be!**

Group: **So Mote It Be!**

Again, the HPS and HP should both have finished, and be at the east, before saying together, *So mote it be!* Since the HP is a step or two ahead, he should stop at the east, turn, and face the HPS as she finishes. They'll make eye contact before saying *So mote it be!* Then the entire group will repeat the phrase. Only then will they return to the altar together.

Calling the Quarters

Quarter-callers were chosen prior to the circle. Each caller will walk to his/her direction when it's time to call it. Everyone will then turn and face the direction, i.e. the Eastern Caller walks to the east, and everyone else faces east. When the caller raises his/her athame to make the invoking pentagram, everyone raises their athames. The caller can make the invoking pentagram alone, or everyone can do it. When the caller makes a final salute with his/her athame, everyone salutes.

As one caller returns to his/her place, the next caller steps up. That is, after the east is called, the Eastern Caller returns to his/her place *while* the Southern Caller walks to the south.

Eastern Caller: **Greetings, Wise Sylphs** (Draw invoking pentagram)
I call you in the East! (Strike bell)
O flying ones, O thoughtful ones
Bring your inspiration to our sacred circle!
In the names of the Lady and the Lord come to us
Guard and balance our holy rite! (Strike bell)
Blessed be!

Group: **Blessed be!**

Southern Caller: **Greetings, Passionate Salamanders** (Draw invoking pentagram)
I call you in the South! (Strike bell)
O fiery ones, O brilliant ones
Bring your willpower to our sacred circle!
In the names of the Lady and the Lord come to us
Guard and balance our holy rite! (Strike bell)
Blessed be!

Group:	**Blessed be!**
Western Caller:	**Greetings, Lovely Undines** (Draw invoking pentagram)
	I call you in the West! (Strike bell)
	O loving ones, O flowing ones
	Bring your intuition to our sacred circle!
	In the names of the Lady and the Lord come to us
	Guard and balance our holy rite! (Strike bell)
	Blessed be!
Group:	**Blessed be!**
Northern Caller:	**Greetings, Mighty Gnomes** (Draw invoking pentagram)
	I call you in the North! (Strike bell)
	O supportive ones, O constant ones
	Bring your stability to our sacred circle!
	In the names of the Lady and the Lord come to us
	Guard and balance our holy rite! (Strike bell)
	Blessed be!
Group:	**Blessed be!**

Wait for the Northern Caller to return to his/her place, then everyone faces east for a final salute, and final strike of the bell (it isn't necessary for the Eastern Caller to return to the east for this).

Invoking the Gods

HP lifts the wand and faces HPS. They exchange a kiss. The HPS grasps the wand so that they're both holding it, facing each other.

They turn together, face north, and raise the wand into the air.

HPS: **Most Gracious Goddess, Mighty Horned One, Beloved Lord and Lady— hearken unto us!**
Great Mother of many aspects. Lady of the Moon, Mother of the Earth, Maiden, Mother and Crone. Glorious bringer of fertility, source of our very lives! Be here among us.

HP: **Mighty Horned One of many aspects. Father of the Hunt, Lord of Death and Rebirth, bright and dark, the Two-Faced One. Wondrous bringer of light; He Who fertilizes all! Be here among us.**

Both: **Lord and Lady, we ask Your acceptance of this sacred rite.**

HPS: **Be Thou our guide and protection as we, your children, worship you in the ways of old. Welcome and Blessed be.**

Group: **Blessed be.**

HP and HPS turn back to face each other, bring the wand between them, nod to each other and/or exchange a kiss, and put down the wand.

Giving Offerings to the Gods

Note: It's my custom to vary the offerings—it is one part of the ritual that I **don't** do the same way each time. In the ritual script I use at home, I keep this part open, with just a list of suggestions.

HPS: **The Lord and Lady have joined us. It is time to give our love and worship to Them.**

HP: **As the smoke rises, so rise our thoughts. As the gods enjoy the sweetness of the incense, so They will enjoy our prayers to Them.**

HPS lifts the censer and the HP lifts the dish of incense.

HPS takes a pinch of incense. She holds it for a moment and gathers her thoughts, perhaps holding the incense over her third eye or her heart while she sends her energies into it. When she's ready, she places it on the censer, saying:

HPS: **To the Lady and Lord. Blessed be.**

HP: **Blessed be.** (Kisses her)

Group: **Blessed be.**

The HPS and HP now switch. He hands her the censer, she hands him the incense dish.

HP takes a pinch of incense and gathers his thoughts. When ready, he offers it, saying:

HP: **To the Lady and Lord. Blessed be.**

HPS: **Blessed be.** (Kisses him)

Group: **Blessed be.**

Now everyone else will make their offerings by walking around to the censer. Beginning with the person nearest the southeast, each person will walk up to the south of the altar. Each will take a pinch of incense from the HP, say, **To the Lady and Lord. Blessed be,** or some other statement, or offer in silence, and place the incense on the censer held by the HPS. The HPS and HP say, **Blessed be.** The entire group echoes. The person who made the offering will then embrace both the HPS and HP, and move deosil past the altar to make room for the next person, who steps forward.

When all offerings are finished, a final **Blessed be!** or **So mote it be!** is pronounced. This can be followed by a chant and/or drumming.

Cakes and Wine (Receiving the Blessings of the Gods)

HP: **The Goddess and God have heard our praise and are glad. It is time that we take Their blessings in return.**

HPS: **For They have given us the fruits of the Earth, that we may know neither hunger nor thirst.**

The HPS or HP gestures for the group to sit down. The HP fills the cup and hands it to the HPS, nodding to her. He lifts his athame from the altar.

The HP and HPS, he with athame in hand, she with cup, raise up on their knees, facing each other very closely, making eye contact. Slowly, she lowers herself until she is seated on the floor cross-legged; she doesn't break eye contact while she does this. She lifts her cup to eye level, showing it to the HP (and the group). Still maintaining eye contact, she brings the cup close to herself, so that it's directly in front of her mouth. She lowers it gradually, to her throat, to her breast, and finally resting it in her lap, between her legs.

The HP, already raised up on his knees, straightens his back and brings himself up to full kneeling height. As the HPS begins lowering the cup, he begins raising the athame. He holds it with both hands, point down, and brings it to chest level, then slowly raises it over his head. As the HPS places the cup in her lap, he brings the athame as far over his head as he can.

They hold this pose for a long moment.

HP: **I am the athame, the Horned God, the seed.**

HPS: **I am the cup, the Great Mother, the womb.**

The HP begins to lower his athame, HPS (slowly) begins to raise the cup to meet him.

Both: **Together they bring life. They bring creation. Together, we are all blessed.**

The HP plunges the athame into the cup.

Both: **Behold the act of life!**

Pause for a moment.

   HPS hands the cup to the HP, and the HP either hands his athame to the HPS, or puts it back on the altar, and she picks her own up off the altar.

   The HP picks up the plate of cakes. He'll hold the cakes in one hand and the cup in the other.

   While the following blessing is spoken, the HPS will dip the athame into the cup and sprinkle droplets of wine onto the cakes. Continue dipping and sprinkling throughout the blessing.

HP: **Gifts of the gods**

HPS: **Are ever sweet.**

HP: **May their taste last.**

HPS: **May they bring us**

Both: **The blessings of life.**

A cake is now immediately placed on the libation plate.

   The HP presents the goblet to the HPS, saying:

HP: **My Lady, it is fitting that this cup of life goes first to you.**

The HPS bows her head, makes her libation, and drinks. She toasts the group, then drinks again. Then she hands the cup to the HP saying:

HPS: **The Lady makes life only with Her Consort.**

He bows his head to her and makes his libation, then drinks.

   The HPS now takes a cake and splits it in half. She eats half and gives half to the HP, who also eats.

The cup and libation bowl are now passed clockwise to each person, beginning to the left of the HP, each making an offering, spoken or silent, before drinking and saying **Blessed be**. Each person who makes an offering "has the floor," everyone listens and says **Blessed be** after.

If no magic or meditation is to be done, then pass the cake plate; otherwise wait.

Using the Blessings

A wide variety of things can be done. The following table shows what might be done, a transitional statement that could be made by the HPS or HP, and whether eating or drinking is appropriate.

Action	Statement	Eating and Drinking
Rites of the Season	**It is now time to celebrate/to enact** (fill in the holiday and/or seasonal act, such as "*to celebrate Beltane*" or "*to dance our Beltane dance*").	Not a good idea. Use the second, individual libation to toast the season after the rite of season is done.
Rites of Passage	**We have gathered to** ("*bless this child*") or **We have a special duty to perform tonight . . .**	Again, the second round of wine and the food can be used to celebrate the completion of the rite of passage, and should be saved until after.
Magic	**We have magic to do. Before we begin, let's review again our goal and visualization . . .**	Only afterwards.
Games	**We're going to play . . .** (review the rules and perhaps say why it's appropriate).	Yes, unless it's physical and things will get knocked over.
Handicraft Projects of a Magical Nature	**It's time to work on our . . .**	Yes.
Discussion	Launch right into the discussion.	Yes
Guided Meditation	**We're going to do a guided meditation, so let's pass our cups and get into comfortable positions.**	Yes for wine (hence "pass our cups") because thirst interferes. No for food.

Action	Statement	Eating and Drinking
Dancing and/or Drumming	You can just begin, or you can signal one of the drummers or singers, or you can simply say, **Let's dance!**	Yes, but be careful it's not in the way of the dancing.
Singing, Chanting, or Toning	Use your hands to silence any conversation, and begin.	Yes. Fill cups first so that people can wet their throats while singing.
Divination	**At this time, we will use divination for . . .**	Yes.
Storytelling	Just begin.	Yes.
Mythic Role Playing or Drama	Explanation if needed.	It depends, but probably yes.
Psychological and Interpersonal Work	Explanation.	Yes.

Thanking the Gods

HP lifts the wand and faces the HPS. They exchange a kiss.

The HPS faces the HP and grasps the wand so that they're both holding it. They turn together, face north, and raise the wand into the air.

HPS: **We thank you, Great Mother of many aspects. Lady of the Moon, Mother of the Earth, Maiden, Mother, and Crone, for attending our rites and blessing us, and now we say: Farewell!**

Group: **Farewell!**

HP: **We thank you, Mighty Horned One of many aspects. Father of the Hunt, Lord of Death and Rebirth, bright and dark, the Two-Faced One, for attending our rites and blessing us, and now we say: Farewell!**

Group: **Farewell!**

Dismissing the Quarters

Eastern Caller   Walks to the east. All face the east.

Hail Wise Sylphs of the East! (Strike bell)

Our holy rite is finished.

We thank you for your protection and aid.

Now it is time to go. (Draw banishing pentagram)

Thank you and Farewell!

Group: **Farewell!**

Southern Caller Walks to the south. All face the south.

Hail Passionate Salamanders of the South! (Strike bell)

Our holy rite is finished.

We thank you for your protection and aid.

Now it is time to go. (Draw banishing pentagram)

Thank you and Farewell!

Group: **Farewell!**

Western Caller   Walks to the west. All face the west.

Hail Lovely Undines of the West! (Strike bell)

Our holy rite is finished.

We thank you for your protection and aid.

Now it is time to go. (Draw banishing pentagram)

Thank you and Farewell!

Group: **Farewell!**

Northern Caller Walks to the north. All face the north.

Hail Mighty Gnomes of the North! (Strike bell)

Our holy rite is finished.

We thank you for your protection and aid.

Now it is time to go. (Draw banishing pentagram)

Thank you and Farewell!

Group: **Farewell!**

Everyone turns to the east for a final salute. (Do not draw another banishing pentagram.)

Uncasting the Circle and Declared Ending/
Reconnecting to Earth

The HPS goes to the east. She faces out, with arms spread out at shoulder height, as if pressed up against the circle. Walking quickly deosil, she "slices" through the circle with her body, saying:

HPS: **What has here been made is now unmade. What has here been conjured may now fade. We who were between the worlds now are in the world.**

(Ending at south of altar, she raises her arms, gesturing for all to do the same.)

HPS: **The circle is broken and the rites are ended.**

Group: **Merry meet and merry part and merry meet again!**

All now turn around and slap the nearest wall, hard! (If no wall is handy, use the floor or ground.)

---

1. There should be a prearranged signal, such as a broad nod from the HPS, indicating that everyone should say this together. The HPS and HP will make eye contact and start together, and anyone who didn't catch the signal will join in.

INDEX

☾ ORDER LLEWELLYN BOOKS TODAY!

Llewellyn publishes hundreds of books on your favorite subjects! To get these exciting books, including the ones on the following pages, check your local bookstore or order them directly from Llewellyn.

Order Online:

Visit our website at www.llewellyn.com, select your books, and order them on our secure server.

Order by Phone:

- Call toll-free within the U.S. at 1-877-NEW-WRLD (1-877-639-9753). Call toll-free within Canada at 1-866-NEW-WRLD (1-866-639-9753)
- We accept VISA, MasterCard, and American Express

Order by Mail:

Send the full price of your order (MN residents add 7% sales tax) in U.S. funds, plus postage & handling to:

Llewellyn Worldwide
P.O. Box 64383, Dept. 0-7387-0301-X
St. Paul, MN 55164-0383, U.S.A.

Postage & Handling:

Standard (U.S., Mexico, & Canada). If your order is:
> Up to $25.00, add $3.50
> $25.01 - $48.99, add $4.00
> $49.00 and over, FREE STANDARD SHIPPING

(Continental U.S. orders ship UPS. AK, HI, PR, & P.O. Boxes ship USPS 1st class. Mex. & Can. ship PMB.)

International Orders:
> **Surface Mail:** For orders of $20.00 or less, add $5 plus $1 per item ordered. For orders of $20.01 and over, add $6 plus $1 per item ordered.

> **Air Mail:**
> *Books:* Postage & Handling is equal to the total retail price of all books in the order.
> *Non-book items:* Add $5 for each item.

Orders are processed within 2 business days. Please allow for normal shipping time.
Postage and handling rates subject to change.

In the Circle
Crafting the Witches' Path

ELEN HAWKE

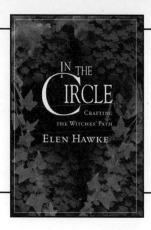

Are you new to witchcraft, or are you looking for fresh ideas to enliven your practice? Whatever your age or level of experience, this book is for you. Take a step-by-step journey through the Moon's phases, the eight seasonal festivals, an understanding of Goddess and God, building a shrine, collecting or making magical tools, performing ritual, exploring sacred sites, and many other aspects of modern witchcraft.

Containing nearly thirty of the author's own beautiful illustrations, *In The Circle* combines Elen Hawke's personal accounts of sabbats and Moon rites with a clear, common-sense approach that makes witchcraft accessible to anyone. Whether you want to practice alone, with a partner, or in a group, *In the Circle* will be a wise guide, providing answers that are inspirational and empowering. Each section takes you deeper into your inner core, the place where you can connect to the spirit of Nature and to your innate knowledge.

For advanced students, this book will rekindle your interest in and love for the Craft, reminding you of why you began practicing witchcraft in the first place.

- Learn how to apply the practical tools of the Craft to shape a way of working that is both rewarding and sacred
- Discover how another witch experiences ritual and the wheel of the year
- Get thoughtful answers to almost every beginning-level question you might have

1-56718-444-8, 192 pp., 6 x 9, illus. $12.95